Dignity or Death

Dignity or Death
Ethics and Politics of Race

Norman Ajari

Translated by Matthew B. Smith

polity

Originally published in French as *La dignité ou la mort. Ethique et politique de la race* © Editions la Découverte, Paris, 2019

This English edition © Polity Press, 2023

This book is supported by the Institut français (Royaume-Uni) as part of the Burgess programme.

Polity Press
65 Bridge Street
Cambridge CB2 1UR, UK

Polity Press
111 River Street
Hoboken, NJ 07030, USA

All rights reserved. Except for the quotation of short passages for the purpose of criticism and review, no part of this publication may be reproduced, stored in a retrieval system or transmitted, in any form or by any means, electronic, mechanical, photocopying, recording or otherwise, without the prior permission of the publisher.

ISBN-13: 978-1-5095-4865-1
ISBN-13: 978-1-5095-4866-8 (paperback)

A catalogue record for this book is available from the British Library.

Library of Congress Control Number: 2022936290

Typeset in 10.5 on 12 pt Sabon
by Fakenham Prepress Solutions, Fakenham, Norfolk NR21 8NL
Printed and bound in the UK by TJ Books Limited

The publisher has used its best endeavours to ensure that the URLs for external websites referred to in this book are correct and active at the time of going to press. However, the publisher has no responsibility for the websites and can make no guarantee that a site will remain live or that the content is or will remain appropriate.

Every effort has been made to trace all copyright holders, but if any have been overlooked the publisher will be pleased to include any necessary credits in any subsequent reprint or edition.

For further information on Polity, visit our website:
politybooks.com

To Josiane, for the past.
To Nabile, for the present.
To Assata, for the future.

CONTENTS

Acknowledgments	ix
Introduction	**1**
Part One: Dignity Re-embodied	**19**
1 Decolonizing Moral Philosophy	21
2 Indignity	39
3 Our Dignity Is Older than Us	65
Part Two: Caliban the Political Theologian	**87**
4 The Universal by Accident	89
5 A Theology of Black Dignity in North America	113
6 Ubuntu: Philosophy, Religion, and Community in Black Africa	137
Part Three: Forms-of-death in the European Necropolis	**157**
7 Recognition and Dignity in the Era of Global Apartheid	159
Conclusion: Black Political Ontology and Black Dignity	**183**
Notes	201
Index	226

vii

I looked at the moon, so full and so bright,
And then at the fireplace, with its flickering light,
And realized why this world will never be right
Then I threw another log on the fire.

The Watts Prophets, "What Is a Man" (1970)

ACKNOWLEDGMENTS

It is customary today in academic works to begin by paying tribute to one or more prestigious institutions that provided, in the form of stipends, grants, or sabbaticals, the funds, conditions, and time necessary to carry out the research for the book in the best possible conditions. This book can claim nothing of the sort. It was funded by a temporary teaching and research assistant position at the Université Toulouse Jean-Jaurès and by governmental assistance in the form of unemployment compensation and, to a lesser extent, a family allowance. To aspire to the impossible profession of Black scholar or intellectual today is to all but condemn oneself to a life of precariousness and poverty. This is because, for many, this presents a contradiction in terms.

Despite these reasons for despair, I remain immensely grateful. I would like to thank Philippe Pignarre first and foremost for encouraging a young, unknown Afro-descendant to publish his first work and for his continued support throughout the various stages of bringing this unlikely endeavor to fruition. Throughout the writing process, his generosity and respect remained genuine and unwavering. It is a great honor not only to be published by La Découverte, but in their collection *Les empêcheurs de penser en rond* [*Preventers of Stultified Thought*], which, belying the colonial myth of modernity, has paved the path for new theories to emerge. I'd also like to thank the first readers of early drafts of various parts of this manuscript: Lou Hanna Baerenzung, Julien Hammann, Marianne Koplewicz, Isabelle Stengers, Gábor Tverdota. If, as the saying goes, any errors in this book are my sole responsibility, there is no question that the meticulous attention of these readers prevented what could have been many more.

ACKNOWLEDGMENTS

One's first work of philosophy is the achievement of a long intellectual journey. I would like to pay tribute to my teachers, mentors, and colleagues, as well as various collective bodies, who taught me valuable lessons when I had so much to learn, who guided my early research and enriched my journey with invaluable advice and much-needed objections: Étienne Balibar, Hourya Bentouhami, Alain Brossat, Grégory Cormann, Tommy J. Curry, Elsa Dorlin, Fabien Eboussi-Boulaga, Arnaud François, Tristan Garcia, Kelly Gillespie, Jean-Christophe Goddard, Benoît Goetz, Lewis R. Gordon, Cleber Daniel Lambert da Silva, Vincent Lloyd, Marc Maesschalck, Mehdi Meftah, Matthieu Renault, Jean-Paul Resweber, Camille Riquier, Guillaume Sibertin-Blanc, Lukas K. Sosoé, Joëlle Strauser, the Brigade Anti-Négrophobie, the Bruxelles Panthères, the Fondation Frantz Fanon, and the Parti des Indigènes de la République.

I would also like to thank those who hosted me or invited me to present early drafts of chapters of this book at various colloquia, conferences, and political or social events: Kader Attia, Manuela Bojadzijev, Claude Bourguignon, Fabio Bruschi, Florence Caeymaex, Maxime Cervulle, Philippe Colin, Mireille Fanon Mendès-France, Paul Mvengu Cruz Merino, Nacira Guénif-Souilamas, Momchil Hristov, Katrin Klingan, Sébastien Laoureux, Sébastien Lefèvre, Lenita Perrier, Geoffrey Pleyers, Nordine Saidi, Enrique Sanchez Albarracín, Patricia Verdeau, Françoise Vergès, the association Toit du monde, the team at Paroles d'Honneur, the Société Toulousaine de Philosophie, the Toulouse chapter of La Ligue Panafricaine Umoja. I'd also like to thank the students at the Université Toulouse Jean-Jaurès for their suggestions and interest in my work. They were the first to hear many of this book's initial ideas.

During the time it took me to write this, I was supported by my family and friends in countless ways. A warm thanks to Henry Ajari, Azzédine Badis, Julienne Bonifacj, Stéphane Cato, Joëlle Greff, Lukas Held, Étienne Oriez, Jean-Michel Rongemaille, Josiane Rongemaille, Marguerite Rongemaille.

The family has been a familiar target of French philosophy over the past century. One thing that is often missed is that for those who are demeaned by a racist society and rejected by the job market— for days, weeks, months—one's family becomes the only reason to continue living. This is why I owe my deepest gratitude to Nabila Hamici. I can't put into words the joy she inspires, the value of her advice and unfailing moral and material support in face of the

ACKNOWLEDGMENTS

difficulties and injustices of this precarious life we share. As much as all the others combined, she made this book possible. Finally, for her existence, which now constitutes the essence of ours, I dedicate this work to our little baby Assata.

INTRODUCTION

Like everything born of the Black condition, this book is the progeny of love and despair: love for my own people and a despair bordering on recklessness. This division is present throughout the book, which is pulled in one direction by modernity's pervasive anti-Blackness and in the other by the unbounded joy of my daughter's laugh. Philosophy will likely never grasp on a conceptual level the intensity of this division. Frantz Fanon, who came as close as anyone to describing it in *Black Skin, White Masks*, struggled to settle on the right metaphor: "The Martinican is a crucified man. The milieu that shaped him (but which he didn't shape) has brutally divided him, and he nurtures this cultural milieu with his blood and humors. The blood of a black man, however, is a fertilizer much appreciated by the experts."[1] *Dignity or Death* sets out to understand, to the extent that understanding is possible, the ethical dimension of Black lives and deaths in the modern period. It is fueled by its political moment, defined by the Black Lives Matter movement in the United States; the global mobilization against anti-Black racism in particular and state violence in general, as seen in the international response to George Floyd's murder; the formation of a radical politics of antiracism and decolonization; the Global North's increasingly vile treatment of exiles forced to flee the ravages of imperialism; and the widespread societal neglect of Black proletariats and lumpenproletariats. While this work doesn't directly take on these overlapping issues, it arose from the same underlying urgency and diagnosis that shapes our contemporary moment: the Black condition is defined today by indignity.

The rise of identity politics and the politics of representation over the past few decades has hardly prepared us for the challenges we are confronting. Whether promoting integration into Western societies or re-embracing African identities, identity politics rose to prominence while neglecting central matters of life and death that are now impossible to ignore. A key argument of this book is that there is a Black condition and a Black history unique to the modern period that is common both to Africa and its diasporas. This condition and history are defined by the political and social violence that disproportionately affects Black people, and by the constant need, in response, to invent strategies of survival in face of this structural violence. Across a variety of cultures, national distinctions, and identity affiliations, there is a shared condition, which can be described as life contaminated by death. The re-emergence of the "Black question" coincides with the decline of a certain phase of critical theory propelled by a radical anti-essentialism. This position is best represented by postwar French philosophy (emblematized by the holy trinity of Derrida, Foucault, Deleuze). It was further developed by a variety of theoretical interventions categorized, within the globalized university, as "poststructuralism," "deconstruction," or "postmodernity." This book springs from the conviction that this phase in philosophy, instrumental as it has been for contemporary thought, can no longer respond to the urgent need to rethink the concept of finitude posed by Black death.

In October 2016, Sébastien Chauvin, a sociologist who teaches at the University of Lausanne, sent me an email in which he characterized my work—while it was still in its early stages—as a "post-constructivist ontology."[2] I am reluctant to use this novel term myself. The prefix *post-* is, in my mind, too bound up with the philosophic tradition we should finally move past. And yet, perhaps no term gets to the heart of the matter better than this one does, which is why it has stuck with me. The notion of a post-constructivist ontology offers, *in nuce*, a lucid diagnosis of the present state of the human sciences. The academic posturing of radical philosophy or sociology is far too often mired in hackneyed banalities and flashy explanations concerning the social construction of race, focusing on the performativity of race or its problematic history. Against a backdrop of bodies beaten and battered, corpses washed up on the shores of the Mediterranean like abandoned rafts, and countless cases of rape and humiliation, the unabashed constructivism of this type of discourse betrays a form of magical thinking, at best, and, at worst, a perverse fetishization of a failed conceptual framework. Rather than offer a more precise understanding of our moment, this kind of theory stands between the world and thought, pointing to

INTRODUCTION

the smoke of the fire of violence raging before us to indicate what sparked it.

We have all grown weary of the endless reminders that there is no biological basis to race. The sociologists and activists who never cease to remind us of this believe they are conjuring away the demon of xenophobia. This mantra is at once inconsequential and misleading. Inconsequential, on the one hand, because those who promote this idea stake their political position on a biological science they know little about, except that the concept of race lacks biological proof. Meanwhile, studies are being conducted to create new taxonomies of human races. If these theories someday manage to garner a scientific consensus, what will become of an antiracism built solely on the blind faith of a poorly grasped science, especially if this antiracism remains devoid of an ethical and political framework? Instead of being at the whims of an unsound biological understanding of race and the temporary half-truths of any given science, a critical theory of race of any consequence won't place at the center of its political program a discovery based on statistical patterns. A critical theory of race isn't a matter of biological anthropology since it doesn't concern facts. It is first and foremost a question of values. The mantra of race being a pure social construct—which culminates in the bizarre fetish of putting the words *race*, *Black*, or *white* in scare quotes—is also misleading in that, in spite of this incessant warning issued from French social scientists, these same scholars are no better equipped to fend off the pernicious effects of such dubious terms. Quite the opposite: the ostensible dismissal of these notions shows just how entrenched they remain in the public imaginary, especially in studies that cast themselves as objective and impartial. Never are such warnings issued around notions of gender, class, or even sex. Numerous scholars and activists act as though the words *race*, *white*, and *Black* were charged with a malevolent yet irresistible aura, which only the precautions they heed in their speech and writing can keep at bay. Their retreat into an anti-Black epistemology in which words are infused with illusory obscenities is thus understood as mere methodological prudence. The bad faith behind these avoidance strategies attests to an unspoken belief in Black abjection, which appears most pointedly in their very critiques of racism.

It is state violence and global structural inequality that produce race, not the discipline of sociology. It is death and dehumanization that produce Black people, not an "essentializing" discourse. *Dignity or Death* offers a philosophical approach to Black experience that breaks with this counterproductive posturing. I am striving for a

3

theoretical approach that is sharp and solid, like the blade of a machete. This book is informed by two philosophical traditions: decolonial thought and politics, on the one hand, and, on the other, Africana philosophy (the intellectual traditions emerging out of Africa and its diaspora). Both of these perspectives spring from a renewed interest in the neglected but invaluable work of slaves, the oppressed, the colonized. I am calling this hybrid approach *Afro-decolonial.*

Toward an Afro-Decolonial Approach

Before being debated in academic institutions across the world, the notion of "the decolonial" was developed by an interdisciplinary group of critical theorists known as "Modernity/Coloniality/Decoloniality" (MCD) in 1998.[3] The main argument advanced by this group of Latin American and Caribbean theorists was that colonial violence is not some negative externality of a modern project considered in its totality as emancipatory, but that it is integral to its very operation. Building on this argument, the principal contribution of the MCD group is its development of a new philosophy of history, whose central focus is modernity or, to be more precise, what many have called the dark side of modernity. According to the Argentine philosopher Enrique Dussel, this didn't begin with the Enlightenment or with the Industrial Revolution. It started in 1492 with the so-called discovery of the Americas. Dussel argues that this conquest marks the beginning of both European consciousness and of modernity. Viewed thus, the notion of modernity refers to Europe's self-designation as the center, with the rest of the world its periphery. "In this violent relationship the conqueror was pitted against the conquered, advanced military technology against an underdeveloped one. At this beginning of modernity, the European ego experienced a quasi-divine superiority over the primitive, rustic, inferior Other."[4]

Modern Europe's supposed ontological superiority was reinforced and refined during the Valladolid debate of 1550, during which non-European and non-Christian modes of existence, forms of living, and manners of thinking were methodically delegitimized. It was here that the Aristotelian philosopher Juan Genés de Sepúlveda debated with the bishop and theologian Bartholomé de las Casas over the conditions of colonization in the Americas. Underlying this larger question was another one concerning the nature of American Indians.[5] The positions of both parties are well known: Sepúlveda, a strong proponent for maintaining a strict hierarchy, held that

4

INTRODUCTION

there was an insurmountable division between the two peoples. Las Casas, for his part, anticipating the myth of the "Noble Savage" à la Diderot, advocated for a less aggressive conversion of the indigenous population, whose stable and frugal lifestyle he admired. Dussel holds up Las Casas as the apostle of persuasive reason, one that recognizes the dignity of indigenous cultures and is committed to the belief that a nonviolent model of integration is only possible through rational argument.

Another member of the MCD group, the Puerto Rican philosopher Nelson Madonado Torres, approaches the Valladolid affair from a different angle, viewing it as a display of "misanthropic skepticism."[6] Indeed, criticizing Sepúlveda's obsession with hierarchy by comparing it to Las Casas's generous reasoning is misguided. The more pressing and problematic issue is the conceptual framework they both rely on. More than a mere doctrine, then, this concerns the very structure of an emergent modern thought, which is contingent upon the sovereign and supposedly neutral assessment of rational jurors. This is presented as a sort of subjective soliloquy where the testimony of "those concerned," which is to say the Indians, is ignored, and where the grievances of the victims are dismissed if they aren't expressed in the respectable idioms of the white man's theology and philosophy. The notion of misanthropic skepticism argues then that the act of bracketing the Indians' humanity is no less cruel than Sepúlveda's explicit accusations of savagery. Instead, the two go hand in hand.

According to the MCD group, rationalization, secularization, and other synonyms of progress represent only one side of modernity. Its other side, its dark side, shows how these so-called advances are inextricably tied to the exploitation, expropriation, and dehumanization of non-Europeans. But the image modernists project of themselves neglects this reality. Denouncing savagery is integral to its value system, as can be seen in Voltaire, Kant, and Hegel.

Yet this notion of savagery rests on a fundamental ambivalence: it can at once refer to the arbitrary violence of an iniquitous sovereign and to foreign ways of living, which, seen as exotic and uncivilized, naturally elicit disdain. The ambiguous condemnation of savagery isn't an accident or a regrettable excess of modernity, but a direct consequence of its emancipatory vision. Make no mistake, modernity harbors the potential for liberation, and the notions of freedom and individuality shouldn't be entirely abandoned. But the use they have been put to raises many questions. Separating the wheat of liberation from the chaff of colonization within modern thought proves difficult. And let's not forget that it was the work of slaves that gave their masters leisure time to devote to philosophy: the former makes the latter possible. Similarly, the European ideal of emancipation is defined against a denunciation of the savagery of Amerindians and Africans.

However, as Lewis Gordon has argued, if the decolonial perspective has brought to light the dark side of modernity, it has failed to acknowledge the position that Africa and Africans have occupied— and continue to occupy—in relation to it. Dussel's panegyric of Las Casas is a telling case in point. His account makes no mention of the role the latter's *History of the Indies* played as early as 1517 in encouraging the Spanish Crown to use the labor of Black slaves in its American colonies.[7] A half a century before 1492, the date that supposedly ushered in modernity, Prince Henry the Navigator created the first market of Black slaves.[8] Whereas the humanity—or lack thereof—of the Indians called for a so-called rational debate at Valladolid, the enslavement of Black people raised no moral scruples among European intellectuals before the eighteenth century. In their view, Black abjection seemed, all other things being equal, entirely natural.[9] The Afro-decolonial perspective I am adopting here will place this long history of dehumanizing violence against Black humanity—a history that undergirds modernity—at the center of an ethical approach inspired by Africana philosophy.

The notion of internal colonialism exercised over the people of the African diaspora in the Americas is well known.[10] It draws an explicit analogy between the fate of native populations conquered by European empires and the descendants of slaves subjected to racial segregation. But if we acknowledge that racial slavery predates the Conquest of the Americas and that it was a driving force in the emergence of modern Europe, we are forced to consider this the other way around. It may be that conquering, commodifying, exploiting, and dehumanizing the Black body constitute the *fons et origo* of coloniality. Kwame Ture's and Charles Hamilton's description of colonialism as the dispossession of political power and agency in their classic work on Black power is what has defined modernity at its outset and what has best withstood the vicissitudes of time.[11] Indeed, 600 years after the Portuguese established the first slave market, Black life is still seen as without value on a global scale. This is why the Afro-decolonial approach I am advancing here hinges on the *ontological question of Black being*.[12] This approach demonstrates that, in the modern period, as decolonial philosophy has shown, the definition of the human being is not self-evident.

INTRODUCTION

An Ethic of Dignity

The ethical stance of *Dignity or Death* has been shaped by the experience and reality of dehumanization. In turning to the venerable notion of ethics, I am not referring to the observation of moral laws, as modern philosophy defined ethics,[13] nor to the fashioning of one's own subjectivity, as it is often construed by contemporary philosophy.[14] Obeying laws and self-fashioning are only possible once the constant threat to one's existence is contained. For an Afro-decolonial approach, acutely aware of modern history and its constant abuse of the bodies of slaves and the colonized, ethics confronts the deliberate division between humanity and its outcasts. As the theologian of Black liberation James H. Cone, whose work will be explored at length in a later chapter, has explained:

> Resistance was the ability to create beauty and worth out of the ugliness of slave existence. *Resistance* made *dignity* more than just a word to be analyzed philosophically. Dignity was a reality that could only be dug out of the shit of the white environment; and it was based on the slaves' relationship with their black brothers and sisters. White people achieved what they called dignity by their enslavement of black Africans; they measured their importance by the number of Africans they enslaved.[15]

In Cone's argument, the term *dignity*, the cornerstone of ethics, takes on two distinct but related meanings. The first is the primordial notion of political ontology which draws a line between the human and the nonhuman. In this understanding, knowing who possesses dignity amounts to knowing who is taken to be authentically human. The second understanding, which is derived from the first, is made explicit by the politicized demands for dignity. These demands stem from the lived and embodied experience of one's own humanity, as well as that of the marginalized group one is consigned to. Politics, in the sense of political engagement, is a constitutive part of a Black ethics. Dignity is part of the conceptual arsenal of an engaged politics. It is an expression of the radical demands such a politics makes bearing on the human condition itself. As the theologian Vincent Lloyd reminds us, dignity has played a major role in the history of Black social activism in the United States. It is at the center of the philosophy of figures as diverse as Marcus Garvey, Langston Hughes, and Martin Luther King Jr.[16]

7

Lloyd shows that the notion of Black dignity transcends the conventional boundaries of political thought and is taken up by movements widely perceived as moderate as well as by a more radical Black tradition. Indeed, it appears in the concluding remarks of an unsparing editorial published by the Black Panther Party's leading press organ: "No! *The Black Panther Black Community News Service*, is not an ordinary newspaper. It is the flesh and blood, the sweat and tears of our people. It is a continuation of the story of the middle passage, of Denmark Vesey, of Nat Turner, of Harriet Tubman, of Malcolm X, and countless other oppressed people who put freedom and dignity beyond personal gain."[17] Here, the demand for dignity draws on a deeper history, rewritten by suffering and revolt, as proof of the possibility of freedom precisely where nothing seems to support it. In the manifesto that opens his work *Revolutionary Suicide*, the co-founder of the party, Huey Newton, even makes dignity the defining feature of every revolutionary, declaring that what matters is to live "with hope and dignity; and if premature death is the result, that death has a meaning reactionary suicide can never have."[18] For Newton, dignity means taking action to dismantle the present order, and that action begins from the social death imposed on Black America. Dignity makes revolutionary action a natural extension of the widespread misery and despair that characterize Blackness. As Lloyd has shown, even today the notion of dignity is central to any mobilization in support of Black lives.[19]

The frequent appearance of the same term throughout a variety of distinct but similar circumstances seems more than just a lexical coincidence. It points to a shared existential sensibility, born of the necessity of confronting violence. The origin of this book springs from my conviction that when the word *dignity* resounds in the streets, chanted by protesters fed up with police violence, when it is wielded by activists moved to lift up a trampled humanity, it takes on a meaning that it has never held within traditional European philosophy and political discourse. Speaking from the margins of humanity, the Afro-decolonial point of view makes it possible to ask in radical terms what it means to be human. The meaning of dignity considered from this position stands in stark contrast to the definition given by European philosophers who never questioned their belonging to a glorious humanity. One of the principal objectives of Afro-decolonial thought is to make visible the limitations of European thought, ethics, and politics.

In the past decade, countless social movements throughout the world have used *indignation* as a rallying cry. "Indignation from the

INTRODUCTION

experience of these frustrations, from the lack of respect and from the feeling of not being heard has turned into an affirmation of dignity in many protests and uprisings. It is at once a personal affirmation, a demand to be acknowledged by institutional powers and to be heard by governments."[20] One of the goals of *Dignity or Death* is to show that dignity takes on a new urgency in the context of the history of dehumanization where the oppressed are routinely denied a voice. My aim is to complicate, and thereby complement, European genealogies of dignity, which have deemed it—despite its oppositional or paradoxical nature—constitutive of liberal democracy.

The bell hooks Dilemma

In today's universities the most significant Black mass movements of the nineteenth and twentieth centuries—from both conceptual and organizational standpoints—are given marginal treatment, especially in philosophy departments.[21] For all their differences, Black nationalism, Panafricanism, and the Back-to-Africa movement have mobilized millions of Black activists throughout the Americas, Africa, Europe, and beyond. But research affiliated with Black studies, Africana studies, and African American studies in no way reflects the centrality of these movements in the political and intellectual history of the African diaspora. These movements are confined to the periphery, while debates focus on the finer points of Black feminism, cultural studies, queer studies, and other trends heavily influenced by continental philosophy, most notably postwar French thought.

To understand the reason for this state of affairs, it is worth turning to a work that has done much to shape the field of Black studies. Bell hooks's first book, *Ain't I a Woman: Black Women and Feminism*, opens with a dilemma posed by the cumulative pressure suffered under racial and gender oppression. The Black woman is presented as a victim of both sexism and anti-Blackness. This dilemma, which has afflicted Black women since the nineteenth century, is expressed by the following alternative: "to choose between a black movement that primarily served the interests of black male patriarchs and a women's movement which primarily served the interests of racist white women."[22] This clear pathologizing of Black men, who are described as atavistic phallocrats, is not unlike other types of racist anthropology,[23] but this is not my main point of contention. The bigger concern is that hooks's parallel between sexist Black men and white racist women doesn't hold up under scrutiny.

9

Indeed, while she rejects outright the political legacy of Black radicalism from the mid-twentieth century (Malcolm X, the Black Panthers, etc.) for its inherent misogyny, she refrains from condemning feminist politics for its inherent racism, despite the overwhelming proof that early women's rights activists didn't directly target the patriarchy, nor did they resist taking part in the *mission civilisatrice* alongside white men as they subjugated Black, Native American, or Muslim "predators."[24] Hooks delegitimizes the political heritage of African Americans while absolving feminism of its racist history. Whereas the Black project was inherently misogynistic, the racism of the feminist project was merely incidental, which allows hooks to embrace it as the core of her political and social project: "Although the focus is on the black female, our struggle for liberation has significance only if it takes place within a feminist movement that has as its fundamental goal the liberation of all people."[25] While, from hooks's perspective, an independent Black political movement seems to pose a threat to women, feminism is seen only as a positive force for the larger society.

Thus, the bell hooks dilemma, which pits a politics of Blackness against a feminist politics—a seemingly Cornellian position— manages to find an unambiguous solution: "Radical groups of women continue our commitment to building sisterhood, to making feminist political solidarity between women an ongoing reality. We continue the work of bonding across race and class."[26] For hooks, neither class nor race pose any obstacle to sisterhood or to the formation of a uniform feminine political subject. In the context of what I am trying to achieve here, the problem with this strategy is less a matter of making feminism and sisterhood the cornerstones of solidarity and of a larger political movement. The problem lies with the doubt it casts on any affirmative conception of race in general and of Blackness in particular. Forging solidarity through sisterhood at the expense of everything else assumes that race and class can be transcended, a dangerous illusion which the radical Black tradition has repeatedly cautioned against. Throughout hooks's writing one finds the same refrain, namely, the idea that "black nationalism is more a gesture of powerlessness than a sign of critical resistance."[27] This delegitimization of Black nationalism and, by extension, the major tenets of African and diasporic political thinking, has become the *doxa* in Africana studies. Not only is hooks's false dilemma, which casts Black men as irremediably sexists and white women as only superficially racists, rarely criticized, but it is also always resolved in the same way: by minimizing the Black archive.

INTRODUCTION

This intellectual attitude which unthinkingly accepts that racial subjugation is an inessential dimension of reality, a mere social construct that can be overcome, is also what allowed European philosophy to occupy a preponderant place in the study of Black life. As the political thinkers Martin Delany, Marcus Garvey, Harry Haywood, Kwame Nkrumah, or Patrice Lumumba have been all but forgotten, Foucault, Lacan or Derrida stand in place of Black voices or, for the more radically inclined, a superficial and tone-deaf Marxism is adopted over a century and a half of Black criticism. Our intellectual moment is so caught up in its own illusions that an attack leveled against Black nationalism such as that found in Asad Haider's *Mistaken Identity: Race and Class in the Age of Trump* can come across as an iconoclastic critique of identity politics. In reality, this book simply rehashes a fashionable post-structuralist identity constructivism, sprinkled with Marxism for good measure, whose heroes are Judith Butler, Paul Gilroy, and Stuart Hall. The routine apology of hybridity, creolization, and anti-essentialism, which is the *lingua franca* of the progressive humanities and NGOs, is used to criticize of the heritage of Black nationalism, which is caricatured as an ideology for elites.[28] As a result, organizing large masses of people around a common cause, which far exceeds any achievements made by the white left in the United States,[29] is written off. Forgotten too is the repression of the Black liberation movement, which was proportionate to the threat it posed to America as well as Africa.

Not only is the archive of Black activism neglected, but fighting for its neglect is seen as a radical and audacious act. Attacking Black nationalism, Pan-Africanism, even the Black radical tradition as sexist, backward, bourgeois, even racist, has become one of the most widespread, predictable, and unchallenged forms of iconoclasm in the Anglophone university. In response, the Afro-decolonial critique of dominant trends of social philosophy and contemporary political theory figures prominently in this book. I have tried to approach each work in good faith, seeking answers to questions that have plagued me from my position within the Black condition: racism, the history of colonialism and slavery, social death. I had to face the facts. It wasn't a matter of white authors avoiding these problems. It was the fact that they spoke about them as if in spite of themselves, while grossly misrepresenting them in the process. The colonized, and especially Black life, are rarely studied in and of themselves in contemporary critical theory, and never without some ulterior motive. They are the collateral victims of arguments that treat them, at best, as supporting actors and, at worst, as mere extras meant to

11

fill space in a historical narrative, appearing here and there in order to prove a minor point or provide local color. This is something I first lived, then considered on a conceptual level, and, finally, theorized.

Pan-Africanism, Black nationalism and the radical tradition tied to the African diaspora will, at some point, rise again to prominence in intellectual debates and political movements. But an indispensable first step will require what Frank Wilderson has described as metatheory: the questioning of "the unspoken, assumptive logic of Marxism, post-colonialism, psychoanalysis, and feminism through rigorous theoretical consideration of their properties and assumptive logic."[30] The notion of dignity offers in this respect an exemplary arena for this questioning. *Dignity of Death* shows how this concept—one of the most universal in the history of European philosophy—has been used throughout Black history to provide a systematic justification of the specificity of Africans fighting against oppression. Throughout this work, key trends of contemporary continental philosophy will be examined from an avowedly Black perspective. Subjecting continental philosophy to this kind of scrutiny is the first act in freeing Africana thought from its yoke.

Frantz Fanon, like many writers from the radical Black tradition, had to fight for his place within the ranks of philosophy. In *Black Skin, White Masks*, he spars with Sartre and Hegel, takes on Octave Mannoni, René Maran, and Mayotte Capécia, tangles with Adler and Freud. This is because there is no place for Blacks in the realm of the intellect; they must force their way in. As much as I value the contributions of postcolonial and poststructuralist theorists and their use of post-Lacanian or deconstructionist philosophical paradigms, and as much as their work has inspired and made possible my own, my work sets out in a different direction. As Lewis Gordon has argued, to prove their theoretical value regarding the Black condition, one must first ask what relations these theories have with racism and coloniality, which is to say, these theories must first pass through the scrutiny of Black critical theory.[31] It isn't a matter here of ostracizing or dismissing European philosophy, but rather of learning to read it with our own eyes, our own bodies and intelligence. As Fanon wrote in his thesis in medicine: "philosophy [is] the risk that the mind takes to assume its dignity."[32]

Chapter Summary

The first chapter, "Decolonizing Moral Philosophy," seeks to identify the main tenets of the dominant understanding of dignity. To this

INTRODUCTION

end, a brief critical history of dignity in the thought of a few major figures in European philosophy—Pico della Mirandola, Kant, and Habermas—is sketched. My aim is to show how the problem of racial dehumanization is not only neglected in definitions of dignity but how, by their very design, these definitions can never directly confront this problem, thereby only further exacerbating it. Consider Pico della Mirandola, whose conception of human dignity, for example, is based on the complementary notions of autonomy (i.e., man's ability to establish laws outside of all dependencies) and the power of appropriation. One won't fail to recognize here the *ego conquiro*, the conquering mentality of a burgeoning colonial Europe.[33] Kantian ethics can be understood as an attempt to rein in this approach by subjecting autonomous and appropriating individuals to the rational rules of morality in order to limit the reach of their power. However, a careful examination of Kant's writing from the angle of race reveals that Black people are held as an exception to these rules. They are beings the moral law is incapable of protecting, those who force it to be re-evaluated. The chapter closes with a discussion of how this moral philosophy, unknowingly based on a colonial episte-mology, gets inscribed and constitutionalized in the founding laws of European nation states. No matter how much one insists that dignity is what defines the human, the question remains as to whether these nation states, these institutions that police borders and citizenship, can be considered legitimate guardians of this supposed universal concept. History would suggest otherwise.

Starting from the premise that dignity is defined against negative social experiences, especially that of violence, the second chapter, "Indignity," interrogates the lived experience of race and the politics that produce it. Arendt, Foucault, and their successors tied to "Italian theory,"[34] analyzed racism's role in the construction of modernity. In their influential accounts of this political history, they contend, more or less explicitly, that race is a construct founded on violence. Their argument takes the Nazi genocide as its paradigm. This decision has two major consequences: the first is that extreme racial dehumaniz-ation is shown to arrive late in European history; the second is that extermination appears as its most essential and characteristic form. The aim of this chapter is to show how shifting the paradigm to center on the slave trade and slavery has significant theoretical conse-quences for thinking through dehumanization. Indeed, these events, which ushered in modernity, represent a form of destruction of life that doesn't take the form of genocide, but instead work by system-atically depriving human life of what makes it worth living, in other

13

words, by depriving it of its dignity. I am calling this destruction of life a *form-of-death*. In so doing, I am deliberately drawing on Achille Mbembe's notion of necropolitics, whose understanding of state-sponsored death closely aligns with what Italian philosophers such as Giorgio Agamben or Roberto Esposito have called "thanatopolitics." But it seems to me more apt to apply the term *necropolitics* to the blurring of the distinction between life and death. This results in a form-of-death, like the counterpart of the daily life of white people under capitalism, characterized by a seemingly endless series of setbacks, aggressions, and prohibitions that "necrose" existence and provoke a loss of faith in the world.

The third chapter, "Our Dignity Is Older than We Are," frames dignity as a necessary response to the necropolitical attack on Black existence. However, although dignity is produced as a powerful negation, it isn't empty of content. It isn't what post-Lacanian political theorists call a "floating" or "empty" signifier. Rather, it is a product of history or, more accurately, an overlapping set of histories bound to the Afro-descendant condition. For the oppressed, dignity signifies entering the realm of politics on their own terms, which implies questioning the very livability of life. Dignity appears then as an effort to live an authentically human life, while recognizing and claiming as one's own the history of this effort. A striking example of this will be discussed with the Negritude movement and its deliberate renewal of the intellectual, political, and artistic legacies of Africa and its diaspora. In contrast with the "outmoded" argument made by Sartre and Fanon about Negritude, I will discuss the importance of its theoretical gesture, which goes beyond simply reclaiming or forging a new identity; it consists rather in the critique it makes against the colonial West from an exterior position. In solidarity with this effort, I am reclaiming the much-disparaged idea of essentialism through what I am calling a *deep historicity*. To accomplish this, I draw a clear distinction between essence (understood as a memory and bundle of lived affiliations) and norms (the modalities of social and political constraints which make possible their implementation). This analysis calls attention to the political and ethical limits of an anti-essentialism obsessively advanced by deconstructivists: the dignity of the oppressed, as a historical phenomenon, will be defined as an indeconstructible part of their existence.

The fourth chapter, "Accidental Universalism," offers a critique of contemporary universalist doctrines by examining their relation to political theology. For all their differences, we will see what philosophical discourses on secularism have in common, namely, a

INTRODUCTION

post-deconstructivist longing to restore the universal, as attested to by theorists such as Slavoj Žižek, Alain Badiou and, in less obvious ways, Étienne Balibar. These philosophical positions depend on a narrow understanding of the relation between politics and theology, summed up in the facile contrast between particular identity markers deemed by their very nature reactionary or regressive and the saving universality of a political subject. For some, the subject is figuratively embodied by the state; for others, by revolution. But all devalue the role of the particular. The main contention of this chapter is that critical theory would be better served if it stopped unquestioningly privileging the universal at the expense of the particular. A rich history of radical uses of Christianity in Black thought and action makes a compelling case for an alternative approach.

The fifth chapter, "A Theology of Black Dignity in North America," presents an ethics of dignity as practiced by a politically active religious tradition. This ethics is shown through the prism of the work of the late James Cone. Contrary to popular opinion, Black people were not converted to Christianity through a brazen act of brainwashing. Their adoption of this religion wasn't a passive endeavor at all. Nor did it fill a spiritual void. The Black church became a privileged site of assembly, action, and creation—rather than of pure and simple alienation—where critical thinking was fostered. At the end of the 1960s, when Cone put forth his new revolutionary theology, he was able to build on this legacy, which framed the Civil Rights and Black Power movements in a new perspective. This chapter gives special attention to the practice and thought of prophetism, understood as a radical democratic discourse and a privileged vector of Black dignity.

Debates over the existence of an "African philosophy" that animated the global Black *agora* of the mid–twentieth century[35] set the stage for the sixth chapter, "Ubuntu: Philosophy, Religion, and Community in Black Africa." Rather than dwell on the most pronounced matter of these debates, namely, the opposition between an ethnophilosophy that accorded an ontological dimension to African linguistic structures, and a critical school that lambasted this approach, the focus here will be on the quarrels that divided the critical school. This chapter will thus set the positivism at play in the work of the young Paulin Hountondji against the existential and hermeneutical approach of Fabien Eboussi Boulaga. I will show how Boulaga's approach prefigured Desmond Tutu's liberation theology and his reinterpretation of the Bantu concept of *ubuntu*, which, among other things, is synonymous with human dignity. This parallel provokes a shift in the meaning of dignity, as it ascribes it to a collective being rather an individual. And let's not forget the role ubuntu played in the Truth and Reconciliation Commission at the end of the 1990s during the post-apartheid transition, a point that will be explored further in this chapter. What emerges through this exploration of South African thought is a conception of dignity that foregrounds ethical reparation and is attentive to human finitude and vulnerability in the face of extreme conditions.

The seventh chapter, "Recognition and Dignity in the Era of Global Apartheid," begins with a reflection on the so-called migrant crisis in contemporary Europe. I offer here an uncompromising assessment of the status quo, focusing in particular on the production of expendable lives that goes hand in hand with European immigration policies and the instrumentalization of state violence, which is deliberately intensified as a strategy of deterrence. But this chapter will also explore deeper issues at stake in this crisis, such as the multicultural politics of recognition, long held up by the liberal left as an effective way of combatting racist asylum policies. I will turn to the work of the German philosopher Axel Honneth to illustrate the latent coloniality in this ideal of recognition. Whereas Honneth never doubts the benefits of recognition, Frantz Fanon had a much more nuanced understanding of the problem, showing that there are, indeed, many shades of recognition. To be clear, recognition often does entail valuing the life of the individual; but, more frequently, it legitimizes the alienation and subjugation of the individual by making the end goal integration into a colonial society. Fanon saw recognition as a corollary to dignity. In other words, authentic recognition stems from the oppressed laying claim to dignity on their own terms, which forces the dominant society to break with its traditional models of recognition. This chapter will also call attention to the driving force of displacement, which is above all imperialism and the coloniality of power. Fanon sees a direct relation between dignity and sovereignty, revealing how a strict line drawn between humanity and inhumanity underlies dominant normative definitions of human dignity. Today's migrant problem isn't only a matter of an accelerating necropolitics within host countries; it reflects above all the long history of dismantling African sovereignties.

It is hardly surprising that the current of Black thought that has elicited the biggest international response—met at once with fervent interest and fierce resistance—goes by the name "Afropessimism." Despite debates over the marketing of a school of thought with sometimes deliberately pithy and provocative claims,[36] I am convinced that its success stems from its resonance with the lived experience of

INTRODUCTION

young Black people in the twenty-first century. "Afropessimism" provides a vocabulary to express our lack of trust in the world, our structural inability to project ourselves into the future, our endemic precariousness. The philosopher Calvin Warren sums it up clearly: the slave trade, its "violence, transport, and rituals of humiliation and terror,"[37] is what transforms African existence into Black being, which is deprived of ontological status, negated. Henceforth, Black life becomes the abject pillar of a symbolic order against which all other identities will be defined, a sort of backdrop of absolute ontological ignominy serving solely as a point of contrast. "The world needed a ~~being~~ that would bear the unbearable and live the unlivable; a ~~being~~ that would exist within the interstice of death and life and straddle Nothing and Infinity. The ~~being~~ invented to embody black as nothing is the Negro."[38] The aim of the eighth and final chapter, "Black Political Ontology and Black Dignity," which recapitulates the principal arguments of this book, is twofold. Despite some recent and relevant criticisms of the paradigm of Afropessimism, there remains a core concept, which has been immune from attack and which is worth spelling out: the idea of a Black political ontology. This is the first goal, which is directly related to a fundamental question concerning political ontology: namely, what does it mean to be born into a world of Black dehumanization? To answer this, Afropessimism's use of the notion of "social death," originating in Orlando Patterson—who in turn borrowed the term from Claude Meillassoux—must be re-examined. The concept of Black dignity, which expresses an ethical and political need to defy the negation of Black being, has been able to draw its strength from the form-of-death itself. I will illustrate this by defending the racial dimension—routinely left out or played down by the conventional left—of the riot, a political expression of necessity at its purest. Finally, Black dignity will be defined by its ability to occupy the space between death and life, which is to say, to welcome the obscure ghosts of the past. Afropessimism argues that Black life emerged out of the calamitous destruction of the African wrought by slavery and colonialism. This diagnosis of the "usurpation of subjectivity, of life, of being"[39] is often countered by pointing to the persistence of certain singular traditions and practices surviving the diaspora and postcolonial Africa. My argument marks a departure from both of these positions. It is the *relationship itself to this destruction that defines Africanness*. This is what Black dignity implies. The Africanness of the Black diaspora is neither a treasure forever lost, nor what may have survived ontological obliteration. It resides in its unique and singular way of experiencing the catastrophe, of living and engaging with it.

As I make clear in the final chapter, I find the most flawed argument of Afropessimism to be its insistence on the absolute unity of Black suffering. I think it is misguided to speak of the abject structural position of Black people as representing an absolute singularity or unprecedented intensity in modern ontology and history. I hold the Black experience of violence to be *absolutely comparable*. In other words, Black life's unceasing exposure to every order of social and political violence is precisely what makes it generalizable. It is what allows us to consider it in relation to a totality. A key argument of *Dignity or Death* is that only scrupulous attention to individual experience can lead to action or utterances that can be generalized. I hope this book will lead to multiple confrontations and encounters between singularities, for it is these encounters that serve as a prelude to ethical liberation and to the development of a new politics of necessity.

Part One

Dignity Re-embodied

We have experienced forced labor in exchange for pay that did not allow us to satisfy our hunger, to possess decent clothing and housing, or to raise our children as cherished beings.

Morning, noon, and night we were subjected to jeers, insults and beatings because we were "Negros." Who will ever forget that black people were addressed with "tu," not because they were friends, but because the polite "vous" was reserved for white people?

We have seen our lands seized in the name of ostensibly just laws, which recognized only the right of might.

We have not forgotten that the law was never the same for whites and blacks, that it was accommodating for the former and cruel and inhumane for the latter.

We have suffered the atrocity of imprisonment for political opinions or religious beliefs; exiled in our own country, our fate has been worse than death itself.

Patrice Lumumba, Speech of June 30, 1960[1]

— 1 —

DECOLONIZING MORAL PHILOSOPHY

The notion of dignity has a long history. Its story has mainly been the one Europe has wanted to tell about itself. In this first chapter, to better understand the origins of today's debates, I will look at some significant stages in this journey of the Western imagination. After a brief discussion of the classical and medieval origins of the term *dignitas*, attention will primarily be given to three philosophical conceptions of dignity: that of Giovanni Pico della Mirandola, Emmanuel Kant, and Jürgen Habermas. Each of these thinkers represents a key moment in Europe's imagined identity as a world power bearing the torch of the universal spirit: the humanism of the Renaissance for Pico della Mirandola, the German Enlightenment for Kant, and today's deliberative democracy for Habermas. Three fortresses of moral righteousness. These writers, and the periods they represent, were instrumental in creating a conception of the human that continues to underpin the Western understanding of ethics, law, and even common sense. Their writings thus shed ample light on how dignity is understood today: namely, as an apolitical, or pre-political, and supposedly neutral concept. This is in stark contrast to the way anticolonialist and antiracist movements have used it as a demand, a rallying cry, or as a critical tool in combating the injustices of our era. These movements expose the limits of the widespread understanding of dignity in the modern Western world. Its limits are being further exposed and called into question by our current situation, in which nation states of the Global North (where the concept of dignity was first formulated) continue to mire their racial "minorities," especially Afro-descendants, as well as those living in a neocolonial Global South, in structural violence. The work of these thinkers is best seen when set against other contemporaneous events: Pico della

Mirandola's in the context of the conquest of the Americas; Kant's ethics in juxtaposition to the appalling moral portrait the Prussian philosopher painted of Black Africans at the height of the slave trade; and Habermas's flawed notion of dignity alongside its reductive use by nation states that have laid claim to it.

Apologists of these canonical philosophers are quick to remind us that what may appear as racist judgments made by these "great thinkers" must be understood "in the context of their period" rather than evaluating them from an anachronistic "anticolonial" position. They lived at a time when, we must not forget, contempt for Native Americans and disdain for Africans were rather widespread. This argument has a basic flaw: it assumes as its primary context that of the bourgeoisie of western Europe, as though the only context available to us is that of white conquerors and the learned men who sympathized with them. There is no recognition that a global context, with multiple actors, is at issue, and that we might allow the perspective of indigenous populations or Black people to shape this context. Not only is it possible, but it may be incumbent on us, to situate philosophy in the context provided by slaves, specifically their demand for an all-encompassing humanity. At the end of the eighteenth century, while Kant was committing to paper his famous metaphysical musings in Königsberg, the freed slaves Ottobah Cugoano and Olaudah Equiano were publishing their philosophical autobiographies in Great Britain, where they outlined, with considerable insight and depth of thought, a new African humanism.

In order to undertake a systematic critique of Eurocentric definitions of dignity, two overlapping ideas call for close examination. The first is the notion of autonomy: the power to make one's own laws. This notion, closely tied to that of emancipation today, will be shown to harbor a darker side. Once seen in its greater colonial context, it becomes inseparable from the will to conquer and an anthropology of dominance. The second idea, which follows from this vision of autonomy, is that of "respect for others." However, in Kant, what passes for respect appears strikingly compatible with an affect that, from an Afro-decolonial perspective, could easily be seen as contempt. In European thought, from Pico della Mirandola to Kant, recognizing, on a superficial and formal level, the dignity of the "rabble," the "savage," and "the Black person" coexists with a deeper, truer, and more virulent animosity that these figures provoke. Contemporary understandings of dignity are still beset with this contradiction, despite the widespread adoption of this term in the legal statutes and constitutions of Western states. It is the very

Premodern *Dignitas*

The term *dignity* comes from the Latin *dignitas*. Although etymology can only tell us so much about the contemporary use of a term, the history of this concept does shed light on some aspects that would otherwise remain obscure. The Italian philosopher Giorgio Agamben has focused on the meaning given to this term in antiquity in many of his works. In particular, he discusses how it was defined in Roman law: "Already in the Republican era, the Latin term *dignitas* indicates the rank and authority that inhere in public duties as well as, by extension, those duties themselves."[1] For individuals belonging to the magistrature (consuls, prefects, senators, etc.), *dignitas* was their office. It was thus synonymous with social rank and authority. In other words, it conferred on individuals who held *dignitas* a certain power, but also duties relative to their social rank: their decisions, actions, and public image were to conform at all times with their dignity. One might say they had to keep rank.

In Agamben's interpretation, *dignitas* divides, so to speak, the life of its holders. On the one hand, they have their ordinary, daily lives, their lives of living human beings. On the other, they embody their social function, but this social function could also be embodied by someone else. Grievances are addressed to the consul *as* consul, which is to say as the possessor of a clear and precise duty, not as a singular individual. As the historian Ernst Kantorowicz has shown in his influential work, this remained the meaning of *dignitas* up until the medieval period, at which point it began to refer principally to a specific social position: that of the king, or, more precisely, his sovereignty. The proverbial expression *Dignitas non moritur* (dignity never dies) signifies that the social and political function of the sovereign doesn't disappear with the death of the individual who embodies it. "The king is dead, long live the king!" is how the succession of monarchs and the continuity of the royal figure used to be announced in France. This medieval conception therefore stressed at once the necessary continuation of *dignitas* and the division of the personality of its bearer as a mortal individual and an immortal king. "By maintaining the fictitious oneness of the predecessors with potential successors, all of whom were present and incorporated in the actual incumbent of the Dignity, the jurists constructed a fictitious person, a 'corporation by succession' composed of all those vested successively with that particular Dignity."[2] Acceding to a *dignitas*, individuals inherit those of their predecessors; they dress in the uniform of their office. The dignitary is thus the contingent holder of an immortal and necessary duty.

A final characteristic of the premodern *dignitas* worth noting was its use in maintaining hierarchy. In the Roman republic, magistratures held by senators, the dignities, were rigidly hierarchical. But, although *dignitas* included other factors that the state valued (such as personal virtues and merits), it was often evaluated by comparing two men. Thus, Roman *dignitas* was a matter of competition and a privilege, an aristocratic distinction. Equating royal dignity with sovereign power in the medieval period only accentuated its status-conferring power. In its premodern conception, then, dignity was a duty defined in strict opposition to those without, or with the least, dignity. In this respect, little changed in its modern conception.

Pico della Mirandola and the Deification of European Man

Although key components of its premodern understanding remained unchanged, the meaning of *dignitas* did undergo a shift during the Renaissance. Giovanni Pico della Mirandola's 1486 text, *Oratio de Hominis Dignitate*, known in English as *Oration on the Dignity of Man*, demonstrates a clear turning point in the understanding of this term. Pico's core idea is the following: humans were created by God as exceptional beings compared to the rest of the animal kingdom. In his argument, humans are born without predetermined qualities and are capable of self-fashioning. In essence, man has been granted the ability "to obtain what he desires and to be what he wills."[3] From this point on, human dignity would reside in individuals' unlimited power to fashion themselves and possess the world. But, following Agamben's lead, we might say that the title of Pico's text is misleading, since its content seems to contradict the received meaning of the term *dignitas*. Indeed, Pico's focus on the undetermined nature of humans appears to mark a radical departure from the premodern idea of dignity as social rank, or a codified and clearly defined standing: "The humanist discovery of man is the discovery that he lacks himself, the discovery of his irremediable lack of *dignitas*."[4] While the classical understanding of *dignitas* implies a restricted set of duties relating to a given magistracy, the humanist conception seems to free individuals from these responsibilities by inviting them

DECOLONIZING MORAL PHILOSOPHY

to become what they want to be and to seize whatever they'd like for themselves.

Although the extent of power he confers to humans is indeed without precedent, contrary to Agamben's argument, *Oration on the Dignity of Man* doesn't represent a rupture with premodern thought. Hierarchy and competition still govern his understanding of *dignitas* just as they did in the premodern conception. Pico's work is filled with tiers, degrees of elevation, and consequently various depths of abjection and indignity. And there is a pervasive hope that, through a deeper understanding of science and art, man can one day make himself the equal of God ("borne outside ourselves like ardent seraphim, filled with the godhead, we shall no longer be ourselves, but He Himself Who made us."[5]). The contribution of humanist thought isn't solely a matter of having placed man at the center of creation; it also put him in direct competition with the Creator. This rhetorical rise to divinity suggests that, as man ascends to omnipotence, he leaves behind the beings deemed unworthy [*indigne*] of ascension: "having been born into this condition; that is, born with the possibility to become what we wish to be, we must take the greatest care, lest people say of us that we, although held in high esteem, did not realize that we had turned ourselves into brutes and mindless beasts of burden."[6] Forced to choose between beast and god, this so-called humanist anthropology paradoxically ends up erasing the human from its reasoning, as though the only alternative was that between brutishness or omnipotence. Pitting the human against the inhuman, this new conception of dignity only accentuates the status-conferring power that defined premodern *dignitas*.

In Pico's view, the human soul itself is divided in this way, leaving no middle ground whatsoever for the ambiguities of humanity. He sees it divided between two natures: one turned toward the heavens, the other toward hell. This worldview, widespread during the Renaissance, fueled the conquest and colonization of the Americas (*Oration on the Dignity of Man* appeared less than a decade before the fateful date of 1492). It was what drove Alejo Venegas, the Spanish humanist, to advance a greatly influential, dualistic view of writing: there was writing that served as a vehicle for the words of God, and that which promulgated diabolic and creaturely ideas. The modes of writing, symbolizing, and transmitting knowledge unique to Native Americans were seen as a case of the latter.[7] The superior individual, standing apart from all others due to his mastery of the liberal arts, towers over the two figures of indignity, the beast of burden and the beast of the Apocalypse. By drawing a clear line

25

between divine humans and creaturely beings, Pico was unwittingly laying the anthropological groundwork for colonial and imperial Europe.

Pico's division between deities and demons is also expressed in his interest in magic. In spite of his insistence on reason being man's principal faculty, Pico pushes his heroic vision of the odyssey of the human spirit so far that he imagines man as a master of the occult. He pits white magic, which he describes as "the absolute perfection of natural philosophy" against black magic, which "is based entirely on the deeds and powers of demons (and is, in truth, an execrable and monstrous thing)."[8] Here too, Pico's position on this matter is emblematic of the worldview of his century. Indeed, one finds this view expressed in Shakespeare's *Tempest* in the opposition between Prospero the magician, and his slave Caliban. The playwright introduces Caliban as the son of Sycorax, a witch from Algiers who was banished from the city "for mischiefs manifold, and sorceries terrible to enter human hearing,"[9] and exiled on a distant island that Prospero would soon colonize. Shakespeare depicts Caliban as a telluric cave dweller who casts spells with the spirited magic of his master. The evil curses Caliban wishes to cast on his enslaver bear a striking resemblance to the chthonian incantations that cause Pico so much concern. "As wicked dew as e'er my mother brush'd / With raven's feather from unwholesome fen / Drop on you both! A southwest blow on ye, / And blister you all o'er!"[10] The occult powers of Sycorax and Caliban—the banished Maghrebin and the child stolen and shipped from Africa—derive directly from the filth-laden, disease-stricken South. Prospero's magic, on the other hand, as well as his defining features, represent the pinnacle values of humanism, which are also the pillars of the colonial worldview: the godly man's subjugation of nature to his own desires and the enslavement of savages, both of which pass as forms of civility, even nobility.

Colonial witchcraft is synonymous with domination. From Pico's white magic to Shakespeare's Prospero a single and unified conception of dignity is at issue. It is best represented by the notion of *autonomy*. The ideal man of the early modern period, the dignified man, pays little heed to his relations with others. He draws his strength only from himself. His ontological solitude is what allows him to show the extent of his power. Seizing lands and goods he believes rightfully his is a display of this. To achieve this level of appropriation, he transforms himself into an unparalleled master. In this respect, it is telling that Pico, for all his insistence on man's divine ascension, devotes more attention to self-fashioning and appropriation than creation.

This is no act of kenosis, with God withdrawing from the world he created to make his presence felt through his very absence. Quite the opposite: modern anthropology, in its deification of European man, is complicit in the old continent's vast enterprise of pillage and destruction, its project of colonial expansion. Colonial deification thrives by taking rather than making. For making—the act of creation—presupposes a separation from what one has created. But the godly man of the Renaissance cannot tolerate separation: all of the world must be his. Thus, contrary to what Agamben maintains, *dignitas*, in Pico's conception, hardly abandons its association with "rank." In fact, it only reinforces it by elevating European humanity to a divine rank. What's more, it envisions this humanity as a *causa sui*, a totality devoid of any alterity.

Kant: Dignity of Office and the Illusion of the Person

Eighteenth-century philosophy inherited its conception of autonomy from Renaissance humanism. This can be seen in Kant's attempt to pare it down and refine it. In his short essay "What Is Enlightenment?" he builds on Pico's reflection while stripping it of its religious sentiment. His conception of the mind's progress no longer depends on the divide between the demonic and the divine, but rather on that between minors and adults, which is to say humanity's state of dependence is set against its absolute independence. Those who borrow their thoughts from others are dependent, as are those who seek a doctor for medical care, or who grant too much credence to knowledge found in books, or who turn to a spiritual advisor for guidance. In short, he or she who counts on another is dependent. It isn't entirely lost on Kant that an underlying anthropological structure is at the origin of these behaviors, which, following Louis Bolk, we might call *human neoteny*. Indeed, as opposed to many other species, a human newborn enters the world as though always already premature: incapable of getting around, feeding itself, coping alone. Given this primordial dependence, providing the infant with a favorable social environment where it can receive constant attention from others is absolutely indispensable for its survival and development. In this respect, every human being must be adopted, and not necessarily by his or her own progenitors. Pico paid little heed to this fact and considered that humans come out of the womb, so to speak, fully autonomous. For his part, Kant didn't believe autonomy was granted to everyone at birth but rather that it was achieved in maturity. He considered that reaching adulthood marked a break from all the dependencies that allow a child to survive during its first years of life.

He likens the prolonged interdependent state of pre-adulthood to a sort of social pathology, defined principally by two emotional predispositions: laziness and cowardice. This is exploited by tyrants, leaders, and spiritual advisors to keep the masses in a state of subjugation. While this is self-evident in certain circumstances, such as with work that requires an obedient employee, the unreasonable expansion of restrictions on contractual work is condemned by Kant. He calls for a public space, a place where opinions can be freely shared, oriented toward the intellectual and moral progress of the political community. Passing into adulthood permits everyone to think for themselves, to make use of their own reason. Prior to this the human is reified, mechanized, dehumanized. Hence, the ultimate goal of the Enlightenment, according to Kant, is "to treat the human being, who is now more than a machine, in keeping with his dignity."[11]

From Pico to Kant, we witness the gradual shift in meaning of *dignitas*. Modern dignity is no longer a specific social office, profession, or magistrature. It is now a human magistrature, "unique to man"—though always envisioned, as we'll see shortly, from a Eurocentric point of view.[12] In his moral philosophy Kant attempts to elevate this notion to the heights of metaphysics. In *Groundwork of the Metaphysic of Morals*, he defines dignity as the property of that which possesses a value in itself, and not only a relative value in the manner of exchangeable goods. What "has a price can be replaced by something else as its *equivalent*; what on the other hand is raised above all price and therefore admits of no equivalent has a dignity."[13] And according to this theory, what has its own value is the human person. If commodities have a price, these reasonable beings have a dignity.[14]

For Kant, dignity is a function of autonomy. Indeed, only those bound by no other legislation than that of their own reason are truly autonomous. They owe nothing to tutelage, to the opinion of others, or even to their own experience and predispositions. As rational— which is to say, moral—beings, humans bear within themselves eternal laws that can alone govern their conduct. These are not the same as social laws that govern customs and traditions. Nor are they customs created or adapted by certain groups over time. It is an ahistorical moral law decreed by reason alone, since this law derives from the principle of noncontradiction. In this respect, the laws of

Kant's ethics are less like laws in the legal sense of the term—codified, amended, or overturned by jurisprudence—than laws of nature that are absolute and necessary. By this measure, the immorality of lying or stealing belongs to the same regime of validation as the boiling or freezing point of water. According to Kantian morality, an action isn't wrong because it is uncustomary or causes suffering. It is wrong only insofar as it is irrational or contradicts reason. For example, the thief who takes someone else's belongings denies through his action the very idea of possession: for possession to mean anything an object must *belong to someone*. As a result, the thief's action is self-contradictory and self-destructive insofar as it denies the idea of possession (by depriving others of their property). But it also reinforces the idea of possession by claiming to appropriate the desired object. This presents a contradiction in terms. According to Kant, one can't feel the desire to possess and also the lack of this desire at the same time. In other words, a reasonable being can't desire to possess something for himself alone and deny this desire on the part of his reasonable neighbor. Similarly, a promise would be devoid of meaning and purpose without the moral obligation to keep it, and so on. Any immoral act is by definition contradictory.

Man's ability to grasp this law, this principle of noncontradiction which is the basis of his own reason, is what allows for his autonomy. If human beings who reach adulthood are no longer in need of spiritual advisors, it's because they know themselves to be bearers of an eternal law and believe they need only follow it to act morally. The role of education then is not to teach them morality, but to help them to discover it, to reveal to them their own rationality. In this Kantian conception, all autonomous, that is, rational, beings, or those wishing to be, are endowed with dignity. In short, autonomy is man's innate possibility to act according to moral law; and his dignity derives from his being recognized and treated as a moral being. Autonomy and dignity are the two main features of what Kantians call "personhood": the abstract, ordinary individual, stripped of any singular qualities and reduced to a bearer of moral law. As the Kantian Éric Fiat explains, "respect isn't directed at any particular quality of myself. It is directed at me because the moral law is found within me. In no way is it an approval of my individual qualities— that is what goes by the name of love."[15] As Agamben notes, this idea more than any other connects Kant's conception of dignity to its premodern understanding. "Both in the case of legal *dignitas* and in its moral transposition, dignity is something autonomous with respect to the existence of its bearer, an interior model or an external image to which he must conform and which must be preserved at all costs."[16] For Kant, respecting the dignity of others means respecting this distinct abstraction. Kant's personhood idealizes a fully rational conduct that is mapped onto a real individual. It is precisely this sort of abstraction that invites an Afro-decolonial critique of Kant's philosophy, which becomes all the more urgent in light of his comments about Africans. Formal respect for the abstract person isn't incompatible with genuine loathing of the real human being. It is worth investigating how this cunning hypocrisy, this pseudo respect, came to be considered, and continues to be considered, the peak of moral philosophy—the most just and rigorous ethics created by modern thought.

A Disembodied Ethics

In his last work, *The Wretched of the Earth*, Frantz Fanon calls into question the Kantian morality just described, in particular the conception of dignity that underlies it:

> For a colonized people the most essential value, because the most meaningful, is first and foremost the land: the land, which must provide bread and, naturally, dignity. But this dignity has nothing to do with the dignity of the "human person." The colonized subject has never heard of such an ideal. All he has ever seen on his land is that he can be arrested, beaten, and starved with impunity.[17]

Fanon critiques the Kantian conception of personhood for its lack of concreteness and its tendency to ignore the real violence afflicting social life. In so doing, he exposes the limits of a disembodied conception of ethics, one that fails to account for the variety of human experience, its precarity, its affiliations. For Fanon, dignity means nothing if it fails to address the being who suffers or if it doesn't identify the causes of suffering and put an end to them. In this respect, the idea of "human person" seems wholly inadequate, as it neglects social relations and the lived experience of the individual. Fanon warns against equating morality with rationalism. Held up as an absolute rule, the principal of noncontradiction excludes the existence of those—such as slaves and their descendants—whose lives are fraught with contradictions that they have no choice but to confront. The laws of reason aren't the same in a racist world as they are in a world without strife. Each relies on a different moral compass. In reality, we are dealing with a world where a slave deciding "to use his own fingernails to rip open his throat was an entirely rational response to landing on a slave ship."[18] A world where the only concern the slaveholder has over the death of a Black slave is his return on his investment. Under the pressure of extreme situations, filled with brutal and daily violence, logic buckles. In these cases, the autonomy of reason, its independence from the voice and actions of the oppressed, doesn't represent the pinnacle of human dignity but rather the cruel indifference of the masters.

It is true that by virtue of his conception of morality, and the distinction it draws between value and dignity (between what can be purchased and what is invaluable), Kant was by necessity an opponent of the slavery of his time: a man or woman, he claimed, could not be for sale. But the divide between the juridical-moral "person" and the real individual—a divide Fanon criticized—pushed Kant to side with abolitionists *despite* his feelings about Black people. In his view, Black people are humans *in spite of everything*. They are reasonable beings *regardless of* their intrinsic abjection. Kant was an early example of the liberal racists who, "out of principle," were opposed to slavery, lynching, and anti-Black violence of all kinds, but who made no effort to hide their deep-seated racial hatred—as long as it had the veneer of scientific truth. Kant is by no means an isolated example. Frederick Douglass called attention to this same attitude among abolitionists in 1856: "Opposing slavery and hating its victims has come to be a very common form of abolitionism."[19]

Influenced by David Hume, Kant viewed Africans as innately inferior beings. In his *Observations on the Feeling of the Beautiful and Sublime*, he writes: "The Negroes of Africa have by nature no feeling that rises above the ridiculous. [...] While among the whites there are always those who rise up from the lowest rabble and through extraordinary gifts earn respect in the world. So essential is the difference between these two human kinds, and it seems to be just as great with regard to the capacities of mind as it is with respect to color."[20] Elaborating on these thoughts in his *Geography*, Kant depicts Africans again as shameless thieves with religious practices as absurd as they are cruel. In his view, they are filthy and licentious savages whose stench he repeatedly imagines to be revolting. In short, his thoughts about the Black continent are summed up in his comments about the Cafres, whom he says "are not only horrendous, but [...] as misshapen and wicked as the other Negroes."[21] Forever the armchair philosopher, he adds in his essay on the "Different Human Races": "the Negro is produced, well-suited to his climate;

that is, strong, fleshy, supple, but in the midst of the bountiful provision of his motherland lazy, soft and dawdling."[22] And, as noted above, laziness is the opposite of autonomy, as surely as wickedness is the opposite of morality. In Kant's view, the African is thus by nature at the other extreme of what constitutes a moral disposition.[23] This mindless, repulsive, and morally deprived being must be treated, in spite of one's feelings, more or less humanely, for the sole reason that the law of morality requires it.

For Enlightenment philosophers, it is only once this anthropological abjection has been bracketed that the purity of the abstract "person," humanity's neutral substratum, can be discovered in the African. Recognizing the African's dignity entails negating the abhorrent image created by the European gaze: one can have dignity *in spite of* being African, which is to say, slow-witted, foul-smelling, dishonest, violent, and lazy. However, by itself, being Black doesn't make one worthy of dignity. The contradiction between African and "person" couldn't be starker. The whole social life of Africans, their beliefs and rituals, are subject to ridicule; but their status as "persons," their belonging to humanity, is grudgingly acknowledged insofar as all of their defining qualities are ignored. Kant's conception of dignity demonstrates an effort to move past the racial loathing that made slavery possible without ever questioning the very validity of this loathing. This moral position sets the purity of the "person," which seems to dwell within Africans, against the impurity of their own lives. But it is also in the name of dignity of the "person" that Europeans judged the lives of Africans abject. This conception of dignity helped legitimize Europe's *mission civilisatrice* and its wish to abolish the aberrant ways of Africans. "Respect yourselves," they were told. "Behave like civilized people." Black people regularly contradicted human dignity just by being themselves. And so the "person" must eradicate any trace of Blackness. Prospero the Pure must eliminate Caliban and his unholy—and characteristically Black—penchant for magic.[24] For all his trumpeting of the principle of noncontradiction, Kant's approach toward dignity attests to an existential contradiction inflicted upon Africans, who suffered a vital division during the time of the slave trade. And this division was imposed even by abolitionists themselves. This kind of paternalistic ethics judges itself not by any real consequences, which is to say, by the useless suffering and injustices it helps to alleviate or prevent, but only by the degree of self-satisfaction it provides. Kant's morality is never inspired by blatant displays of injustice, but only by the discovery of the moral law itself, before which one stands in awe.

Kant's approach isn't the only one to indulge in this sort of moral onanism.

Today, Kant's ethics are often portrayed as rigid, cold, implacable. Even to save lives, even to save a dear friend pursued for no reason by assassins by hiding him in your house, this morality forbids lying in any way. Kant was well aware of his morality's unbending stance. This is why, in spite of the law's severity, at times "we take the liberty of making an *exception* to it for ourselves (or just for this once) to the advantage of our inclination."[25] Herein lies the paradox of Kantian moral philosophy concerning the question of race. Allowing for such an exception, that is, being exempt from the moral law, is tantamount to submitting to evil. But, at the same time, when it comes to Black people, beings whose abjection is exceptional, even quasi-transcendental, there could hardly be a more legitimate reason for such an exception. The dissonance created between a disembodied morality, a demeaning view of Africans, and the right to an exception lays the groundwork for a theory of racist exoneration. This is how it presents itself: any well-meaning person will readily grant that Black people are "persons" in the Kantian sense of the term, which is to say ordinary human beings deserving to be treated as such. But your everyday racist will also allow that, given their frightening appearance, their behavior, their history and ways, the repulsion or fear they provoke, the Black man sometimes all but forces any good citizen to make an exception, to avoid treating him as morality would require since he doesn't look or act like a person truly worthy of dignity. A striking example of this can be seen in the testimony of Darren Wilson, the Ferguson police officer who had to justify murdering an eighteen-year-old Black man—Michael Brown— before a grand jury. This testimony, along with help from some overly lenient judges, was enough to exonerate him. He described Mike Brown as a sort of monster, a "grunting demon" with superhuman strength, more beast than man.[26] Killing is justified by the white man's seemingly natural contempt for the nonwhite person. The Black man's monstrosity is such that it allows for exceptions to the law and to morality. The Black man's killer can be forgiven for his act: he didn't neglect his duty toward the person, but he was driven by the circumstances to make an "exception." Of course, Mike Brown possessed dignity as a "person." But when a bullet is fired into his body, this dignity momentarily fades before the existential indignity of race. The young man died with his arms up in a gesture of surrender.

In the end, it is Officer Wilson's dignity that is respected rather than Mike Brown's. Wilson emphasizes his own dignity by publicly presenting his murder of Brown as an act of self-sacrifice and courage. An Afro-decolonial ethics seeks to break with this moral tradition that continues to consider Black people as part of humanity *in spite of everything*, that continues to accord them a certain dignity in spite of their lack of intelligence, in spite of their savage nature. Humans in spite of the abjection, terror, or contempt they elicit; humans who must be treated as "persons" in spite of their stench and ugliness. Humans for whom, gun in hand, one is free to make an exception even as they have their back turned. Kant sought to moralize the deification of Western man in the humanist anthropology of Pico and his contemporaries by curtailing this godly man's power. All he could do was find excuses for his own moral failings. In both cases we witness the moral legacy of a racist vision of the world, a vision that becomes crystallized in the European—or, more precisely, Eurocentric—conception of dignity.

From the Nationalization of Dignity to Ethical Conflicts

European moral philosophy tends to focus on ahistorical ethical questions. To consider dignity as an abstract property detached from experience and context and set apart from the violence and dangers that plague existence is a case in point of this deeply entrenched habit of modern thought. While Kant remains the most emblematic figure of this tendency, the German philosopher Jürgen Habermas has proven to be, in many respects, his twenty-first–century successor. This is most patently displayed in his article "The Concept of Human Dignity and the Realistic Utopia of Human Rights." The argument he advances aims to strike a balance between Kant's norm-based morality and that adopted by his critics, such as Fanon. He evokes his earlier work where he defined dignity as existing in a perfect middle ground between its premodern conception, which is too narrowly conceived, and Kantian rationalism, which too readily overlooks the fact that dignity is "embedded in concrete forms of life and their ethos."[27] However, despite his wish to account for social suffering and to move away from Kant's tendency toward abstraction, his approach falls into the same abstract logic as Kant's by relying on a legal framework. His theory thus stands as a telling example of the next stage of dignity's historical depoliticization through its nationalization. In Habermas, dignity is exclusively defined by the legal norms and statutes of European nations.

Indeed, Habermas repeatedly points to the postwar adoption of the term *dignity* in many nation states' constitutions as part of a political strategy to stave off another global conflict like World War Two. However, throughout his discussion, Habermas makes no distinction between the legal definition of this term and its use by activists. From his perspective, if activists take up this term, they are drawing directly on its legal understanding, just as their ideals are modeled by the state. Demanding dignity, then, is always done in the language of power. Habermas ignores the very means by which dignity is demanded, and thus remains oblivious to its force and urgency. There is little reason, though, to assume that the dignity demanded by activists is the same as the one codified in a legal framework. Habermas's argument falters under his belief that morality—which gives meaning to the notion of dignity—seemingly stands outside of conflict, and that the only goal of social and political struggle is to codify morality in law, allowing particular cases to be absorbed into the working order of modern democratic states. In other words, in Habermas's view, activists' demands for dignity cannot confront the current law head-on, but only highlight its shortcomings or imperfections, with the aim of making progress possible.

> The experience of the violation of human dignity fulfils an inventive function in many cases, be it in view of the unbearable social conditions and the marginalization of impoverished social classes, or in view of the unequal treatment of women and men in the workplace or of discrimination against foreigners and against cultural, linguistic, religious and racial minorities, or in view of the ordeal of young women from immigrant families who have to liberate themselves from the violence of a traditional code of honour, or in view of the brutal expulsion of illegal immigrants and asylum seekers. In the light of historical challenges, *different* aspects of the meaning of human dignity acquire urgency and relevance in each case. These features of human dignity specified and actualized on different occasions can then lead both to a more complete exhaustion of the normative substance of existing civil rights and to the discovery and construction of *new* ones.[28]

This rehearsal of cable news talking points robs the notion of dignity of its historicity in two ways. First, by indiscriminately juxtaposing incompatible situations of indignity; then, by adopting an external point of view in order to explain how these experiences should be interpreted and, above all, addressed. In effect, Habermas places state violence that targets minorities—regardless of their legal status—on the same level as supposed misogynistic traditions, which we can safely assume are nonwhite. The former are cloaked in the euphemisms of "discrimination" and "cruelty"; the latter, unabashedly described as "torment" and "violence," are cast in a harsher light. Habermas belongs to an intellectual tradition that sees Black men, and more generally nonwhite men, as virile, patriarchal beasts who, in the minds of these intellectuals, represent a "depository of negativity."[29]

By juxtaposing contradictory interests, in which non-Europeans are in turn the victims of minor abuses and the cruelest of executioners, Habermas depoliticizes the concept of dignity. He ends this tally by instructing his readers that laws such as those enacted by European liberal democracies are what is needed to remedy these problems. The state becomes the neutral arbiter through which all conflicts are resolved. Habermas goes on to define *dignity* as the bridge that links morality (in the sense of behavioral norms) and law. In this way, the presumed universal and egalitarian matter of morality finds expression in positive law. Thus, the only trace of historicity that can be found in Habermas is his admission that ahistorical moral norms such as Kant's should be turned into laws, thereby creating a sort of legal history. From an Afro-decolonial approach, dignity, rooted in its historicity, is what binds ethics to politics, not law. And this approach could never subscribe to Habermas's giddy embrace of liberal democracy, under which Michael Brown, George Floyd, and countless others have been—and will continue to be—killed.

The Western history of the concept of dignity is one of avoidance tactics devised to divert attention away from human suffering and, above all, its social causes. Whether by conjuring an abstract "person" or by advocating for the monopolization of dignity by the state, no one wants to admit that the blood of history's victims is on their hands. In strict opposition to the approaches outlined above, a theory of Black dignity adopts by necessity a relational ethics grounded in history. But for such a theory to be viable, it must take care to avoid indulging in the sort of naïve historicism that grants each period its own moral standards, which ultimately amounts to a dressed-up relativism. In reality, each period isn't characterized by an ethics, but by *ethical conflicts*. An ethical conflict arises when the moral standards of a group have the effect of establishing, consolidating, or rendering imperceptible the domination, control, or power of some of its members over others—whether through negligence, omission, or deliberate action. In such situations, individuals relegated to a subaltern position by this dominant morality can no longer abide by its rules. As a result, the oppressed are forced to counter the ethics that is hostile to them by imposing their own.

Habermas expresses as much when he writes that "'Human dignity' performs the function of a seismograph that registers what is constitutive for a democratic legal order—namely, just those rights that the citizens of a political community must grant themselves if they are to be able to respect one another as members of a voluntary association of free and equal persons."[30] In his view, the experience of indignity only reveals the intrinsic value and perfectibility of the model of liberal democracy. In other words, demanding dignity for myself compels me to subscribe to this model, which is to say, to keep it at a distance from both myself and the violence I am subjected to. Dignity is thus not conceived as *a* property (which is to say, a characteristic) of oppressed individuals, but rather as *the* property (the possession, the product) of Western democracies. An ethical conflict is being staged, then, between those, such as Habermas, who consider the model of modern liberal democracy to be the most conducive for honoring dignity, and those who feel threatened by the model itself, who even regard it as criminal. The assumption that the European democratic model is virtuous and desirable ignores the violence that takes place in its name. What's more, the widespread adoption of the notion of dignity as a legal right in modern states serves only to blunt its force and stifle its potential to galvanize and mobilize the oppressed. The legislative case for dignity and the one made by rioters hardly refer to the same notion; two distinct concepts are at play, as are the ways of living they imply. For his part, Habermas does concede that "human rights are the product of violent and at times revolutionary struggles for recognition."[31] But he always separates these struggles from the dignity they are demanding. He sees these struggles as a necessary step toward state recognition rather than as an immanent expression of dignity. The latter is naturally tied to "the legitimate claim of marginalized and underprivileged sections of the population who want to be included in liberal social conditions."[32] But it would be more accurate to see these struggles as a rejection of the dark side of the "liberal social conditions,"[33] namely, the ravage and violence of imperial states that impose these conditions.

From Pico to Kant and Habermas, ethics is stripped of its historicity as well as its conflictual tension. In contrast, the ethics I'm advocating for here accounts for its own position in relation to these various conflicts. It also engages with, and expresses, its own historicity. Much is to be gained from studying and describing the world and lived experiences in which an ethical discourse is rooted, especially since this discourse is a manifestation of political engagement. In the Afro-decolonial ethics I am proposing, the experiences of racial dehumanization play a decisive role. It is only by bringing this dehumanization into focus, by attending to its affective register, and by seeking to understand the necessity of the revolts provoked in response to it, that we may hear what slaves, colonized peoples, and their descendants mean when, staring down their oppressors, they demand dignity.

— 2 —

INDIGNITY

The question of dignity always arises in the face of humiliation or insult, the threat of violence, or the specter of death. In other words, dignity becomes a matter of consideration as soon as one is deprived of it. Indignity logically precedes the conceptualization of dignity: negative experiences and attacks on vulnerable existences bring dignity to light and make it tangible. This chapter will trace and describe the affective and conceptual shift that takes place as one passes from enduring indignity to demanding dignity. To be clear, even liberal thinkers, Habermas among them, readily recognize human finitude and vulnerability as constituting the foundation of dignity.[1] But, rather than settling for mere recognition—as is the case with these thinkers—an Afro-decolonial approach interrogates the consequence of this foundation: namely, that *dignity can only be fully grasped from the perspective of the oppressed, which is to say, the most vulnerable humans of any society.*

To see this at play, I will turn to the experience of slavery and the transatlantic slave trade, both of which continue to haunt our contemporary moment. This experience will be treated as paradigmatic. A serious assessment of this history—and the accounts made of it by the oppressed—necessarily calls into question the dominant forms of social critique. Emancipated slaves and Afro-descendant thinkers invented new forms of writing and discursive practices, mixing philosophy, autobiography, and theological-political reflection to address their unprecedented conditions. This writing will be the focus of this chapter. Understanding this writing as it was lived and experienced in history requires two simultaneous theoretical operations, which may appear contradictory at first glance. The first is a matter of drawing a distinction: namely, singling out specific forms of racist

39

political violence by isolating them from other historical models of repression and cruelty. The second, on the other hand, draws parallels, identifying a relative consistency in the way racial violence—and the epistemology that justifies it—has operated across historical periods and settings. The concept of indignity gives expression to this family resemblance, this continuity of experience among victims spanning colonial, neocolonial, and postcolonial contexts.

But as I make this case, I am reminded of Frantz Fanon's remarks in *Black Skin, White Masks*: "I am a black man, and tons of chains, squalls of lashes, and rivers of spit stream over my shoulders. But I have not the right to put down roots. I have not the right to admit the slightest patch of being into my existence. I have not the right to become mired in the determinations of the past. *I am not a slave to slavery that dehumanized my ancestors.*"[2] This could be interpreted to be at odds with my project here. Those who look down on Black people and their history read—and will continue to read—this passage as an invitation to let bygones be bygones, to leave behind a painful past that will only mire Afro-descendants in resentment. But this couldn't be further from the point Fanon is making. One can hardly be liberated from haunting memories and emotional strife by ignoring their causes and suppressing their effects. On the contrary, liberation is the result of anamnesis and of acting upon one's knowledge. One stops being a slave to slavery by knowing it inside and out, by understanding the inner workings of its bloodstained, gruesome machinery. It is by identifying what makes the demands for dignity among slaves still feel so urgent today, in spite of the major historical changes we have since endured. It is only by being aware of this memory and of what it has bequeathed to the present that a liberation from slavery can be realized. In other words, avoiding becoming "mired in the determinations of the past" isn't a decision one can simply choose to make as an act of free will. It takes a united front of intellectual, social, and political forces, all acting together to bring about a decolonized world.

The aim of this approach isn't only to formulate a notion of indignity by drawing on the voices of the oppressed. It is also to debunk the commonplaces propagated by the social sciences and contemporary philosophy which, like faulty evidence, prevent us from thinking through colonial difference and the specificities of racial experience. Although race isn't central in their respective works, Hannah Arendt and Michel Foucault are two philosophers whose thinking has had a major impact on theories of racism. And for this reason, they stand in the way of achieving a more careful understanding of racism by contemporary critical theory. It is time to leave aside a conceptual framework built around the mass violence tied to the genocides of the twentieth century—a major occupation for these two thinkers and their followers—and turn to the everyday suffering of indignity where the distinction between life and death has become profoundly blurred.

Writing a Life of Indignity: An Epistemology

According to Gilles Deleuze, the act of thinking always springs from a violence suffered, from a disturbance that interrupts the continuity of everyday life from the outside, arousing reflection from its "natural stupor."[3] This is perhaps nowhere truer than in the autobiographical accounts of slaves whose lives were interrupted in the most abrupt and cruel way imaginable: by being stolen and wrenched away from everything that defined their lives. But it is worth pointing out that if violence compels the mind to think about its current situation, it also, at the same time, prevents it from doing so. Extreme violence is paralyzing and stupefying. It rattles thought and disturbs the senses, depriving them of the calm needed for reflection. Slave narratives always convey this: they are accounts of extreme violence made in retrospect, expressing both the need for reckoning and the impossibility of doing so. It is as though reflecting back on this moment allows one to recover dignity, a dignity discovered in the firsthand experience of indignity, which is to say, in the stupor caused by enslavement. To take on a life of indignity in writing, one has to experience it and know it intimately. But this haunting experience must be in the past tense, at a slight remove from the present, which otherwise could never bear its weight. Ottobah Cugoano's account is exemplary in this regard:

> The grievous thoughts which I then felt, still pant in my heart; though my fears and tears have long since subsided. And yet it is still grievous to think that thousands more have suffered in similar and greater distress, under the hands of barbarous robbers, and merciless taskmasters; and that many even now are suffering in all the extreme bitterness of grief and woe, that no language can describe. The cries of some, and the sight of their misery, may be seen and heard afar; but the deep sounding groans of thousands, and the great sadness of their misery and woe, under the heavy load of oppressions and calamities inflicted upon them, are such as can only be distinctly known to the ears of Jehovah Sabaoth. [...] Thus seeing my companions and

DIGNITY RE-EMBODIED

countrymen in this pitiful, distressed and horrible situation, with all the brutish baseness and barbarity attending it, could not but fill my mind with horror and indignation.[4]

The slave is a paradigmatic figure of indignity. The slave's cry gives voice simultaneously to dissent, indignation, and reflection, but through its very expression this voice remains inaudible. Slave narratives strive to render this cry, which is provoked by the conditions of indignity. The stories and autobiographical accounts of Black slaves from the eighteenth and nineteenth centuries emerge from a world where the harshest servitude was the norm and where keeping captives in terror and ignorance was, in the eyes of the masters, an indispensable form of control. The mere fact that some slaves were not only able to escape their shackles but also acquire enough education to put their stories down on paper is, needless to say, no small feat. But the admiration that this heroic effort elicits is frequently undermined by a patronizing attitude toward the slave's intellectual capabilities. Historically this writing was primarily fueled by abolitionist movements to sway public opinion and advance their own cause (some members of these movements recorded and transcribed the stories of illiterate slaves). Slaveholders defended themselves against the damning portrayal of plantations these testimonies painted for the larger public and contested their authenticity.[5] For the contemporary reader, however, this writing appears devoid of any political stakes, serving only as a valuable resource for scholars. Framing them as autobiographies also causes them to be read as tales of heroic deeds rather than as significant contributions to theoretical and philosophical debates. This is what unites the abolitionists of yesteryear with the well-educated public of today: they both have a utilitarian relationship to these texts and share the false assumption that testimony is incompatible with philosophical thought. After all, what could the white scholar learn from Blacks with only the lowest level of education, apart from a few picturesque details and some historical curiosities? Putting these commonplaces behind us, a more probing and meaningful consideration can be gained by adopting a geopolitics of knowledge.

There is no *epistemological point zero* in slave narratives as there is in the dominant work of European philosophy and social sciences. In other words, there is no "point of view that hides and conceals itself as being beyond a particular point of view, that is, the point of view that represents itself as being without a point of view."[6] Slave narratives are not under the illusion of objectivity. Rather, they possess a knowledge and a way of thinking that involves the writers' bodies, experiences, and geohistorical situation. As Walter Mignolo puts it: "Our being and our sensibility—I am there where I think—is rooted in the place where we think."[7] This isn't a matter of pointing to a place on a map or tracing a correlation between thought and geographic location, but rather of identifying a position among the play of racial, economic, and political forces and of understanding how one is affected by the power dynamic between what is often referred to today as the Global North and the Global South. This sheds new light on a body of writing that expresses the experience of servitude. No longer is this writing a mere vehicle for communicating an uncontested set of facts and curiosities, albeit in imperfect form. Instead, these slave narratives, these hybrid texts that defy classification, can serve as guides for reimagining how social philosophy might be written today. Foregrounding the author's experience, drawing on a wide range of registers, adopting a perspective from the dark side of modernity—all of these can serve to expand thought rather than be glossed over as deficiencies or oddities.

The challenge is to learn how to appreciate in this writing what only appear as shortcomings from the Eurocentric perspective of an epistemological point zero: its lack of objectivity, methodological rigor, theoretical self-reflection, and so on. A certain sophistry underlying the official ideology of Western social sciences admits as a matter of course that a dry, descriptive, impartial style is needed to achieve universal communication, a style in the mold of the natural sciences which is as devoid of literary value as it is of conceptual import. From this perspective, Ottobah Cugoano's manner of blending autobiographical details, impassioned disquisitions, theological arguments, and philosophical speculation violates every tenet held by today's social sciences. Cugoano's writing is seen as an artifact for the historian or the academic theorist, but surely not as a relevant statement on today's state of affairs or a model to be emulated. Paring down language to a set of recognizable protocols— i.e., limiting its function to an expository presentation of facts—is supposed to make it more accessible to a wider audience and facilitate dialogue. Slave narratives—and more generally the entire history of Black social critique—prove, on the contrary, that bringing into play a diverse and unrestrained set of registers and modes of thought (philosophical, poetic, novelistic, theological, militant, or scientific) is a rational decision with more universal appeal. This is because such a discursive practice reveals human existence in all its ambivalence as opposed to serving only an instrumental rationality. And it has the potential to impact readers in all aspects of their being: informing them but also moving them, giving rise to knowledge at the same time as anger, provoking reflection as well as religious sentiment. The most universalizing discourse is not the most pared-down one, but one that refuses to limit itself to a narrow, rigid, and caricatural vision of rationality. Only then can it address the entire human being.

Scholars in the humanities and social sciences in Western Europe and North America are thus grossly mistaken when they assume that the empiricism, realism, and positivism they practice regularly constitute a universally accepted body of knowledge from which any speculative endeavors are by necessity excluded. As the anthropologists Jean and John Comaroff rightly point out, "For the global south, the refusal of theory has long been an unaffordable luxury."[8] The same holds true for minorities in the Global North. These methods, which seek to hem in discourse rather than expand it, reinforce the intellectual, economic, and political dominance of the North over the South. They are worthless for those who strive to express the inexpressible, who seek to imagine another social order rather than describe, imitate, and bolster the status quo. Dignity is at the core of this Afro-decolonial approach to writing theory.

Indeed, for slaves, dignity was the driving, though invisible, force behind their struggle, their thinking, and their writing. Before any definition of dignity, before it can even be conceptualized, this is how it acts in practice and produces its effects. The writing of slaves presents the first Afro-descendant demand for dignity expressed in print in the modern era. It is a translation into European languages of long-fought struggles and rebellions.[9] This offers a clear advantage. As this writing bears witness in vestigial form to these struggles, and the political thought that propelled them, one can bypass the second-hand accounts of historians altogether. These texts intertwine philosophical meditation and testimony. And, as we saw with Kant, there is no place for the first-person philosopher in European moral philosophy. Such a perspective defies the protocols of point zero epistemology, which perhaps explains why European philosophers have shown no interest in this writing. It is hard to overstate the importance of this perspective in the history of abolitionist and anti-slavery struggles and the demand for Black dignity. Needless to say, the attention it deserves is long overdue.

The fact that the slave trade is now a matter of the past is a poor reason to become indifferent to it. Olaudah Equiano's conflicted feelings expressed at the beginning of his autobiography from 1788 speak as much to our current moment and the Black intellectual's place within it as anything written since: "did I consider myself an European I might say my sufferings were great: but when I compare my lot with that of most of my countrymen, I regard myself as a particular favourite of Heaven, and acknowledge the mercies of Providence in every occurrence of my life."[10] Equiano was a slave, but he acknowledges throughout his account that he was lucky in his misfortune, that his journey was incomparably happier than that of many Black people of his time. But he also notes that the racial position of white people always prevented them from experiencing the suffering he had to endure. Measured against the Black condition, Equiano was privileged; but when measured against the European condition, he was cursed. This intermediary position is precisely what makes an Afro-decolonial social philosophy possible. It is where the necessity of thinking through and expressing indignity coincides with the material conditions that allow one to do so. One must no longer be in a state of servitude, under duress, or threatened by severe violence in order to speak up. But for one's words to be meaningful and truthful, it is necessary to have been—or potentially be—the target of this cruelty. There is a sort of existential solidarity one must adopt which stems from the awareness of a relative interchangeability of respective situations. This keeps one from becoming apathic.

Borrowing W.E.B. Du Bois's concept of double consciousness, Paul Gilroy speaks of the difficulty of calling oneself both Black and European at a time when these two identities are defined in political discourse as mutually exclusive.[11] Lacking a clear place and denied legitimacy, the double consciousness of Black Europeans struggles to express itself. What Equiano shows is that not only does this double consciousness point to a divided and wounded state that prevents one from fully inhabiting the world, but it also gives one a mission. Make no mistake, the emancipated, having made it out of the most brutal submission, can use their new position to serve their own interests at the expense of their own people. They can subscribe to the narrative of an advanced European civilization and see themselves as superior "evolved" beings. But the emancipateds' new condition can also serve as a portal between worlds, allowing them to lend voice to an otherwise silent Black suffering and Black consciousness. The emancipated are not exceptional beings. They are simply those who can speak, write, and make themselves heard; those who continue to feel the weight of indignity, but are not overwhelmed by this and can think through it. "Let the groans and cries of the murdered, and the cruel slavery of the Africans tell!"[12] Cugoano cries out. A century later, Du Bois would look at how the free Black man laid the groundwork for abolition through his cultural practices. "His religion became darker and more intense, and into his ethics crept a note of revenge, into his songs a day of reckoning close at hand. The 'Coming of the Lord' swept this side of Death, and came to be a thing to be hoped for in this day. Through fugitive slaves and irrepressible discussion this desire for freedom seized the black millions still in bondage, and became their one ideal of life."[13] This triumphant narrative of the free Black man who, after discovering the rising sun of freedom, descends back into the dungeon to bring the good news to his people, reads like Plato's allegory. Du Bois exaggerates the prophetic role of the "free Black man," which is almost a contradiction in terms given the precarity and revocability of his newfound status.[14] Du Bois gives in to the tendency to romanticize this figure as privileged, but he does rightly call attention to his role as a cultural messenger, which, in this case, is expressed through religion.

As Charles T. Davis and Henry Louis Gates Jr. have shown, the act of writing offered former slaves a way out of the zone of nonbeing. It allowed them to bear witness to their irrefutable humanity, providing an opportunity to display the existence of their reason, which had been denied them for so long.[15] But it would be wrong to limit the testimony of slaves to this function alone. Their undertaking also represents a riskier and more complex endeavor: that of expressing the fundamental inhumanity and racism of modern white civilization and its systemic production of indignity. Without this effort, Black speech cannot be heard.

The Hidden Horror of Colonialism: A Memory

Slave narratives attest to the vital importance of memory. The need to never forget infuses their accounts. These writers strive to remember their African childhood—if they had one—but also the details of their capture, deportation, imprisonment, or liberation. Everything must be said, recovered, repeated. And this very desire to remember seems inextricable from the conditions of servitude. In his seminal study of different institutionalized practices of slavery throughout history, the sociologist Orlando Patterson notes that the slave's condition is characterized by possessing a past while being deprived of the right to remember, to belong to a community and to a particular cultural lineage.[16] Natally alienated, slaves have a past, a history, but they have no *right* to that past. They have to erase everything that binds them to their pre-capture existence. The testimony of freed slaves is thus of supreme importance, as it not only has an immediate political impact, but also provides a model for demanding dignity by collectively reclaiming memory. Telling Afro-descendants to stop "bemoaning" and "agonizing over" a past marked by racial dehumanization belongs to a slaveholder tradition of forcing slaves to forget their ancestors and origins. This factor of the slave's condition—the devastation of memory—has survived abolition better than any other, but it garners far less attention than the iron laws and beatings of the plantocratic order. The slaveholder's desire to destroy alterity can still be seen in vestigial form in a certain progressive discourse today, especially concerning Black communal memory. And the push to abandon the past has little to do with the desire to move beyond conservative traditions. It is because these pasts reveal ways of living that differ dramatically from those of a Eurocentric modernity, offering a promise of different futures and struggles than those made available by the current order.

The memories recounted in slave narratives, then, need to be considered carefully, as they are constantly subject to the risk of erasure posed by readers and critics alike. These Black memories are at times deliberately effaced; at others, neglected or misunderstood. This second scenario is taken up by the Italian philosopher Adriana Cavarero, who attempts to think through indignity with her concept of "horrorism." She does this by returning to Hannah Arendt's notion of dignity, which implies participation in a political community. Arendt writes: "Man, it turns out, can lose all so-called Rights of Man without losing his essential quality as man, his human dignity. Only the loss of a polity itself expels him from humanity."[17] In Arendt's formulation, dignity is thus achieved by engaging in public life and participating in a larger political arena. But such a political existence assumes one will be recognized by the community as a singular and unique being who actively participates as an individual. This last point is central to Cavarero's reading: the negation of human dignity she calls "horrorism" is not foremost a question of expelling individuals from their community of belonging but, on a much deeper level, a matter of denying them their singularity and wholeness. For this is the very condition that allows participation or engagement (be it postmortem) in any given political community.

Contemporary forms of terrorist violence—suicide attacks being perhaps the most vivid example—exemplify horrorism's brutal creation of indignity: "The body undone (blown apart, torn to pieces) loses its individuality. The violence that dismembers it offends the ontological dignity that the human figure possesses and renders it unwatchable."[18] The negation of dignity is thus the negation of everything that allows a body, an individual, or a personality to be recognized in its singularity. Additionally, Cavarero speaks of a second category of horrorism that she calls an "ontological crime" (i.e., as Arendt makes clear, a crime that impacts the ontological integrity of a human, or its dignity). This pertains to *defenseless* victims. The picture horrorism paints is fundamentally asymmetrical. Its protagonists are not warring parties, but defenseless and anonymous victims thrust into the void of depersonalization by extreme violence. The event of "Auschwitz" is the most illustrative embodiment of its paradigm. If, for Cavarero, ontological crime is understood as the dispossession of the individuality of the defenseless, then the death camps, which perfected a system for turning victims into defenseless creatures who were subjected to all kinds of humiliation, stand as the quintessential form of horrorism in the twentieth century.[19] Indeed, the two defining characteristics of horrorism are clearly at play in this example: the destruction of the figural unity of the body (due to the cremation chambers), and, at the same time, the creation of defenseless victims.

This is where Cavarero's analysis shows its limitations. There is a blind spot here that is not unique to her thinking but shared by a whole host of European critical theorists from Horkheimer to Agamben. The underlying issue stems from their approach to extreme political violence, which designates some historical examples as paradigmatic while willfully neglecting other no less important historical moments. Extermination camps are seen to mark a definitive shift, a ghastly plunge into a whole new level of horror. But the inaugural events of modernity, such as the massacres of Native Americans in the "New World" and the transatlantic slave trade, remain outside the purview of social critique. There is no place for these memories. And yet, before Auschwitz, a thinker as influential as Walter Benjamin hadn't shown such blindness to this long history of extreme violence. "The colonial history of European peoples begins with the appalling event of the *Conquista* of the Americas, which transformed the newly conquered world into a torture chamber."[20] In their obsession with the mass crimes of the twentieth century, thinkers such as Arendt and Cavarero are able to preserve a refuge of clear conscience against tormenting guilt. It is certainly easier to level a radical critique at a single massacre engendered by European political thought than to understand the horror of Nazism as the resurgence of tendencies inherent in modernity since its beginning. Viewing Auschwitz as a singular event supports the argument that European political culture collapsed in this late stage of development, rather than seeing this inherently brutal culture as doomed at its outset, a position impossible to ignore if, like Benjamin, one takes the long view by starting in the fifteenth century rather than the twentieth. This is precisely the argument being made by the freed slaves Equiano and Cugoano.

It should be noted that Cavarero, still taking her lead from Arendt, acknowledges the existence of colonial massacres. She first does this in passing,[21] before approaching the matter in an appendix where, again in the manner of Arendt, she discusses the work of Joseph Conrad. But this decision raises two problems. The first derives from Arendt's conceptual approach itself. Cavarero points this out: "There is, in Conrad's story, a gaze upon Africa 'with Western eyes' if not an outright racial prejudice, which Hannah Arendt's reading risks reinforcing."[22] But she fails to note that this strategy only bolsters a racist perception of the world that Arendt never manages to overcome. For Arendt, racism in the colony seems to have arisen as the "barely conscious reaction"[23] of white pioneers who, upon settling in South Africa, confronted a wild, inhospitable land inhabited by a vile indigenous population.[24] Thus, racism appears to be the consequence of a degenerate group of Europeans gone astray from their national community, and, therefore, from their dignity. The forced labor mercilessly inflicted upon the indigenous populations of South Africa by the Boers is nothing other than the consequence of white misery: the inhumanity of the Black populations, though shackled and chained, surely must have drawn the bearers of a rich European heritage into their own world of vice and laziness. Racism, the cause of Black suffering and the product of a well-established European intellectual tradition that goes back at least to Las Casas's *History of the Indies*, becomes in Arendt an almost unconscious consequence of white misery. Her unabashed embrace of the "Western perspective" is all the more indefensible given that, as Frantz Fanon has shown, the colonized has a much wider and more truthful perspective than the colonizer. Whereas the former have no choice but to understand the humanity of those who are oppressing them, the latter are forced to deny the humanity of the colonized in order to establish their power and legitimacy.[25] If the colonized's perspective appears fairer, it is because their world is richer, vaster, and less limited, as it leaves room for an open exchange of views. Adopting the perspective of the Black man, Fanon sees beyond—without overlooking—Arendt's interpretation of the origin of racism, expressed from the perspective of the colonizer. Arendt and Cavarero have thus walled themselves off from the memory of the colonized and, therefore, are incapable of considering its truth value.

The second problem lies in her reduction of a vast colonial history to a single moment—namely, the "partitioning of Black Africa" (seen through the lens of Conrad's Congo and Arendt's South Africa). Cavarero describes the negation of dignity as the death of the individual's originality, arguing that the genocides of the twentieth century are unprecedented instances of this. And yet, can there be a more striking negation of singularity than the transatlantic slave trade's sweeping transformation of human existence into liquid assets? Achille Mbembe reminds us that "within colonial capitalism's mode of functioning, there was a constant refusal to institute the sphere of the living being as a limit to economic appropriation."[26] This state of commodification and expendability[27] that marks Black lives characterizes the entire history of Eurocentric modernity. The fungibility of slaves, their exchange value, clearly shows how they are doubly stripped of dignity according to Arendt's understanding of the term: first, by making them interchangeable and thereby undermining any claim to singularity; and second, by assuming they circulate freely in the manner of any market commodity in global capitalism, which denies them any sense of community belonging since they can be sent away at any time. Neither Arendt or Cavarero give any consideration to this radical negation of the modern conception of citizenship.

Arendt and Cavarero illustrate how reflections on genocidal violence in the twentieth century—in spite of the unquestionable need for thinking through these events—are given pride of place over a wider vision of the politics of dehumanization that would account for the conquest of the Americas and the ravages of the slave trade. As a result, indignity has become too narrowly defined, as it relies on a vision insensitive to, among other things, the history, memories and struggles of Native Americans and deported Africans, which are part and parcel of the creation of the modern world. This insensitivity inevitably impacts the way we understand the racist violence of our contemporary moment. In slave narratives such as Cugoano's, *insensitivity* becomes its own political category that acknowledges the indignity of the Black condition.

> And as well then might we not expect tenderness and compassion from those whom the goddess of avarice has so allured with her charms, that her heart-sick lovers are become reversed to the feelings of human woe; and with the great hurry and bustle of the russet slaves employed in all the drudgeries of the western isles, and maritime shore, in the cruel

and involuntary service of her voluptuousness, having so dazzled their eyes, and bereaved them of all sensibility, that their hearts are become callous as the nether millstone, fierce as the tygers, and devoid of the natural feelings of men? From all such enchantments we would turn away, and fly from them as from the ravenous beasts of prey, as from the weeping crocodiles and the devouring reptiles, and as from the hoary monsters of the deep.[28]

In fact, this understanding of insensitivity runs through the work of many writers, from Cugoano to Césaire (notably his *Discourse on Colonialism*). Contrary to its etymology and privative prefix, for these writers in-sensitivity is seen as a positive quality. Of course, this doesn't mean that it is beneficial or desirable, but only that it is possible (and extremely profitable) to cultivate it and develop it in oneself. *Insensitivity is the ability to inflict suffering on another human being, or to witness it, without feeling any desire to stop it or attenuate it.* In any racist social organization, this quality is highly valued, if not indispensable.[29] Understood in this way, insensitivity is one of the conditions of possibility for producing indignity. Far from being a barely conscious reaction in the manner Arendt describes, racist cruelty requires the stubborn obstinacy of political subjectivation: the creation of the self, institutionally constructed as an agent or insensitive spectator of violence, humiliation, and insults.

Pitting the social philosophies of Arendt and Cavarero against those of the Afro-descendant tradition throws into relief an ethical conflict bearing on the perception of social violence and the sensitivity to its effects. To understand what is at stake, consider the dark story of Nat Turner. *Confessions of Nat Turner*, which was first published by a white lawyer in 1831, is a singular document in the history of slave discourse. This short text claims to be a faithful reproduction of the words of the leader of a violent slave revolt that took place in Virginia on August 21 and 22, 1831 (40 years to the day after the Haitian revolution). Historians have generally accepted the authenticity of Turner's words as reported by Thomas Gray, who strives to assure the reader of his credibility. But although the "confession" itself makes up the bulk of the work, it is Gray's preface and postface that shape its final interpretation. And, at a time when white America relished stories of slaves' misdeeds, its tone is unmistakably horrorist: "It will be long remembered in the annals of our country, and many a mother as she presses her infant darling to her bosom, will shudder at the recollection of Nat Turner, and his band of ferocious miscreants."[30]

DIGNITY RE-EMBODIED

Turner's *Confessions* are indeed chilling. Unlike Augustine's or Rousseau's spiritual or moral musings, these confessions speak of cold-blooded murders. They force the reader to confront questions of life and death and to grapple with the most profound ethical dilemmas. Born a slave, Nat Turner's extraordinary intelligence and abilities were recognized by his family at a young age. He learned to read early, became familiar with the Bible, and, in his own words, was viewed by the Black community that surrounded him as a prophet straight out of the New Testament: a mouthpiece for the apocalyptic word of God. Called upon by the Holy Spirit and witnessing what he interpreted to be signs of Providence, he assembled a small group of slaves that continued to grow as plantation owners steadily lost land. This group embarked on a violent mission to dismantle the institution of slavery. During their campaign, any white person who crossed paths with this slave rebellion was mercilessly murdered, regardless of age or sex. As Gray notes, there are passages that are sure to astound even those who are the most committed to the Black cause. Consider Turner's unsparing account of what happened after killing his own master and his master's entire family: "there was a little infant sleeping in a cradle, that was forgotten, until we had left the house and gone some distance, when Henry and Will returned and killed it."[31]

Add to this the fact that Turner's group was wielding axes and swords, decapitating their masters or slitting their throats, and you have a textbook image of Cavarero's horrorism: defenseless killings (in addition to infanticides, these slaves generally attacked masters while they slept) and mutilations that destroyed the body's figural coherence. Turner never turns away from these ghastly scenes: "I sometimes got in sight in time to see the work of death completed, viewed the mangled bodies as they lay, in silent satisfaction, and immediately started in quest of other victims."[32] But the matter becomes less clear-cut when we consider his motives. This isn't to say that the "ends justify the means" but to recognize that Turner's story exposes potential blind spots of social critique. Taking into account his motives complicates our reading of his story and forces us to grapple with conflicting, even contradictory, interpretations. It is worth noting how Turner recounts the origin of his rebellion: "Since the commencement of 1830, I had been living with Mr. Joseph Travis, who was to me a kind master, and placed the greatest confidence in me; in fact, I had no cause to complain of his treatment of me." He goes on to share a conversation he had with his future brothers-in-arms: "I saluted them on coming up, and asked Will how came he there, he answered, his life was worth no more than others, and his liberty as dear to him. I asked him if he thought to obtain it? He said he would, or loose his life. This was enough to put him in full confidence."[33] The slave owner who would soon be brutally murdered and have his entire lineage down to the newborn baby wiped out is thus described as a *kind master*. But the conversation Turner shares immediately shows the meaninglessness of his master's kindness. The very conditions of slavery, the abjection and inhumanity of existing as a captive, create a life—the word is hardly appropriate—that is not even worth living. The slave owner's kindness is as abstract and nonsensical as a crown of flowers hung on the gallows.

Nat Turner's story calls attention to the limitations of Cavarero's approach and, more broadly, to those of traditional social critique. Maintaining that "the point of view of the defenseless must not only be adopted here, it must be adopted exclusively; that is what really matters"[34] isn't tenable in Turner's case, which would amount to solely adopting the point of view of a slave-holding family, in the same way that Arendt adopted without reservation the perspective of racist colonizers in South Africa. By adopting the perspective of the defenseless one assumes the role of spectator.[35] Horrorism unfolds on the level of the visible and elicits empathy, not unlike the way the 24-hour news cycle invites its audience to behold with awe the shocking images of an attack carried out in Europe or North America. To "see" indignity without tangibly feeling it from the position of the oppressed, to seek an objective point of view by walling oneself off from the geopolitics of knowledge, is ultimately to endorse a willful blindness and to accept numbness as a natural response. It also puts aside the fact that this ostensible sensitivity to certain forms of indignity creates, as though in perfect reflection, an insensitivity to others. Nat Turner's story draws a line between those who wish to keep the world as it is and those who feel compelled to tear it down and make it anew.

As a system of oppression, the reality of modern slavery goes beyond its spectacular manifestations (torture, rape, mutilation, etc.). Though *The Confessions of Nat Turner* speaks little about the abuse endured by slaves, it gives a granular description of the masters' suffering once they become the targets of the slaves' vengeance. This raises an important ethical question: is it possible to understand the daily persecutions of an existence characterized by indignity without indulging in spectacle? Can we see indignity not as a singular event or an exception, but as a condition of existence? Or are we inclined to take the side of the masters, given the sensational media coverage that amplifies any level of suffering they may endure? The notion of insensitivity found in Cugoano and Equiano also speaks to the political conditioning that can make us sensitive to some spectacular forms of violence while remaining absolutely indifferent to others. The casual indifference to non-Western experience shows the prevalence of this political insensitivity. This can be seen as much in media coverage as in the field of critical theory, or in the latent Eurocentrism of everyday discussions. Moving past this insensitivity to everyday atrocities—as opposed to their more spectacular forms—requires a new perspective.

Make no mistake, I don't believe there is any way of justifying the killing of a newborn. On the other hand, taking into account the fuller picture shows that the opposition between life and death doesn't have the same meaning for the slave as it does for the master. And this is only natural given the master's total control over the life and death of his "possessions." Even Hegel made note of the fact that slaves have stared death in the face;[36] having suffered *"Angst"* and fear, they are thus capable through this experience of inflicting the same fate on their masters whose vanity has made them complacent and unguarded. They have experienced in their consciousness "the fear of death, of the absolute lord. In this [consciousness] has been internally dissolved, has trembled through and through within itself, and everything fixed has quaked in it."[37] Like Toussaint Louverture before him, Nat Turner embodies this ambiguous figure of the slave fighting against indignity. The understanding of indignity I am proposing here designates a *condition* more than an event—in this case, the Black condition. Life and death are inextricably linked in it. As Cugoano writes, "our lives are accounted of no value, we are hunted after as the prey in the desart, and doomed to destruction as the beasts that perish."[38] Due to its very ordinariness, indignity lacks the spectacular quality of the suicide attack or the extermination camp. It expresses itself more insidiously and perniciously by repeatedly denying the right to memory and community. To be sure, a life of indignity is all the more exposed to sudden outbursts of extreme violence and displays of horror. But its suffering occurs primarily on the day-to-day level: indignity results from a life that is no longer, or *almost* no longer, worth living.

The Necropolitical Production of Indignity: A Critique of Power

For all their respective and profound differences, there is one thing that Native Americans during the time of conquest share with

African slaves of the eighteenth century, Algerian *indigènes* at the start of the twentieth century, Palestinians after the Nakba, or with today's Black populations in Europe and the United States. To very different extents, under distinct regimes and carried out on extremely variable levels of intensity, all have directly experienced indignity. In spite of these differences, how can indignity be given a precise definition that speaks to all of these situations? Given this chapter's focus on questions of life and death, it is impossible to ignore the subject of biopolitics (i.e., the power exerted over the biological existence of populations), especially since, in addition to its influence on contemporary social philosophy, it began as a social critique of racism. Or, more accurately, it started as a Eurocentric critique of racism, one that was widely adopted after Michel Foucault gave it its first formulation. While its popularity never ceased to grow, rarely was it subjected to careful scrutiny.[39]

By Eurocentric, I don't just mean the tendency of taking European matters—historical or otherwise—as one's principal object of study. Every philosopher or theorist has the right to pursue what most appeals to them. An approach becomes Eurocentric when its analysis of Europe becomes unduly generalized or seen to represent phenomena on a global scale. In such instances, no basis of comparison or diverging points of view are provided to relativize such sweeping claims. And when race or racism is at issue, this oversight is felt all the more acutely. In a lecture at the Collège de France in the 1970s entitled "Society Must Be Defended," Foucault defined racism primarily as a "way of introducing a break into the domain of life that is under power's control: the break between what *must* live and what *must* die."[40] In short, for Foucault, racism operates in two phases. First, it segments the living into different groups, then it introduces a political struggle whose existence is ultimately dependent on the elimination of one or more of the other groups. The old notion of political enemy is rehashed in racism to present a biological threat. Framed in this way, the survival of one race depends on the extinction of another. "If genocide is indeed the dream of modern powers, this is not because of a recent return of the ancient right to kill; it is because power is situated and exercised at the level of life, the species, the race, and the large-scale phenomena of population."[41]

The long history of colonial racism, which predates the social Darwinism underlying Foucault's argument, belies the assumption that racism begins with the modern invention of race as a construct. But the principal problem with Foucault's argument is that he

55

arbitrarily frames racism within a *genocidal teleology*. Without citing the specific historical event he is referring to, he expresses as much himself: "Racism first develops with colonization, or in other words, with colonizing genocide."[42] If colonization can be equated to genocide, then colonial violence can no longer be identified and defined as racist unless it is part of a genocidal campaign targeting a specific population. The United Nation's Convention on the Prevention and Punishment of the Crime of Genocide (1948) defines genocide as a set of acts (murder, subjugation, sterilization, etc.) "committed with intent to destroy, in whole or in part, a national, ethnic, racial or religious group." The key word in this definition is *intent*. Defined thus, it excludes the vast majority of colonial violence. This is either because colonists intend to keep the colonized alive—at least in theory—due to their indispensability to the means of production, as is the case with slavery or forced labor; or because their killing is without intent, as is the case with systems of segregation and apartheid. Killing a native inhabitant—rarely done out of necessity—causes no moral scruples, and, in some circumstances, is even done for sport.

Foucault projects onto colonial racism categories from a completely distinct historical-political moment, namely that of the eradication of the Jews and the Romani, on which the UN definition of genocidal crimes is based. At a time when a Zionist ideology seeks to legitimize the occupation of Palestine by reclassifying the category of genocide as an inconceivable and exceptional crime against humanity, this sort of historical error has great political ramifications.[43] Foucault's gesture has the unintended consequence of minimizing colonial crimes, which become reduced by way of contrast to ordinary military operations. Although he wishes to expand colonial history as though it were in a Procrustean bed, Foucault's genocidal teleology—the hypostasis of racism—falls in line with colonial discourse by designating genocide as the "crime of all crimes" against which all other political violence will ultimately be measured. But viewing the history of mass violence solely through the lens of genocide backs one into an ideological corner. "Depriving the enslaved individual of the 'natural' right to freedom and self-ownership constitutes the crime against humanity. [...] Saying the slave trade and slavery sought to accomplish different goals than the European genocide of the Jews, and that therefore they are not comparable, doesn't mean they weren't both crimes. Such obscene comparisons are hardly worth discussing."[44] An Afro-decolonial approach must take into account the variety of experiences and political constructions of indignity.

The philosopher and Auschwitz survivor Jean Améry took the opposite approach to that of Foucault: drawing on the work of Frantz Fanon, he allows the colonial experience to provide a framework for understanding his own experience, without collapsing the two into one experience.[45] In his seminal work, *At the Mind's Limits*, he distinguishes between two figures of violence who maintain a direct relationship to death through their position within a defined political space. There is, on the one hand, the soldier whose focus on survival imbues him with heroism. On the other, there is the prisoner of the concentration camp whose ultimate duty is death.[46] A third figure should be added alongside these two: that of the colonized Black subject (which includes the plantation slave) who unceasingly inhabits the almost indistinguishable space between life and death. This third figure is the one excluded from a biopolitical approach. Foucault's genocidal teleology leads him to identify the greatest threat of his period as a reigning power that "is exercised in such a way that it is capable of suppressing life itself. And, therefore, to suppress itself insofar as it is the power that guarantees life."[47] Perhaps alluding to the risk of nuclear apocalypse, Foucault is outlining here a conceptual framework for thinking through social violence, one that, in the work of Giorgio Agamben and Roberto Esposito, takes the name of *thanatopolitics:*[48] the extermination of expendable lives becomes the flip side of any politics of care developed by privileged populations.

As the African American scholar Jared Sexton suggests, Achille Mbembe's concept of necropolitics may "provincialize"[49] a current of biopolitical thought that is under the sway of Eurocentrism, which is to say, it may bring its limits to light and transcend them. But Sexton, who is otherwise highly critical of Mbembe's skewed vision (with its neglect of the North American context) ignores the profound ambivalence of this notion in the work of the Cameroonian thinker. Whereas, in his well-known article "Necropolitics,"[50] this term is synonymous with thanatopolitics à la Foucault or Agamben, elsewhere Mbembe gives a definition richer in interpretive possibilities. This broader definition springs from the belief that "what lies beyond death deserves to be considered in and of itself, as a prerequisite to inhabiting the world of history."[51] From this idea a new conception of the relationship between life, death, and politics emerges. Moving past the principle of noncontradiction that holds death and life as inexorably and mutually exclusive, this approach is deserving of more attention, especially given that the principle of noncontradiction is foreign to the vast majority of African cosmologies and experiences, as well as those inherited from Africa. As the

Cameroonian writer Léonora Miano has compellingly argued, it is when Mbembe's concept is seen from this angle that its full heuristic potential becomes apparent:

> Death is thus a resource, since it is part of experience, of the cultural baggage that makes up one's identity. Clearly, the diversity of Sub-Saharan writing doesn't seek to revive the past for its own sake. This writing is ruffled by the past, just how the living are ruffled by the breath of their ancestors who watch on from the land of the dead, and come marching through the dreams of their descendants. This writing gives body to what has disappeared, examining it as a tracker does animal tracks, to read their signs and share with the world the science of survival that Sub-Saharans and Afro-descendants have mastered. This writing performs a veritable archaeology of pain.[52]

Miano's sentiment echoes the Christian eschatology advanced in an African context by another Cameroonian, the philosopher and theologian Fabien Eboussi Boulaga: "The cleft between life and death is minimal and closing so rapidly that human persons now pass from the one to the other with ease. The dead are among the living, who will soon be dead."[53] By way of contrast, the thanatopolitical alternative between those destined to live and those destined to die seems too simplistic. Beyond the rigid opposition between these two ideal-types—the hygienic, normalized life promised by a certain biopolitics and the genocidal annihilation of thanatopolitics—lies a zone of existence where the distinctions between life and death become blurred. This necropolitical space is the space of indignity.

Agamben distinguishes between two conceptions of life: the first is βίος (*bios*) or form-of-life, which is to say, political existence, immanent in the norms that govern it; the second is ζωή (*zoe*) or bare life: life seized by the law, killable without reprisal. Following this model, the mechanics of indignity can best be understood by considering two opposing conceptions of death: θάνατος (*thanatos*) and νεκρός (*necros*).[54] *Thanatos*, as the Epicurean philosopher has shown, is what isn't: the nothingness derived from the absence of sensation, the absolute and unquestionable interruption of life. This is bare death—death as a limit—from which one is always already certain never to return. An assured death, and therefore a docile and reassuring one. On the other end of the spectrum, *necros* refers to the interstitial space between death and life inhabited by slaves, gladiators, tragic heroes, and those buried alive. It is a life under a form-of-death. This defines in large part the Black condition today, which is perhaps what Jared Sexton means when he says "black life is lived in social death"[55] or when Steve Biko claims: "All in all the black man has become a shell, a shadow of man, completely defeated, drowning in his own misery, a slave, an ox bearing the yoke of oppression with sheepish timidity."[56] Black life has been ravaged, made uninhabitable. This notion of form-of-death isn't only a descriptive concept, defined by the social relations unique to slavery; it is also part and parcel of African and Afro-descendant imaginaries, cosmologies, and ontologies where the distinction between life and death isn't as clearcut as it is in the white world. This opens up a field of inquiry that no longer concerns the production of life or death, but, rather, the production of the unlivable, which is perhaps the best synonym for indignity: that which makes life no longer worth living *in the present*. The past, felt as a spectral haunting, and the future, insofar as it harbors even the slightest possibility of a radically different existence, are oh so much more real and prevalent than the present in lives defined by indignity. More radical still is the reality of political violence that necropolitics makes visible: it isn't only a matter of extinguishing life or deciding who gets to live and who doesn't, but, more importantly, a process of *constantly blurring the very boundary between life and death*.

Daily Indignity: An Existence

This necropolitical approach to indignity raises perhaps more questions than it answers. What does it mean, for instance, to experience indignity? As mentioned earlier, this experience doesn't concern torture or mutilation any more than it does genocide. Indignity is a condition. To grasp it on both a conceptual and affective level, one must imagine the experience of the form-of-death as an everyday phenomenon. Such an understanding of indignity avoids the pitfalls of the conceptualization of the everyday in European philosophy, which invariably frames it as nonthreatening. In that conceptualization, the everyday is "everything in our surroundings that, by virtue of its regular presence, is immediately accessible, understandable and familiar. [...] It is the regular course of things, the routine order of the world which causes no inconvenience and is accepted for this very reason as unquestionable."[57] This *carefree* definition smacks of leisurely brunches, Sundays idled away on a sunny café terrace or in the comforting boredom of one's family. Like any vision of the world that masks a harsher reality, this particular view is ethically suspect for what it ignores. Racist insults, constant police harassment, and countless other daily aggressions are all the more easy to neglect due to their "regular presence." The habit, acquired at a young age, of being humiliated, or subjected to violence, doesn't attenuate the inadmissible scandal, just as Nat Turner's story reminds us. The everyday life of the white *petit bourgeois*, characterized by its hypostasis of *insensibility* as defined by Cugoano and Equiano, is at the very root of the problem of indignity. In its indifference and insensitivity, the everyday white life ignores the inherent brutality of the social world. This experience of daily life isn't at odds with the daily indignity and violence endured by Black people. They are merely two sides of the same coin. As Steve Biko has made clear, the violence and indignity is the shadow cast by the experience of the white everyday: "The racism we meet does not only exist on an individual basis; it is also institutionalized to make it look like the South African way of life."[58] This means that, while institutionalized racism is primarily a function of the state, it can only work on this structural level precisely because it is constantly embraced, reinforced, and practiced by ordinary individuals. Racism is imperialism crystallized into a lifestyle.

Frantz Fanon has provided the clearest description of this divide between the white everyday and the everyday of victims of racism. In *Black Skin, White Masks*, he lays bare the constant moral insecurity felt by Black people in Europe. Even just speaking up and thereby exposing one's African or West Indian accent makes one a target of ridicule or contempt. Black people must therefore constantly police themselves. If they have internalized this into a form of self-aggression or self-distancing, it is because the default behavior of white people is to treat them as foreigners, or children, or both at the same time. "Yet, we'll be told, there is no intention to willfully give offense. OK, but it is precisely this absence of will—this offhand manner; this casualness; and the ease with which they classify [the black man], imprison him at an uncivilized and primitive level—that is insulting."[59] The white everyday, which "causes no inconvenience" and remains "unquestionable," is experienced by Black people on another register altogether: that of indignity. And, in their indifference and insensitivity, white people unknowingly insult, ridicule, and belittle. The most banal exchange reveals, from a Black perspective, predatory behavior. This is because the everyday, regular relationship white people maintain with Black people is one of surveillance: "not only must the black man be black; he must be black in relation to the white man."[60] This reality of experiencing the everyday as a threat is thrown into stark relief in the context of legal apartheid or settlement colonies where, as Fanon has shown in *A Dying Colonialism*, passing through a checkpoint is a mere formality for the colonizer but presents a life-threatening risk for the colonized.[61] This is always how the police checkpoint is felt in Black neighborhoods throughout the West: a threatening risk that demands constant vigilance. Black people live *in* the same world as white people, but they don't live *the* same world. Each world has its distinct language. Black people are the suckers who inevitably die in the first thirty minutes of an action film; they are the ones portrayed in the media as originating from a savage no-man's-land in Africa; or the ones who are paternalistically caricatured in textbooks. What white people perceive as entertainment or news or knowledge is felt by Black people as an insulting and explicit attack on their dignity. The experience of the checkpoint—a defining feature of apartheid and colonial regimes—is today a widespread phenomenon felt throughout the world.

Daily life for Black people is a hostile experience. It almost goes without saying that the reason for this is a pervasive racism. For Afro-descendants, racism is the grammar of indignity. Of course, when considered on a global scale, racism appears to be another effect of the North-South divide. It is the metastasis of capitalist pillaging, institutional control, or orchestrated demolition of Africa, Latin America, and the Caribbean. In other words, the product of an imperialism or coloniality that has penetrated the spheres of knowledge, politics, and the economy. But its impact is existential. Indeed, this structural inequality is most acutely felt on the level of the everyday. Racism is the *embodied experience of coloniality*, which compels one to question imperialism's oppressive totality. However, the mechanisms of racism are subtler than many believe. Racism is not restricted to the set of beliefs it is often reduced to, such as "Black people are lazy" or "Arabs are terrorists," and so on. It is a way of thinking, a manner of framing matters, as though the Valladolid debate were endlessly restaged with every new encounter with a Black person: Who is this person? Where does he come from? What is he doing in my neighborhood? Does he speak my language? Is he dangerous? Should I clutch my purse? Hold on to my wallet and my phone? These questions are only asked in the rarest of circumstances when two white people meet.

Racism is the ceaseless questioning of people's very legitimacy to be where they are and to do what they are doing. This is why it is so easy to downplay it or to not see it at all. In its relentless interrogations and experiments, it displays the spirit of rationalism. In other words, racism isn't a body of knowledge; it is a form of inquiry. But that inquiry stems from a series of misconceptions, and the comfort and satisfaction with these misconceptions is what underlies white supremacy. Seen in this way, even the most trivial situations are revealed in their true light. If so many French Afro-descendants are bothered when a white person asks them about their origins, it isn't because they view the Republic as their only legitimate identity marker and seek to forget their place of origin (such an effort would of course be in vain). This seemingly innocuous question is but another instance of an endless interrogation over their fundamental legitimacy. The regular worries or odd questions of white people are in fact the everyday operations of a racist totality. Being "black in the relation to the white man" on a daily basis entails being under his supervision, subjected to his questioning, and standing out to him as a problem. Ceaselessly questioned, Black people begin to question themselves. This is what explains their unease and insecurity with the everyday.

If, in the European imagination, Black people are still viewed as mysterious and strange, it isn't because they are infrequently encountered (a point that is increasingly harder to make in big cities) or even "exotic." As Fanon once again points out, it is because they have been invalidated and negated, their whole beings voided and therefore they present no tangible reference. Under the watchful gaze of white people, Black people have "no culture, no civilization, and no 'long historical past'."[62] They appear vacant, which is why they elicit countless questions. As W.E.B. Du Bois has argued, Europe and North America have debased the older civilizations on which they were built. To lend credence to the myth of their intellectual and scientific superiority, they destroyed or appropriated all the forms of knowledge they could glean from the indigenous populations they colonized (fortunately, they could only glean so much), even though their rise to power was based solely on their carefully honed practice of wiping out populations. Making white civilization the unique and uncontested source of knowledge came at the expense of eradicating countless cosmologies and epistemologies.[63] It took a large-scale and persistent effort to create a world where "the black man has no ontological resistance in the eyes of the white man."[64] White people hollowed them out, effacing entire histories and symbolic orders. Marked as illegitimate, Afro-descendants live in a present where they are not welcome; they are haunted by the specters of innumerable ancestors who lived and died scorned and disdained (soldiers or colonized subjects sacrificed for empire, slaves sacrificed for capital, victims of police violence killed with no repercussions, and so on). In these cases, life and death are impossible to disentangle. Indignity comes from the ceaseless act of interrogation, which is to say the continuous delegitimization of life. This delegitimization is at the core of the daily experience of victims of racism. It is the experience of a life under the form-of-death.

This constant questioning is made manifest in a repressive state primarily through police violence, which targets Black people everywhere throughout the world. Another constitutive characteristic of the condition of everyday indignity is its vulnerability to a thanatopolitical death sentence or to necropolitical conditions under which it is literally impossible to live. This can occur in at least two ways. The first is through the state's deliberate use of oppression; the second, through its absence of involvement or refusal to uphold its own principles, which results in a failure to protect its people from privatized forms of violence. The first immediately evokes an over-zealous police force, which finds expression in a myriad of ways, most notably in officers trained to kill, harass, and resort to violence.[65] But this also includes elaborate methods for creating unlivable conditions. The architect Léopold Lambert has called attention to this. He describes how the state of Israel uses bulldozers as war tanks to lay waste to Palestinian neighborhoods while carefully constructing unlivable spaces designed to be transformed into battlefields. Thus, he observes, "the meticulous attention given to the conditions of destruction is so thought-out and controlled that the process of demolition becomes a mirror image of its opposite, namely the design and planning of any regular architectural project. The chaos usually associated with demolition and destruction is in fact entirely absent. Rather, it resembles the precision and long-term planning of a military strategy. Like any other architectural project, it aims to exercise both control over the environment as well as over the disposition of bodies in space."[66] The second way concerns countless forms of violence perpetrated in direct and indirect ways by capital. A prime example is the structural adjustment programs imposed on Africa by the World Bank and the IMF. With these programs, mining operations are protected by private military contractors (i.e., mercenaries). In these cases, profit-seeking multinational corporations hold the sovereign power to decide who lives and who dies.[67]

In every case, the escalation toward extreme violence, in the form of killing or the construction of unlivable conditions, is merely a more manifest realization of the constant drone of social violence. "One cannot say that a given country is racist but that lynchings or

DIGNITY RE-EMBODIED

extermination camps are not to be found there. The truth is that all that and still other things exist on the horizon. These virtualities, these latencies circulate, carried by the life-stream of psycho-affective, economic relations."[68] Of course, this doesn't mean that a genocidal teleology is inherent to racism, but rather that extreme violence can erupt at any moment and without warning. And it does this without upsetting the social order—in fact, it only further consolidates and reinforces it. The daily questioning of Black people's legitimacy anticipates them being put to death at a later date. If young Black people are considered killable, it is because their ordinary lives are marked by indignity. The historian Robin Kelley makes this point when he argues that unpunished police killings are no more outrageous than the ambient violence that plagues daily Black life. Both are bound to the same forms of structural indignity: "[Michael] Brown's life was cut short, but had he lived he would have faced the prospect of a slow death, of bearing enormous debt without the prospect of a fulfilling livelihood while continuing to navigate a world of constant surveillance and harassment."[69] Black death in a racist world is continuous with Black life. One extends the other into what Frantz Fanon called the zone of non-being. A white-supremist, anti-Black world thrusts Black life into indignity and subjects it to a form-of-death. In this world, the Black philosopher himself is doomed to appear like a trained monkey.

— 3 —

OUR DIGNITY IS OLDER THAN US

Dignity defines itself first and foremost against indignity, but its significance isn't derived solely from this opposition in a purely differential manner. The constant violence of indignity makes recourse to the notion of dignity inevitable, but dignity isn't only a response to social violence. Afro-decolonial dignity is a clearly defined concept with its own substance. This goes against its most common understanding. Even in the legal arena, "dignity" is a flexible concept that leaves lawyers considerable, if not excessive, discretion to define it. And current social theory and political strategies deliberately maintain dignity as an ambiguous term. The political philosopher Ernesto Laclau, for instance, a hugely influential figure along with Chantal Mouffe for the contemporary left in Europe, has forcefully argued that the keywords of political organizing should remain indeterminate and malleable.

The central matter of Laclau's approach—which he sees as politically engaged—is that of populism. Rather than view this term as synonymous with "demagogy," he defines it strictly as the product of the people, which stems from a collective adherence to the same affective register. Laclau takes as his starting point the discontent felt in a variety of ways by the poor and middle classes of Western societies. For him, this discontent is an expression of what he calls "popular demands," which are as varied as the people who make them. And it is through these political demands, which aim to redress their grievances, that a community is able to transform itself into a historical subject with agency. This is a deliberate departure from Marxism in that populist politics work by bringing together a varied and disparate set of demands. Of course, Marx was well aware of the fact that revolutionary groups weren't exclusively made up of the

DIGNITY RE-EMBODIED

proletariat. But in his view, it was the duty of the communist *petit bourgeois* to betray their class in order to fully embrace the social project and interests of the proletariat. For Laclau, on the contrary, divergent demands must be given equal attention and common ground must be sought between them rather than letting any one demand take priority over the others.

But how do you aggregate a varied set of demands? Laclau argues that the principle that underlies a set of popular demands should be taken as universal, even though it can never really be so. Framed in this way, the universal is but a symbol of a missing plenitude, the object of desire driven by discontent. It can also be seen as aspiring toward progress as well as demanding equality, freedom, justice, and so on. These terms are deemed "empty signifiers" by Laclau, among which he would likely include "dignity." By virtue of their very ambiguity, they are able to bring together a diverse set of demands and to assemble and unite the goals of different political actors. The empty signifier is emptied of its signified in order to better express plenitude, community, fulfilled promises, which are goals that are unachievable in practice but that remain the primary motivations of political engagement. By deploying these empty signifiers, populism seeks to establish a hegemonic position. [1] It does this by embodying the goals of a section of society larger than any individual group. To exercise hegemony is to meet—or claim to be meeting—a social need. Thus, "a popular identity functions as a tendentially empty signifier."[2] Key terms such as *justice, freedom, equality*, and so on, are devoid of conceptual substance. They simply signify an absent plenitude. It is through these terms that citizens, assembled to form a people, make demands designed to address their discontent. The people, constituted through collective performance, resort to such empty signifiers to intensify and exacerbate the differences between two categories of people: the rich and the poor, the people and the elite, the victims and the perpetrators, and so on. The ambiguity of these concepts is not a sign of their theoretic paucity; rather, this very ambiguity makes them a much more effective—and affective—tool of unification.

To claim, then, that dignity (and more specifically in this case Black dignity or dignity of the oppressed) has a specific content is to exclude it from the economy of the empty signifier. Dignity isn't simply an empty vessel made to hold various desires. In the Afro-descendant tradition, it is the cornerstone of politics. Its purpose isn't to create a hegemonic order or to assemble a majority, but to empower the oppressed and serve as a call to action. As such, it has been an essential resource in countless political and social struggles where it has served as a bulwark against reactionary attacks. A noteworthy example of such use is represented by Aimé Césaire's *Négritude*. Césaire felt compelled to give this collective movement a certain historical depth by situating it in relation to its predecessors. Indeed, underlying the political and existential urgency to reconnect with their past—an urgency that Afro-descendant thinkers believe to be essential to their own sense of dignity—is the notion of deep historicity. This notion challenges many intellectual and political assumptions, especially the anti-essentialism characteristic of post-structuralist philosophical discourse.

The Struggle of Dignity

Beginning with the abolitionist movement, Black liberation struggles have had much in common throughout the modern period. Not only have they shared similar concerns but they have also engaged in the same modes of political intervention. Jacques Rancière's conception of politics sheds some light on this. In short, politics is a matter of making public a certain number of practices and relations that have remained within the domain of the private sphere. It is done by speaking out about matters of so-called personal choice and the arbitrary nature of interpersonal relations, thereby opening these up to wider debate. To politicize a seemingly private issue in this public manner is to argue that the issue in question never was a matter of personal choice of a select few. These choices are, rather, overdetermined; they are shaped and produced by power relations and points of tension that implicate the whole of society. And a decisive factor in this process of politicization concerns "all those who were not entitled to participate in public life because they did not belong to 'society' but merely to the domestic and reproductive life."[3] This refers to women, of course, but also to slaves of all types, as well as the colonized, victims of segregation and racism, the undocumented, and so on. From this perspective, acquiring a slave, for example, is not a private affair, a simple transaction between a buyer and a trader: it is a political matter that implicates the whole social order.

However, despite the consistency of such efforts at politicization, they each present a divergent case. This is where Rancière's analysis falls short. This is because it is impossible to fully account for, and therefore politicize—i.e., make public—the slave's condition, the condition of women or even the human condition as such, as though these represented a set of uniform circumstances. Their impenetrable complexity only allows for a glimpse, or a partial rendering, of their conditions. Homing in on a specific aspect of their conditions is needed to elicit interest and generate a political response. For the history that concerns me here, the effort of politicization has centered on two matters: Black suffering and Black power. It is at the intersection of these two approaches that an ethics of dignity is born.

The politicization of suffering played a major role in abolitionist discourse. The torture endured by slaves who were regularly raped and humiliated was described in intricate detail. This discursive strategy sought to penetrate the wall of white insensitivity and indifference to awaken compassion and spur an uprising against the system of slavery.[4] But, as I have argued, the experience of suffering inhibits speech and reasoning. All one can do is cry out. Politicizing suffering thus always entails speaking in the place of the person who endures it. Even when the speakers are those who directly experienced suffering, they express themselves in the name of a past version of their own selves; they become the spokespeople for a previous "I," for a remembered Ego.[5] Any politicization of suffering, any attempt to make the pain of a group a public matter, cannot escape the structural need of "speaking for" or "speaking on behalf" of another. Within the abolitionist's ranks were many white people who, out of an ignorance of Black suffering or out of contempt for the individuals who endured it, misconstrued the stories illiterate slaves entrusted to them, distorting them to better suit their own tastes or to achieve the effect they were after. This serves as a stark reminder of the structural risk of politicizing Black suffering, which can at any point degrade into paternalism. This sort of confiscation of speech runs through the entire history of Black liberation.

The only way to prevent this is to ensure that the politicization of suffering is always accompanied by the politicization of Black agency. Paternalism represents Black people as passive and docile beings whose only hope for salvation resides in the munificence of white society and the state. They are never portrayed as agents of protest, but only as the passive beneficiaries of white activism. White society has maintained the illusion that it was their political interventions and good will, rather than the long history of slave marronage and their innumerable revolts, that led, for instance, to the abolition of slavery, so generously decreed by the French or American republics.

The politicization of *power* (a deliberate reference to the rich and varied history of use of *Black power*) belongs to an entirely different logic: not that of "speaking for," but that of "speaking with." It is no longer a question of substituting the absent or assumed speech of the oppressed with one's own. It is a matter of emphasizing the political charge—far too often denied—of the actions and protests that are being staged. Spontaneous reactions to violence and exploitation are always already political. Uprisings, riots, protests, calls for action are not thoughtless responses that should be contained. They are a manifestation of politics that must be sustained and prolonged beyond their initial actions. Malcolm X's response to the Harlem "race riots" in 1964 illustrates how Black power can be successfully politicized in this way. Of course, he doesn't condemn the riots; but he also doesn't seek to provide a simple causal or sociological explanation, which would imply that the rioters are no more than the powerless and faceless playthings of social forces beyond their control and comprehension. Far from adopting the social scientist's condescension, he identifies the political rationality of the riot, which remains pertinent to understanding any riot taking place in any low-income neighborhood: by destroying property and storefronts that belong to neither them nor their people, but which they have no choice but to inhabit and frequent, these young Black people are not, as journalists love to claim, destroying *their own* neighborhoods. They are abolishing the most blatant signs of their dispossession and indignity. The owners of the commercial and domestic real estate being destroyed are not part of the community; those responsible for dispossessing the community remain out of reach. The closest one can get is by destroying the symbols of their ideology, their sources of profit, and their instruments of property control.[6]

Where there's oppression there's resistance, and where there's resistance there's politics. This sums up the politicization of power. Contrary to what is often argued, such a politics of power doesn't seek to lead or shape a revolt, but rather to strengthen it. It strives to expand it and have it catch on in strategic places outside its point of origin. For Malcolm X—as for Frantz Fanon, Steve Biko or James H. Cone—this is the theory of riots. To speak in the name of the oppressed, to speak *as* the oppressed, to politicize their power, and hence to say that they are capable of acting and speaking for themselves, is certainly not an impossible act. This presents a performative contradiction that isn't lost on anyone, or, in the very least, rightly raises some political suspicion. "If they can speak, why don't you let them?" But when power is politicized by the oppressed their words are themselves an illustration of this power. This is a fundamental aspect of any struggle for dignity.

An ethics of dignity is formed when these two expressions—politicizing suffering and politicizing power—intersect in the speech and actions of the oppressed themselves. The first denounces indignity, which lays the groundwork for the second, where power asserts itself as the best way to combat it. This recalls a point made earlier: any demand for Black dignity and humanity must first come to terms with the inhumanity and violence of white society. This also shows that dignity, from an Afro-descendant perspective, is not just another concept. For the oppressed, it signifies above all access to the realm of politics. Steve Biko noted as much while also expressing the urgency of keeping the living death of indignity at bay: "The first step therefore is to make the black man come to himself; to pump back life into his empty shell; to infuse him with pride and dignity."[7]

The notion of dignity is perhaps the most radical of all political thoughts, for it calls into question the very livability of life itself: the need to free oneself from everyday suffering and asthenia through the power of the collective. This is why the demand for dignity has figured so prominently in the history of Black movements, and, more generally, in the history of movements led by the oppressed: the demand is made by those whose relationship to the nation-state has been defined by violence and repression. In other words, by those who are taken to be subjects—political, legal, and so on— without being considered human. In this respect, dignity stands in stark contrast to other fundamental political keywords that Ernesto Laclau deemed empty signifiers (which, when held up to scrutiny, never prove to be entirely empty). For example, the demand for equality is by necessity relative, depending on the relationships maintained between individuals and social groups. Similarly, the political demand for freedom implies a certain relationship to institutions from which one wishes to be free. Laying claim to dignity, on the other hand, the oppressed refer to no other point of comparison apart from their own collective being. Unlike the demands for equality or freedom, the dignity of the oppressed isn't defined by comparison, but through a radical affirmation of one's self against the present social order. This allows for relationships to be forged through a shared sense of dignity and common struggle. It is the possession, and sometimes the only remaining possession, of all those who "can only enter into the political arena by trespassing."[8] Although its reach extends in many directions, the ethics of dignity is first and foremost a struggle for a political, cultural, and economic existence in contexts where this existence is uncertain, tenuous, shrouded in obscurity.

This approach is not self-evident. The critic Saidiya Hartman, for instance, sought "to point to the limits of the political and the difficulty of translating or interpreting the practices of the enslaved within that framework."[9] Excluded from public space, slaves were, in her reading, also entirely excluded from politics. Their practices of resistance could thus not be considered political since they weren't carried out by subjects, citizens, or even, strictly speaking, people. Contemporary Afropessimist theorists apply this radical view to our present moment. But such a position seems misguided insofar as it assumes as universal an extremely restrictive conception of politics. Rather than frame the situation of slaves and of the oppressed within a modern paradigm of bourgeois citizenship, the concept of dignity invites a re-evaluation of the very idea of politics by taking Black uprisings, such as that of the Haitian revolution, as its point of departure.

In his work on consequential Black political figures from the United States in the twentieth century, James H. Cone placed dignity at the center of his re-evaluation of politics. He asks us, for instance, to consider the central role Martin Luther King's speeches played in politicizing Black power in the South: "Through prophetic preaching of the gospel of Jesus, combined with fearless civil rights activity, Martin inspired ordinary blacks—maids, cooks, and janitors—to believe in themselves as human beings, to stand up to white bigots and demand that the law recognize their humanity."[10] Cone argues that, despite their different approaches, Malcolm X had the exact same objective as King. But the Muslim preacher's rhetorical strategies and speeches spoke to the needs of the ghettos of the urbanized north: "Malcolm inspired Harlem blacks to walk the streets with dignity and to be prepared to die for it: 'Treat me like a man, or kill me,' he demanded, and blacks knew he meant it."[11] For King, dignity is achieved through a spiritual evaluation of one's self and a reawakening of religious sentiment. For Malcolm X, it is earned by confronting death head-on. In both cases, daring to affirm a Black humanity and forcing one's adversary to recognize one's dignity entails passing from the zone of nonbeing to that of being. Simply claiming a political existence is not without risk, but it can have far-reaching social consequences, as the institutions of racist societies are principally built on the repression and neglect of this humanity. Putting pressure on this pillar makes the whole racist structure falter. Hence the significance of Cone's analysis. He presents dignity as the effort on the part of African Americans to live an authentically human life, a life worth living. More important still, he shows that dignity bears within it the history of this effort, a history that has shaped us and made us who we are.

Negritude's Rational Core

The fight for dignity—for the recognition of a political and cultural existence—was at the heart of a movement that had a profound impact not only on the history of African diasporas but on literature writ large: the Negritude movement. Emerging in 1930s Paris and centered on poetry and theory, this movement was led by young Black students who, from their positions within the most elite establishments in the French capital, launched a radical critique against assimilation and the erasure of African or Afro-Antillean cultural specificity. Césaire expressed its ambitions in these terms: the goal is "to destroy the mechanical identification of races, to tear apart superficial values, to seize the black man [*nègre*] who resides within us, to plant our *négritude* like a beautiful tree until it bears the most authentic fruit."[12] Césaire's call for de-assimilation, understood as the primary truth of Negritude, was echoed by the movement's other figurehead and the first president of Senegal, Léopold Senghor: "I was fighting against the goal of *Assimilation*, and everything this implies and entails—respectfully, but unambiguously."[13] This movement, especially through Aimé Césaire's iteration of it, provides a model for demanding dignity, but it also reveals the pushback and falsehoods such a project is sure to encounter along the way. Despite its critical success, its enduring legacy, and its unforgettable neologism, *négritude* remains nonetheless synonymous with the erasure of Black dignity. To be sure, this is not due to Césaire's writings, nor even to the neocolonial collaborationism that stained the Senghor administration. Rather, it is due to the reductionist interpretations the movement has been subjected to by critics and followers alike.[14]

Césaire's view that Black dignity is part and parcel of the heritage of Black historicity was met with criticism, with some caricaturing his thought as hopelessly folkloric, while others saw it as a first and necessary—though largely insufficient—step in the right direction for the colonized to reclaim a denied identity. Jean-Paul Sartre gave voice to this second interpretation and was perhaps as consequential for the history of Negritude as anything written by Césaire and Senghor themselves. Negritude was in its infancy as a literary movement in 1948 when Sartre signaled its demise. In "Black Orpheus," which served as a preface to an important anthology edited by Senghor,

Anthologie de la nouvelle poésie nègre et malgache de langue française, Sartre forever sealed Negritude's place in the history of ideas by representing it as a mere stage or transitional moment. In Sartre's interpretation, Negritude is death deferred. This interpretation, given by an ostensible, albeit timid, supporter of the movement, was pivotal. This definitively established how the movement would be henceforth received. Negritude was rarely put on trial after this, rarely was it attacked head-on. Rather, people spoke of its moment having passed, of its having run out of steam. Negritude was thus reduced to a short-term tool, a ladder abandoned after reaching the top. One is, of course, grateful for its existence, since "black self-awareness is by necessity born, in the present situation, from poetic experience."[15]Ultimately, Negritude is but a prelude to political action, not political action itself. Indeed, according to Sartre, Negritude is destined to dissolve in its current form only to find full expression in class struggle: the universal struggle of the international working class against the capitalist bourgeoisie. As Fabien Éboussi Boulaga nicely sums it up: "The specificity of the African renaissance was reduced to a mere avatar of the proletariat's struggle, admittedly a kinder struggle filled with pathos."[16]

Sartre's intervention is compelling in that it avoids prescribing a specific course of action: he isn't prodding Black people to adopt a universalist or Marxist position. He frames it as a political necessity: Negritude *cannot not* become Marxism. At the risk of oversimplifying Sartre's argument, it could be best depicted with a syllogism. Negritude is an anti-imperialist movement for liberation; any anti-imperialist movement for liberation is achieved through a universalist Marxism; therefore, Negritude will be achieved through a universalist Marxism. Sartre's failure to see how Black singularity was a cause in itself for liberation presented a problem that Frantz Fanon was quick to highlight. But Fanon's widespread support relies on the same assumptions about Negritude that Sartre made: Fanon is repeatedly seen as having "overcome" Negritude. This reading is marred by an outdated obsession with identity and a narrow focus on the individual that bears no small resemblance to Sartre's anti-imperialist universalism. In such a reading, Fanon's supposed sublation is viewed outside of a dialectical framework, as though he simply *tossed aside* Negritude, preserving nothing else but the obnoxiously banal idea that maybe being Black isn't so bad after all. This strips Césaire's thought of any meaningful theoretical insight, presenting it as a kind of self-help advice for Black people ("Black is beautiful"), urging them just to love themselves for who they are. But

Césaire's Negritude lays out above all else an ethics of dignity. This is why Fanon didn't treat Césaire as washed-up. If he pointed out certain political shortcomings of Negritude, he didn't abandon the movement altogether. In other words, Negritude possesses a *rational core* which also animates Fanon's philosophy. This rational core is the concept of dignity.

To better understand this, one must first grasp the philosophical mechanisms used to reject assimilation. Césaire first expressed this in 1935 but continued to return to it and refine it throughout his life. Much of the misunderstanding around Negritude stems from the mistaken idea that this rejection is motivated by a sort of Black narcissism. In fact, this rejection is rooted in a critical diagnosis of colonial society, in its relentless destruction of memory, and its default mode of pervasive necropolitical violence. Colonial society normalizes violence to such an extent that this violence begins to erupt back home, setting modern European civilization on a course of self-annihilation with racism as the driving force. As the philosopher Jérémie Piolat has shown, the eruption of colonial racism in the *metropole*—with its disdain for popular culture and vernacular knowledge—signals an existential crisis. He describes the sapping of European knowledge "from below," the disappearance of communal dances and songs as bodies are rendered docile in the service of imperialism and capital. The paradox of this historical evolution since 1492 is telling: "In theory, what is supposed to bring glory to Europeans in their own eyes is what, in reality, diminishes them."[17] In other words, the willful neglect of all the popular technologies of self along with a state of emotional distance are usually described by their own victims as the attributes of a superior European rationality that has saved them from their backward ways. But these euphemisms hardly hide the insensitivity underlying Western attitudes or the blind faith white populations have in the propaganda that portrays them as a superior race. These euphemisms do nothing to dispel the indisputable fact that their civilization no longer excels in anything but techno-science and in developing innumerable ways to kill on an industrial scale.

To speak from a point of exteriority, then, as Césaire's Negritude suggests, represents a benefit in itself. Refusing to participate in this murderous society and the raw violence that fuels it is the cardinal virtue of Negritude. When Césaire states, in the very first article he wrote as a young adult, "woe to those who need Descartes's argument of the stick to convince themselves they are none other than themselves,"[18] he is in no way affirming that Blacks are doomed to remain unchanged. In Césaire's view, there are no innate properties unique to Black people, fixed properties that should be accepted and cherished. Far from naturalizing Blacks, Césaire's contribution serves more as a decolonial response to the famous Socratic ethical commandment: "Know thyself as the oppressed." In other terms, liberation can't be achieved by becoming the enemy, by adopting or imitating the attitudes and values of the colonizer. Not only does such an illusion reinforce the colonizer's legitimacy, but, by thrusting one into the heart of the white world rather than remaining on its periphery, it also accustoms one to its practices of violence and humiliation.

Thus, Negritude refuses to participate in modernity's colonial logic. But what does it offer in its stead? Césaire's response is as honest as it is troubling: *ruins*. But sublime ruins. Introducing the Martinican review "Tropiques" in 1941, he writes: "the monstrous atrophy of the voice, the age-old bearing of overwhelming burdens, the prodigious speechlessness. No city. No art. No poetry. No civilization, or no real one, with man projecting himself onto the world, fashioning the world in his image, leaving his signature on the universe. A death more appalling than death, where the living wander."[19] Césaire takes on indignity, this deliberate, necropolitical, confusion between death and life, which imprisons Black people in a form-of-death. In his "Discours sur la négritude" (1987), he defines Negritude as "a manner of living history within history: the history of a community whose experience appears, truth be told, singular with the uprooting of its population, the deportation of men from one continent to another, its fading memory of beliefs, its ruins of massacred cultures."[20] The violence of these negative experiences, of these unlivable histories, is what gives value to everything Black people from Africa, the West Indies, North America, or Europe have preserved. And Césaire suggests that these ruins, these repurposed relics, these intense, haunting memories, interact and cross-fertilize to give rise to a new world, one that escapes the orbit of Europe. This is what Negritude is about.

When Césaire discusses the role of the Black intellectual, he prefigures the late work of Fanon, the political philosopher of such works as *A Dying Colonialism* and *The Wretched of the Earth*: "Our role [...] is to proclaim the coming and prepare the way for those who hold the answer—the people, our peoples, freed from their shackles, our peoples with their creative genius finally freed from all that impedes them and renders them sterile."[21] A single hero: the people. Césaire's politics of ruins draws on the battered pasts of Black populations throughout the world who have endured the unspeakable wrath of racism, imperialism, and coloniality. The twentieth-century Black person is a product of the sedimented history of these political conflicts, shaped within the social sphere as well as that of the imaginary. All Black people inherit this inescapable history; they are haunted by its ghosts, and they can all appropriate these ruins, rediscover their forgotten power, embrace the deep sense of dignity that penetrates and connects their disparate parts. Far from being the vestiges of defeats and humiliations, these ruins possess truths that animate today's social and political struggles, inspiring music, poetry, religious prophecy, and a variety of arts stemming from Black culture. The logic of Negritude is thus thoroughly— albeit implicitly—pan-African. Negritude is nothing more than an invitation to embrace, with all its contradictions, the repressed history of Black dignity.

Deep Historicity

It is important to note that the notion of dignity doesn't only concern the demand of a livable life on the part of the oppressed but also the history of this demand. This argument has theoretical and political implications that shouldn't be ignored. Most prominent among these is the awareness that dignity can't be fully grasped and appreciated without an awareness of its *deep historicity*. My use of this term implies the interplay of three phenomena. The first is the ongoing, first-hand experience of modes of domination that, although issuing from the past, continue to persist as indelible memories: slavery, colonization, segregation, exploitation, alienation. The second concerns the existence and transmission of a history and culture of the struggle against oppression, which inevitably drives today's oppressed. Finally, the third concerns the presence of a habitus and/ or physical markers that betray a subaltern belonging imposed by the social order: language, accent, vocabulary, skin color, facial features, hair texture, table manners, or movement through space, and so on, which demonstrate that to belong to the oppressed is not a matter of choice. Césaire's Negritude provides a clear example for how the deep historicity of Black experience can be recognized, acknowledged, and willfully remembered. This is why it results in an ethical engagement I dare call *essentialist*, a term whose meaning I hope to shift by ridding it of the negative values assigned to it over at least the past thirty years, both in activist discourse and in social and political philosophy. By essentialism, I mean a *politics of essence*. This is a politics that, in Fanon's words, "transforms the spectator crushed by a nonessentialist state into a privileged actor."[22] In other words, a politics of deep history, lived memory, and attachments, which, when derived from the experience of the oppressed, aligns perfectly with a politics of dignity. Needless to say, any critique of this essentialism can't fall back on the overly simplistic idea that social identities are "historical constructs."[23] For, after all, apart from mathematical figures and maybe God, what isn't a "historical construct"? What matters most for establishing a new conception of essence are one's attachments:[24] not the fantasy of an innate substratum of identity, but what gives rise to a community and what a community defends against destruction or deconstruction as a matter of politics. To put it simply, as the Black British sociologist Kehinde Andrews has claimed, "Blackness is a *political* rather than a cultural essentialism."[25]

In my use, the notion of Black essence thus stands in stark contrast to that of Black nature, which suggests that there are intellectual, physical, or mental features biologically specific to "a Black race," conferring upon this race certain social advantages and disadvantages. Even if such features were to exist, it would be ethically problematic to make them the alpha and omega of social organization, as this would amount to erasing individual qualities in favor of a crude statistical norm.

The French philosopher Étienne Balibar has provided a compelling anti-essentialist argument. He begins by diagnosing "the equivalence between essence and norm, the essentialization of social norms and the normative interpretation of the essential characteristics ascribed to human nature (such as the opposition between cultures that requires individuals to *choose* the one to which they belong, or the division of multiple forms of sexuality between masculine and feminine poles, between passive and active, etc.)."[26] His view goes well beyond the crude constructivism often prevalent in the social sciences. But it isn't without its own flaws. Taking the time to distinguish between the notions of essence and norm only to claim hastily that they are indistinguishable poses a logical problem. For Balibar, essence, which is to say a bundle of affiliations not unlike Césaire's understanding of Negritude, is thus identical to norms, merging to the point of confusion with the constraints imposed on individuals and groups. And humanity, in Balibar's view, is defined according to the differential principle of anthropological distinction, which posits that "the human being cannot escape being divided, split into opposite types or models of individuality, even though *the site of this split or opposition can never be settled once and for all*—except, that is, by institutions of a necessarily coercive or violent kind."[27] The concept of anthropological distinction entails the perpetual and differential production of oppositions, from which humanity seemingly cannot escape (evoking Derrida, one might call it an anthropological *différance*, an endless unfolding of singularities). And only institutions, among which the state obviously plays a central role, can interrupt this process of differentiation to establish—by force—codified and uniform norms of identity. This is what Étienne Balibar, and many others, calls essentialism.

It would be more prudent and precise to maintain a clear distinction between essence, which is to say, collective memory, and the norms through which it can be imposed as a single and obligatory reference. This seems all the more necessary with racially oppressed populations—those that possess a deep historicity. Their social position indicates that there are no robust, independent institutions dedicated to their cause or well-being. Two clear examples speak to this institutional vacuum. The first concerns the colonized and postcolonized, who can find themselves at the whims, and under the control, of cheap imitations of traditional institutions, such as those of French Algeria, which Frantz Fanon described as "archaic, inert institutions, functioning under the oppressor's supervision and patterned like a caricature of formerly fertile institutions."[28] But this also concerns the survival of independent institutions—though fragile and small-scale—to which one adheres out of faith, desire, or tradition, but which stand no chance against the state and its repressive and ideological apparatuses. The place of Islam in the contemporary West (despite its opponents' exaggerated sense of the influence it wields) corresponds in large part to this second example. In such cases, the policing of morals and conduct that is sometimes coupled with nonwhite essentialism is precarious, ill-founded, and doomed to failure.

But going on about the inadequacy of these normative institutions that fail to represent the morality and history of the oppressed misses the point. Such a discussion suggests that the most urgent political matter is to reinforce and strengthen these same institutions. In fact, just the opposite is what is needed. The distinction proposed here between essence and norm lays the groundwork for a new political conceptualization of essentialism and offers a fresh take on the historical depth of dignity. The lack of institutional support for the oppressed, their lack of power, should not be seen as an absence but an opportunity. Rather than collapsing essence and norm together,

OUR DIGNITY IS OLDER THAN US

the distance between them should be reaffirmed and politicized. Understood in the light of its deep historicity, essentialism is no longer confining. On the contrary, it enlivens existence by linking it to a community, a history, an imaginary, a narrative. It also serves as a reminder of the interdependence that binds people together. In this respect, relationships aren't opposed to essence. They are one and the same.[29]

My contention is that essence is what binds an individual in the present to a collective past and a political future. By claiming himself to be, *in essence*, Black, Césaire is claiming as an integral part of his being a pan-African history and a philosophy of Black consciousness. Historians and sociologists often retort that laying claim to a past that is infinitely complex and contradictory is an empty political gesture. Worse still, this gesture oversimplifies a rich history.

But this position ignores how Black heritage is consciously handed down from generation to generation. Biko has learned from Fanon, who learned from Césaire, who in turn learned from Du Bois, and so on. Each of these writers makes explicit reference to the political and intellectual legacy of his predecessors. This understanding of essentialism is not reducing the world's complexity; it is affirming that our view of the world owes much to that of our predecessors. It recognizes that there is an ever-evolving, deep historicity that is passed down from one generation to the next. It is not a reductionist view of the world, but one that broadens the world with an inherited perspective. Touting a supposed complexity without tracing a singular path through it is an exercise in intellectual futility, a retreat into a meaningless fantasy. This is why the popular notion of "strategic essentialism," knowingly taken up with no small amount of bad faith, has little to recommend it. Arguing that an essence can be claimed politically only insofar as it is devoid of substance, or that those who lay claim to it never put too much faith in it, amounts in the end to playing make-believe.

Black historical consciousness is a self-conscious consciousness. It is conscious of the import of the previous generation's consciousness. To put it more clearly, to be politically essentialist, to fight for the dignity of the oppressed, is to know that our predecessors, in different contexts unique to their situations, faced the same problems that we are facing: those of social death and survival in a world marked by structural violence, freedom from racial inequality, faith in the oppressed, and so on. Black thought today has inherited the consciousness and ways of thinking of a previous generation, which itself grew out of a legacy of rebellions—but also betrayals. Black essence ensures the constant presence of a family, even in a world that views Black people as illegitimate beings and vagrant souls. It also serves as a reminder of what we owe to those who came before us. For our dignity is older than us. As the black liberation theologian James Cone writes: "We must take the speeches and tales, the blues and the spirituals, the prayers and the sermons of black people and incorporate them into our present existence, relating our parents' strivings to our daily fight to survive."[30] This is how dignity is preserved, this is how it lives on. Such a relationship with the past is not in any way an imprisonment. The past of Africa and its diasporas, a past shaped by crimes and defeats as much as by military exploits and victories, invites a sense of responsibility. A sense of responsibility toward this history but also and above all to our current situation, to those living today. Rather than view essence in conjunction with norms *à la* Balibar, essence should be seen in conjunction with agency. In this respect, my understanding of essence aligns with what the critic Nathalie Etoke calls "diasporic consciousness":

> Diasporic consciousness is a sense of belonging that contributes to an existential fullness. It maintains memory by subjecting it to an archeology riddled with blues. The past fiddles with the present. The past reminds the present of its responsibilities. A present established on the ruins and stelae of what survived the destruction, and what was born of it.[31]

Following this reasoning, essence is not a constraint, but the simple recognition that human memory is finite and that affiliations derive from experience. It isn't possible to simply become whoever or whatever one chooses. This is why the definition of human dignity underlying Eurocentric modernity is suspect. It is no accident that Pico defines man as he who "can rightly acquire what he wishes, and be who he wants to be" just as the Americas were about to be conquered. This hubris, this illusion of grandeur, inaugurates colonialism and the Western belief in its unchecked domination. However, one must not ignore the fact that an individual's or a group's attachments and relationship to the past can become pernicious. The past is never an end in itself and the wish to "remain what one is" satisfies a vain desire and violates the revolutionary drive of human existence. As times change, not everything from the past should be held on to. Some ideas are better left behind. But memory will never be overthrown: no one can abandon his or her memory, nor can it be exchanged for another. Still, it is always possible to modify it, to enrich it. In *A Dying Colonialism*, Frantz Fanon compares this process to the transition to adulthood. Teenagers dream of ignoring all the rules, of being their own authority. But it would be mistaken to believe that becoming an adult means following clear rules and learning how to conform to a specific set of norms. In reality, being an adult entails knowing one's heritage, but also knowing one is free to betray it, which is to say, one can break the rules or establish new ones to better one's own situation. To enliven one's essence—one's memory—without becoming a slave to it: this is an Afro-decolonial position.

Some will object that if Black people and other victims of modernity have a deep historicity, then white people must have one too. This objection is utterly detached from reality. Its principal flaw lies in its narrow view, since it doesn't include colonial Europe as well as white and racist nations in the horizon of its totality. A typical example of this view is found in the old ethno-relativist discourse of the "new right,"[32] which appears to be back in vogue. According to this ideology, each culture is unique and possesses its own specificity which must be diligently preserved. Thus, the very selfhood of European civilization, at once held up as an unparalleled model and described as one ethnolinguistic group among others, is thought to be under attack by the onslaught of American imperialism on the one hand, and the surge of African and Asian immigrants on the other. Fabien Éboussi Boulaga, as though anticipating this superficial position, provided the best response: "to one who lives the destruction of one's own 'world' due to the violence dealt by other worlds and who witnesses the making of cultural hierarchies after the criterion of force, it is permitted, to say the least, not to be satisfied with either the relativism which relishes the equal taste of the various cultures that be or with the pluralism that calls on everyone to tend to the beautiful form of one's original culture, nothing withstanding."[33]

Frantz Fanon makes a similar point in much more concrete terms: "For centuries Europe has brought the progress of other men to a halt and enslaved them for its own purposes and glory; for centuries it has stifled virtually the whole of humanity in the name of a so-called 'spiritual adventure.' Look at it now teetering between atomic destruction and spiritual disintegration."[34] According to Fanon, this is how the white world is viewed by its victims—not from the limited vantage point from which it sees itself, but as belonging to a social and historic totality. Of course, Fanon isn't adopting a point zero epistemology, which confuses one's view of the totality with totality itself. He is offering a critique of the dominant order in its totality from a specific, subaltern position within the geopolitics of knowledge. And from this perspective, the modern West is not one place among others, one culture among others. It is a force of destruction, propelled by slavery and the eradication of alterity throughout its history. The path of ethno-relativism does not lead to dignity for all, because this ideology can't recognize that the dignity of the oppressed entails putting an end to imperial Europe, the European nation-state, whiteness, and all the other signifiers that have served no purpose other than that of asserting the dominance of the West. These obsessions have little to do with patriotism; instead, they reveal an arbitrary lust for power and domination.

The Indeconstructible Part of Ourselves

In the language of contemporary philosophy, *deconstruction* refers to the process of demonstrating that literary or philosophical texts, even institutions, are not coherent and unified totalities but rather are, at their very origins, beset with contradictions they aim to repress. They cast themselves as pure and cohesive, but bear within themselves the seed of their own undoing. The signature move of deconstruction is to identify within the very economy of the text or at the core of its identity an underlying contradiction. We see deconstruction at play, for example, when the queer philosopher Judith Butler argues that no heterosexual man asserting his unbounded virility can ever perfectly align with his self-image.[35] This dissonance reinforces gender norms. Such a theoretical project is an invaluable instrument for social critique, but it shouldn't be fetishized.

The figurehead of deconstruction, Jacques Derrida, considered justice to be "indeconstructible."[36] There are no doubt many ways to interpret Derrida's allusive remarks on the indeconstructibility of justice. One might, for instance, understand justice to be what deconstruction serves. Justice is its core concern and purpose, its *raison d'être*. If institutions should be dismantled, if the ideal of absolute coherency held dear by western philosophy throughout its history should be called into question, it is in the name of justice. And this is precisely what makes it indeconstructible. If justice is removed from the equation, deconstruction becomes what most of its detractors reduce it to: a philosophy of nihilism. But claiming justice to be a guiding principle is fraught with its own contradictions for a philosophy that situates itself on the side of the oppressed. James

OUR DIGNITY IS OLDER THAN US

Cone makes this point in his description of the ethics of Black slaves, which they recognized "intuitively and experientially" since their "mental and physical survival was at stake":

> Right and wrong were not abstract philosophical truths but existential and historical realities defined by black survival and liberation in the social context of servitude. For black slaves, to do the right thing was to do what was necessary to stay alive in bondage with dignity. It had little to do with intellectual discussions about Immanuel Kant's categorical imperative or John Stuart Mill's utilitarianism. Black slaves did not discuss the logic of ethical theory but created ethical structures for behavior in the struggle for survival.[37]

Slaves are not concerned with, or subconsciously guided by, the question of justice. Surviving with dignity is their only urgent concern. However, this doesn't make their ethics unjust. It simply indicates that their ethics is guided by a different principle than that suggested by Derrida. What guides their actions, what fuels the irrefragable part of their beings, is not justice, but dignity. Knowing that deconstruction can be used against the deep historicity of the oppressed, which is to say, against dignity itself, it is hard to overstate the importance of this last point. Despite its considerable intellectual achievements, postcolonial theory often finds itself being used against dignity in just this way. The Indian critic Homi Bhabha offers a telling example of this:

> The language of critique is effective not because it keeps forever separate the terms of the master and the slave, the mercantilist and the Marxist, but to the extent to which it overcomes the given grounds of opposition and opens up a space of translation: a place of hybridity, figuratively speaking, where the construction of a political object that is new, *neither the one nor the other*, properly alienates our political expectations, and changes, as it must, the very forms of our recognition of the moment of politics.[38]

The deconstructivist impulse to abolish the distinction between opposing political positions in favor of what Bhabha calls "hybridity" disables the very form of critique it is striving to achieve. But there is no way of escaping slavery without politicizing the very condition of the slave. Nothing is revolutionary, or even transformative, about identifying the supposed privileges of the slave and the servitude of the master in the name of hybridity. The fluidity of identities in postcolonial discourse undermines the very historical foundation

83

upon which any politics of dignity—that is, any decolonial essentialism—depends. In short, Bhabha implies that those whose existence is hardly visible must become even more invisible in order to enter the political arena. This view fetishizes nonexistence: the more plastic, elusive, and uncategorizable political agents are, the more agency they are given in the discourse of deconstruction. [39] Historically, at least in the context of the transatlantic slave trade, no slave revolt or abolitionist discourse of any consequence thrived by creating a hypothetical "space of translation" between master and slave. They succeeded by abolishing the very place of the master, which is to say, the very possibility of occupying the position of ownership over someone else. In other terms, change was occasioned not by some ideal of a being without quality, of an "enfeebled subject," but from what the Belgian philosopher Marc Maesschalck has called "the return of an empowered subject."[40]

As the queer theorist Sam Bourcier claims, not without provocation, the impulse toward dis-identification was already present in "the anti-identity and, I'd venture to say, anti-minority posture found in Michel Foucault, Gilles Deleuze or Jacques Derrida."[41] He adds that, apart from some significant and meaningful differences, a shared focus of these philosophers on the fluidity of signification and the structural impossibility of any ontological foundation has undeniably allowed for a forceful critique of the state and of identity norms. But they remain nonetheless mired in the dream of human plasticity inherited from Pico and are unwittingly complicit with the ideology—embraced by French republicanism—of colorblindness, which depends on the illusion of objectivity. The anti-humanism that reached a fever pitch in the 1960s only reinforced the core tenet of Eurocentric humanism: the understanding of Western man as a being without substance, defined by the limitless possibilities of transformation and appropriation that lay before him. Is it any wonder, then, that this way of thinking is taken up by dogmatic militants under the banner of a politically hopeless and theoretically sterile anti-essentialism? The overvaluing of difference, *différance*, and a differential system always involves the retreat—ultimately, the indifference—of singularities. It also signals their political impotence. The unceasing multiplication of singularities is thus an unmistakable sign of their insignificance.

Working across methodological divisions and calling into question master signifiers, French philosophy had a laudable and undeniable impact on thought in the latter half of the twentieth century. But it can just as easily lend itself to questionable uses. What's more, half a century later, it has exhausted much of its potential for social critique. Remaining prisoner to the perpetual suspicion spurred on by this philosophical moment ultimately leads nowhere. A new paradigm is overdue. In order to move past an unbridled universalist triumphalism as well as deconstruction's eternal return to difference there is perhaps no better guide than Fanon: "Challenging the colonial world is not a rational confrontation of viewpoints. It is not a discourse on the universal, but the impassioned claim by the colonized that their world is fundamentally different."[42] A poststructuralist approach, which dissolves the particular into a repeating sequence, and an approach that is centered on the fight for dignity, which would stand for nothing without an essentialist identity, are largely incompatible. A politics of dignity can't be a politics of difference. It must be a politics of the particular, of the singular, of originality.

Perhaps the most pointed definition of dignity—the one I am leaning on here—comes from Sadri Khiari. Reflecting on the political thought of Malcolm X, Khiari puts it in straightforward terms: "Dignity is Black power."[43] This power can be expressed in three different ways. First, dignity is above all the power of stepping into the political arena, of affirming the value of one's existence against conditions of indignity. Second, it is the power to demand a livable existence and define it through one's actions. Finally, it is the power to situate oneself within the history of the power of the oppressed, which is to say, within the history of dignity, of its trials and triumphs. This last point is critical. When the dignity of a young Black person is under attack, when this person is raped or killed by state authorities, the whole history of struggle, of political gains and demands for an African humanity, begins to falter. These gains are tenuous and, far too often, the fear of losing them haunts Afro-descendants. The sole possession they are sure to never lose is their dignity. It isn't the object of a demand, but the very ability to make demands: the ability to diagnose indignity and commit oneself to combatting it, even in situations that seem utterly hopeless. This is why one never really fights *for* dignity, but always fights *in* dignity. Our dignity is the indeconstructible part of ourselves.

Part Two

Caliban the Political Theologian

I gave thee a king in Mine anger,
And took him away in My wrath.

Hosea 13:11

— 4 —

THE UNIVERSAL BY ACCIDENT

Early in 1972, a short collection of writings was published in Johannesburg. *Essays in Black Theology* was compiled by the pastor Sabelo Ntwasa, secretary of the University Christian Movement. On February 17, 1972, while the volume was going to press, the South African government "banished" the clergyman.[1] He was put under house arrest, a sentence principally reserved for adversaries of the apartheid regime. In practice, this amounted to a forced withdrawal from all public life. As soon as the book was released, it was taken out of circulation and the Christian University Movement was immediately dissolved. The government's goal was unambiguous: nip the new militant Black theology movement in the bud and bring to a halt its intellectual and social project before it could gain prominence.[2] The book had to wait no longer than a year before being published in London under the title *Black Theology: The South-African Voice*, with important contributions from Steve Bantu Biko and James H. Cone.[3] It would be wrong to read this episode of state harassment against a religious discourse, and those behind it, as a clear instance of religious persecution: there is little doubt that the motives of the "Christian Nation" of South Africa were primarily political. However, framing Black activist discourse in theological terms, whose perceived defiance was enough to elicit significant repression from the state in response, was certainly not just the incidental result of circumstances—even if it is true that the pastor's pulpit was, at the time, one of the few remaining authorized places of public expression for Black Africans. Stepping back from the individual case of Sabelo Ntwasa, it is worth recalling that, though never a coherent body of thought and practice, theology has been a privileged vehicle for the affirmation of Black dignity throughout the course of modernity.

This point is far too often overlooked, especially in contemporary Western Europe, where the words "politics" and "Christianity" either evoke the reviled notion of theocracy, or, in a less harsh light, the few right-leaning "Christian-democratic" political coalitions, which have found acceptance within today's parliaments.

Such clichés ignore the impact religious discourse has had not only in combatting apartheid in Africa, but also in engaging in many other liberation struggles around the world. To return to a Shakespearean figure previously evoked, Christian theology is seen reductively like the figure of Prospero: associated with ideas of purity, nobility, but also sovereignty, omnipotence, and control. So much so that other relations between Christianity and politics have been all but forgotten, with Black theology being a significant case in point. In contemporary social theory, Prospero's defiant servant Caliban is speaking out, as did Black theology in London in 1973. Aimé Césaire's rewriting of Shakespeare's play in 1969, in which a slave gives voice to the revolutionary ambitions of Negritude through a series of tirades, marks perhaps the beginning of this upheaval. At the turn of the twenty-first century, the Antiguan sociologist Paget Henry made Caliban the emblem of an Afro-Caribbean philosophy haunted by the specter of racial violence.[4] A few years prior, the Italian philosopher Silvia Federici cast him as a proletarian and an anticolonial activist.[5] This re-evaluation of Caliban has blazed a trail that the following pages will set out to follow from a theological-political perspective: in my reading, Prospero stands as an allegory of traditional theology whereas Caliban embodies a critical—read *prophetic*—theology.

This distinction comes from the philosopher Cornel West, who drew a contrast between a "prophetic Christianity," which arises during crises when the survival of a people forced into servitude or exile is at stake, and a "Constantinian Christianity," in which religion is at the service of imperialism and state power. But the church and the state make an uneasy alliance, and liberation is unlikely to be attained through their collaboration. "Constantinian Christianity" owes its name to the Roman emperor Constantine I who converted to Christianity in 312. The man who called himself the "bishop over those outside [the church]" was baptized only when at the brink of death. Thus, he was able to live as a pagan and above all as an emperor, which is to say, he was able to wage wars and to kill, with the assurance of seeing, in the twilight of his life, his sins washed away with holy water. West takes this practice of ambivalent faith as his point of departure: "With Constantine's conversion, a terrible co-joining of church and state was institution-alized [...]. As the Christian church became increasingly corrupted by state power, religious rhetoric was often used to justify imperial aims and conceal the prophetic heritage of Christianity."[6] Breaking with pagan pluralism, Constantinian Christianity gave the empire an aura of moral universality, which the modern state still sees itself as possessing. This remains the case even when the state embraces secularism as its official ideology, as in France.

This secularist view of religion, which has an expansionist view of state power and control, is in need of explanation. An approach that favors the oppressed and their demand for dignity requires much more than a simple rejection of the statist and imperialist perspective of the Constantinian approach. The absurd idea that a Gigantomachy is being waged between a Christian Prospero and a secular Prospero should be dismissed outright. Only then can Caliban step forward to assume his rightful place. This also entails re-examining the question of the universal, which is at the core of other forms of political thought centered on emancipation, especially that of the philosophers Slavoj Žižek and Alain Badiou, who have both offered new readings of the legacy of Christianity. This chapter sets out to show that both secular statism and its avowed enemy—a radical social critique that makes strategic use of Christianity—ultimately share the same modernist view of the world. In the name of progress, both hold up universalism as a rejection of the particular and its "barbaric ways." Black theologies offer a different path forward, stemming precisely from a recognition of *the particular*, which has been systematically relegated to a subaltern position by recent critical theory. But, as we shall see, dignity exists only in the particular.

A Constantinian Secularism

Any analysis of the concept of dignity in Black thought would be incomplete without a deeper reflection on the role theology has played in it. But this approach is often met with disdain or misun-derstanding. The main obstacle isn't, as one might assume, an atheism ostensibly hostile to religion, but rather the confidence that a supposedly neutral or more comprehensive approach inspires. In other terms, the problem has little to do with appreciating or failing to appreciate religion, with assessing its claims on truth or its falsehoods. The problem concerns the false assurance of knowing what the term "religion" encompasses. "Secularism,"[7] according to the anthropologist Talal Asad, maintains and perpetuates a gross misunderstanding of the varieties of religious experience, which is all the more egregious as it forms the very condition of possibility of religious pluralism. To understand secularism as it actually exists one must see past the grand narrative presented in textbooks and gushingly praised in political speeches. Secularism isn't an exceptional invention, an epiphany of human reason, the inestimable fruit of Western genius, but a discourse of the nation state.

The function of secularism isn't simply to draw a clear line between private space as the site of religious expression and a neutral public space where one appears as a citizen through the absence of religious affiliations. This framing authorizes the state to define what religion is (i.e., what it *should* be). As Enrique Dussel has pointed out, this satisfies a desire to confer on society a bipartite division between the modern and the premodern, with the former cast in a positive light and the latter in a dark one. Secularism is based on the notion of progress understood as a long transition from the primitive to the autonomous bourgeois individual.[8] In *Qu'est-ce que la laïcité? (What is secularism?)*, the French philosopher Henri Pena-Ruiz offers an unabashed panegyric to this modernist vision, which underscores the importance of Asad's analysis. According to Pena-Ruiz, the privileged place *laïcité* occupies in historical and contemporary society derives from the need to combat what he calls "clericalism," which threatens social unity: "As a belief freely uniting people of faith, religion cannot and should not be confused with clericalism, a markedly temporal ambition for domination that is concretely embodied in the seizure of public power. Understood in this way, clericalism, which imposes its laws on others, goes far beyond the legitimate authority of a clergy whose limits are defined by its community of believers."[9] But how can religion be legitimately defined as a mere belief?

As Asad argues, secularism imposes from an irreligious and modernist perspective an overly generalized definition of religion. This is the exact opposite of freedom of consciousness. Far from granting religious freedom, the state forces individuals to conform to its own conception of religion, which depends on the strict separation of the private interiority of faith and an externalized politics envisaged in the sole manner of the dominant order. It is the secular approach itself that reduces the public practice of religion to "clericalism," which, with its perceived desire for control and influence, can thus be condemned as reactionary. Clericalism is the bogeyman that secularism has itself created, for there is nothing better than the threat of an enemy to legitimize state power. Reducing religion to a set of "beliefs" is thus a way to neutralize this threat. The term *belief* is used to suggest a private spirituality, one that is silent and internal, denoting a sort of inconsequential mysticism. These two constructs of the nation state—"clericalism" and "belief"—legitimize each other and stand as pernicious alternatives, that is, alternatives which "place people before choices that seem as incontestable as the nature of reality."[10] In fact, being held captive by these *pernicious alternatives* precludes the very possibility of a third option.

Yet in spite of how deeply entrenched they are in the European political imagination of the twenty-first century, such alternatives depend on two shaky assumptions. To begin, there is no compelling reason to uncritically accept the inherently modern idea that equates religious experience to "belief," which is ultimately an impoverished and truncated form of theological reflection, a series of vain and vague meditations on the origin and meaning of the universe that goes by the name of "spirituality" today. What's more, it would be naïve to think that "clericalism," that is, the struggle for state power, is the only possible political use of religion. Indeed, as the philosopher Vincent Delecroix has shown, there is a long tradition of the "biblical word" being used "to destabilize the political order, to delegitimize any form of power, to weaken or dissolve any state structure."[11] It is hard to overstate the importance of this last point. Indeed, defending and legitimizing the state is one of the defining characteristics of secularism. This is no surprise, since the state and secularism are seen as mutually dependent.

Black theology, on the other hand, belongs to the religious tradition of challenging the political order, which Cornel West has called prophetic Christianity. For example, when Ottobah Cugoano promised that slaveholders and their collaborators would be mercilessly punished by God, he called into question the theological legitimization of the slave trade while giving the slaves' revolt an eschatological framing. His words denationalized God, privileging a Creator that stands in solidarity with the antislavery struggles lifted from the Old Testament:

> But to set up the ways of the wicked for an example, and to make the laws respecting their suppression, and the judgments that were inflicted upon them for their iniquity, and even the written word of God, and the transactions of his providence, to be reversed and become and precedents and pretences for men to commit depredations and extirpations, and for enslaving and negociating or merchandizing the human

species, must be horrible wickedness indeed, and sinning with a high hand. And it cannot be thought otherwise, but that the abandoned aggressors, among the learned nations will, in due time, as the just reward of their aggravated iniquity, be visited with some more dreadful and tremendous judgments of the righteous vengeance of God, than what even befel to the Canaanites of old.[12]

Cugoano's prophetic speech, which imbues the deep suffering of the defeated with celestial significance, has nothing of the bigoted "clericalist" ambition to impose a new order on the social world. But neither is it reducible to the internalized fervor of faith, since in this case it has a duty to be externalized, to make its rage against the injustices of this world heard. Clearly this is not to establish a theocratic dominion, but to invalidate the iniquitous sovereignty that the slave traders have imposed on Africans with impunity. Secularism fails to recognize that there are at least two ways theological speech wields power. Of course, theological-political discourse can consolidate power, allowing the sovereign—metaphorically equating himself to God—to establish his legitimacy and rule over the world like God rules over the universe. This is the logic underlying Carl Schmitt's *Political Theology*. The critique of clericalism is a response to such an understanding, which is not without merit. But this understanding doesn't account for other ways of wielding power. The notion of an all-powerful God can lead to dramatically distinct conclusions. God's unlimited power can preclude any claim to power on earth. If everything is in his possession, then no mortal has the authority to command another mortal. On the other hand, one has full authority, as Cugoano's prophetic fulminations illustrate, to oust from power false masters and self-proclaimed lords. Blind to this mobilizing power, or even to the very possibility of such a discourse, secularism puts forth a system of oppositions that pits a premodern obscurantism against irreligious emancipation. The latter is falsely assumed to be free of any form of arbitrary or barbaric motivations. The concept of dignity itself is often fitted into this mold. Pena-Ruiz's argument is a clear illustration of this:

> There are indeed secular values, or principles, that derive from a rigorous understanding of human dignity. Religious freedom, equal rights, valuing the common good over personal differences, faith in the principle of personal freedom and independence, which goes hand in hand with a free and independent people, a principle of freedom that allows people to choose freely their own communities of belonging

rather than being alienated from them: the word *laïcité* [secularism] resounds with these ideals.[13]

Dignity is equated with freedom, which is narrowly construed as the freedom of choice. In reality, this pernicious choice between modern emancipation and premodern obscurantism is a prison. Yet, in a context where state racism is pervasive but where, at the same time, everything is done to keep its victims in ignorance of their own condition, affirming the dignity of being Black isn't offered as a choice. Nor is it a matter of being alienated from one's identity. It is a question of knowing oneself as the oppressed in a context where this knowledge is deliberately withheld. Pena-Ruiz's interpretation exemplifies the challenge this form of self-knowledge poses for Black people caught between their present awareness and an understanding of a deep historicity. He performs an odd reversal by presenting the standard model citizen as a memory-less being who takes nothing seriously and for whom *almost* everything is a choice. "The secular idea unites men, elevating them while at the same time detaching them"[14] from their beliefs and ethical stances. The freedom that secularism worships "detaches" citizens from everything—with the notable exception of the rule of law and order, which is to say, the demands of the state. Not a word is uttered about the inherently violent nature of the state. On the contrary, it is idealized, cast in a messianic light, washed clean of any trace of negativity, repression, propaganda: "There are, as we've seen, values unique to *laïcité*, embedded in the juridical and constitutional foundation of society, and which align perfectly with fundamental human rights. The state guarantees these rights and works to actively promote them through the institutions that embody them."[15] This irenic vision, in which the state embodies the human rights that it claims to defend, places it beyond critique, since it seemingly provides the very conditions that allow for the spirit of critique. The European nation-state is the transcendental of secularism.

Through its authoritarian discourse on religion and its embrace of the state, secularism doesn't represent a rupture from Constantinian Christianity but rather a continuation of its ambitions. As Asad points out, with secularism, "the violence of religious wars" was simply replaced by "the violence of national and colonial wars."[16] This is because secularism isn't simply a "fiction," an ideology, or a passing fad. It has a decisive politico-theological function. The discourse of secularism is the theodicy of the modern state, just as Constantine Christianity was the theodicy of empire: a justification of its innately good character, despite the evil that corrupts it.[17] Secularism makes the state an emblem of positivity, ranking it alongside modernity, which is to say, universality, progress, the wealth of nations, rational morality, and individual dignity. In short, secularism characterizes the state in this way to justify the *mission civilisatrice*. This explains in part why critical theory has at times distanced itself from secularism, drawing instead on the history of monotheisms. But withdrawing from the Constantine worldview is easier said than done.

Prospero: Political Theologian

In its propensity to paint itself as an unprecedented emancipatory solution to the dreaded problem of liberticidal clericalism, secularism neglects the many radical traditions of ecclesiastic self-critique where the discourse of faith is turned against itself. Fortunately, the oppressed didn't have to wait for the separation of Church and State to figure out that religion was an unmerciful instrument wielded by governing powers, nor did they ignore the virtues that its prophetic expression could assume for the governed. Mindful of this, as well as of how secularist rationalism has often legitimized the state and capitalism, some communist-leaning philosophers have turned to biblical sources to reinvigorate contemporary political thought. As we'll see, their efforts have been limited for the most part to borrowing strategies for conceptualizing self-mystification while remaining oblivious to the revolutionary uses of religion, uses that can have a real and forceful impact on politics, as the history of Black theology attests. Alain Badiou and Slavoj Žižek are two of the most prominent examples of this tendency. They both organized their philosophy around the concept of universality and the figure of Saint Paul, who embodies universality in the history of Christianity.

For Badiou, Paul the Apostle is the inventor of the very idea of the universal word, which is to say, the universal message. Hence Badiou's interest in this figure. Indeed, according to Paul, the Christian message doesn't belong exclusively to the Jewish communities where it initially took form, but it is also addressed to the Gentiles, that is, the pagan Greeks. Thus Paul takes the message of Christ's resurrection out of its communal or cultural context and downplays the story of Jesus' life, the miracles he performed, and all the feats that made him known in the streets of Jerusalem. "To sharply separate each truth procedure from the cultural 'historicity' wherein opinion presumes to dissolve it: such is the operation in which Paul is our guide."[18] Paul's universalism implies, then, that there are no exceptions, no differences, no communities, only the word of truth addressed equally to anyone and everyone. Badiou is playing one side of identity against the other: a subjective, political identity (which concerns the will and the unshakable conviction that one has truth on his or her side) and an objective identity (made up of memories and collective affiliations). In so doing, Paul, the Apostle to the Gentiles, is depicted as the archetypal figure of the militant.

In reality, arguing that Paul is the creator of a universal message is hardly new and certainly doesn't make Paul a revolutionary. The widely appreciated Protestant theologian Rudolf Bultmann makes a similar argument, claiming that Paul speaks uniquely to each individual in his preaching. Individuals are thus encouraged to step out from behind protective, impersonal institutions such as communal law to forge their own practice of faith and devotion. In contrast, "Jewish piety, the obedience under the law, is in reality a way of escaping from the genuine call of God, from decision."[19] Badiou contributes to this classic argument that casts Paul as a precursor to communism by introducing a new form of subjectivity: a militant subjectivity, which assumes universality by purging itself of the particular.[20] It is worth noting in passing that the idea of a rupture between Judaism and Christianity, central to many theologians and philosophers, is problematic in its own right. Indeed, there is an implicit antisemitism lurking beneath the Pauline perspective. Arguments such as Bultmann's frame Jewish thought as clinging to an atavistic privileging of the particular, which can be overcome by the luminous universalism of Christ's message. Badiou, himself a fierce critic of the radical anti-Judaism of Marcionism, seeks to avoid this problem by situating Paul at equal remove from the people of Israel and the polytheists. He thus disassociates his universalism from Jewish law and, in the same gesture, from the wisdom of the Greeks.

Even if he later reversed his position, we owe to Slavoj Žižek a theological-political interpretation of the universal much richer than that which depends on the complete removal of particularity. This marked a clear departure from Badiou's theory, which falls in line with the *doxa*: "Judaism thus not only belies the common-sense notion that the price to be paid for access to universality is to renounce one's particularity; it also demonstrates how the stain of unacknowledgeable particularity of the gesture that generates the Universal is the ultimate resource of the Universal's vitality: cut off from irredeemable/repressed particular roots, the Universal ossifies and changes into a lifeless, empty, abstract universal form."[21] A more authentic Christian position, then, doesn't attempt to overcome the particular in an effort to accede to the universal. Rather, it undoes the opposition between the universal and the particular made possible by the absoluteness of love, thereby radicalizing the Jewish gesture. Unfortunately, beginning with *The Puppet and the Dwarf: The Perverse Core of Christianity* which appeared three years after the above quote, Žižek abandons this radical conception of the relation between the universal and the particular, moving closer to Badiou's position and embracing "the common-sense notion that the price to be paid for access to universality is to renounce one's particularity," which he had previously derided. "The key dimension of Paul's gesture is thus his break with any form of communitarianism: his universe is no longer that of the multitude of groups that want 'to find their voice', and assert their particular identity, their 'way of life', but that of a fighting collective grounded in the reference to an unconditional universalism."[22] Žižek thus ends up embracing without reservation Badiou's definition of the universal as *that which is shared by all* and which is achieved by *distancing oneself from particularities and communities*. These two defining features are also those that characterize Henri Pena-Ruiz's secularism. As Pena-Ruiz explains, "the state's neutral position regarding denominations is only the flipside of its concern for the universal and for shared values."[23] Although Badiou's and Žižek's conception of the universal is meant to serve a "communist" political project, it maps directly onto the secularist model that governs the modern state. Devoid of any revolutionary potential, it is therefore a far cry from an iconoclastic philosophy.

For Žižek, if our time calls for a return to Paul, it is above all because the only absolute we recognize is a negative one of radical evil in the form of mass killings. "The evocation of the Holocaust serves as a warning of what the ultimate result of the submission of Life to some higher goal is."[24] Finding in Paul a philosophy centered on affirmation, bolstered by a desire to do away with all negativity, demonstrates once again Badiou's influence on Žižek. Indeed, Badiou characterized Paul's approach as *anti-dialectical*: a philosophy that has no place for negativity. For him, grace is an affirmative act that doesn't depend on suffering, humiliation, defeat. Badiou can thus call for founding "a materialism of grace through the strong, simple idea that every existence can one day be seized by what happens to it and subsequently devote itself to that which is valid for all."[25] In other terms, from Badiou's perspective, when Paul famously affirms that in Christ there are no longer slaves or masters, it doesn't mean

THE UNIVERSAL BY ACCIDENT

first and foremost that Christianity delegitimizes the institution of slavery, but rather that the slave and master are held as equals before God's universal word. This means they both legitimately bear witness to, and serve as messengers of, an Apostolic—which is to say, militant—discourse.

In sum, universal truth and the idea of freedom hold that slaves and masters are equals. This abstraction erases the pivotal role played by liberation struggles—whose influence has shaped Afro-descendant thought—and the existential transformation they imply (i.e., the shift of status from object or beast to human). Even if we accept Badiou's argument that Christian discourse is valid "for everyone" and that "any existence" can be "moved" by it, it still doesn't follow that it would be received the same by everyone, or that it would have the same effect when applied to the zone of being or to that of nonbeing. Black theology teaches that once slave and master take up the same religious doctrine, there is no longer one religion, but two: that of the oppressed and that of the oppressors. Let's not forget what slaves do with God's message among themselves and for themselves behind their masters' backs. Nat Turner is a case in point. Badiou's conception of the universality of Pauline discourse assumes that it remains invariable, fundamentally intact, and unaltered by those who receive it. The missionary mindset behind this idea has long been familiar to Africans. It is that of "a Christianity of empire [that] imposes itself only by tearing up its converts by the roots, out of where-they-live, out of their being-in-the-world [...]. The missionary discourse has a habit of propounding God, or the content of the faith, as the irruption into one's world of the purest Strangeness, and conversion as the snatching of the candidate for Christianity from the jaws of perdition, which is confused with one's traditional mode of living and being human."[26] Far from the unmistakable ecumenism that Badiou claims to reveal in Paul, religious institutions of Black America were from the outset political organizations driven by the interests of slaves alone: "at the start of the nineteenth century, insurrection was channeled through, and fomented by, the black church. The church allowed people to gather to discuss these matters, it circulated information, it was the hub of a wider network. The very creation of independent black churches was an expression of the black desire for emancipation."[27]

Turning away from the communal spirit of collective organizations, Badiou describes Paul's apostolic or militant discourse as a self-authorizing truth that resists argumentation and the performance of miracles. Simply put, the naked power of what is given as truth requires either outright adherence or flat rejection. Christ's resurrection is not to be judged according to what it makes possible but simply to be accepted or rejected as a primordial existential truth, but without guarantee. This hollow apostolic acceptance is largely absent from Black Christianity. Not because the discourse of Black Christianity relies on proof or the ineffable. It is based on dignity, which is to say, the astonishing power demonstrated for centuries by the survival of populations whose conditions of existence have been worse than death, conditions, as I've been calling them, of indignity. This survival isn't only attested to by the people themselves, but also by their artistic and intellectual traditions. Badiou fails to recognize that outside the experience of oppression, without the affliction of living under the constant threat of death, there is no *good* reason (which is to say, no ethical-political or unsuperstitious reason) to adhere to Christianity and its belief in resurrection. Outside of these oppressive conditions, and with liberation no longer being vitally sought, there is no need for Christianity.

Badiou does, however, speak of this lack of need in other terms: "Resurrection is neither a sublation, nor an overcoming of death. They are two distinct functions, whose articulation contains no necessity."[28] A politics of resurrection is not the necessary response to the persistent experience of indignity and of living under the form-of-death since, from Badiou's perspective, violence and oppression are more or less indiscriminate. Mehdi Belhaj Kacem has rightly pointed this out: for Badiou, "philosophy is what purges the truth of its blood and grease, elevating it to the canonical eternity of the concept."[29] Kacem adds, "for me, the *abstraction* at the core of Badiou's thinking stems from the idea that Goodness exists as an independent process and is completely detached from all the Evil it opposes (within and outside of politics)."[30] In Badiou's view, evil and death are trivialized. But for slaves, they are hardly trivial matters that can be comfortably ignored. "Of death the Negro showed little fear, but talked of it familiarly and even fondly as simply a crossing of the waters," wrote W.E.B. Du Bois.[31] Death is a traveling companion; at times a relentless adversary, at others, an indispensable ally ready to strangle a master with a death grip. By dismissing it, Badiou condemns himself to a narrow Eurocentrism which views death merely as a matter of choice.[32] Black theology, born of the struggle for survival and liberation as old as modernity itself, counters this interpretation of resurrection with its own. James Cone makes this clear:

> It is within this context that the resurrection is a *political* event. The politics of the resurrection is found in its gift of freedom to the poor

and the helpless. Being granted freedom while they are still poor, they can know that their poverty is a contrived phenomenon, traceable to the rich and the powerful in this world. This new knowledge about themselves and the world, as disclosed in and through the resurrection, requires that the poor practice political activity against the social and economic structure that makes them poor. Not to fight is to deny the freedom of the resurrection. It is to deny the reality of Christ's presence with us in the struggle to liberate the slaves from bondage.[33]

In Badiou's depiction, the figure of Paul is that of a wealthy man who, without apparent reason, grows passionate about an idea (in this case, that of Christ's resurrection) which becomes a truth he preaches throughout the world. To be sure, the idea is universal, but its universality erases the key difference between those for whom this truth stands as a vital necessity and those, following Paul, for whom it merely wards off angst and spices up a dull or splenetic life. These two ways of receiving this truth couldn't be further opposed. When the good news of resurrection is brought to slaves and masters, a new universal subject doesn't arise. Instead, a slave's Christianity emerges on one side and that of the master on the other. They may have a shared vocabulary but not a shared experience. Even when religion was encouraged and supported by the landowners, Black people still practiced it in private at no small risk to themselves, thoroughly reinterpreting and reshaping it in their own manner.[34] Nat Turner is the product of those private nighttime meetings. Slave and master cannot both be touched by grace simply by believing in the same truth; grace can only be experienced by all when freedom is achieved and the institution of bondage is forever abolished. Only then can one stop conspiring in private gatherings and begin to commune freely.

Contrary to what Žižek and Badiou maintain, the problem of our time is not that people are obsessed with negativity, but rather that they fail to see its necessity and its power. It has become so inadmissible to openly acknowledge the unquestionable political role murder plays in some contexts of rebellion or revolution that these murders are reduced to nothing, if not outright denied as murders, as negative operations. Even the existence of negativity is denied, which in fact allows for the possibility of massacres or mass extermination. A clear distinction must be made between a politics of negativity that acknowledges and embraces its negativity (such as with the period of the "Terror" during the French Revolution) and a politics that casts itself as intrinsically positive and beyond reproach, and thereby purely and simply dismisses its victims (such as the National Socialist's

CALIBAN THE POLITICAL THEOLOGIAN

Judenrein defined as a "Final Solution"). The former recognizes its own negativity and, understanding its necessity, must strive to contain and control it *as much as possible*;[35] the latter denies any negativity and presents itself as a positive solution to a problem. James Baldwin alerted us to this: as massacre is an act of self-affirmation for the exterminator, extermination is deemed *innocent*. Those who fail to recognize their own negativity cannot assume responsibility for their actions. We must see past the false alternative between a holocaust-obsessed thinking evoked by Žižek, which accuses any attempt to radically transform society of promoting mass crimes, and the giddy enthusiasm for the "rights of the Infinite, exercising their sovereignty over the contingency of suffering and death,"[36] which, cloaked in angelic innocence, turns a blind eye to the existence of extreme violence it lacks the courage to think through, let alone acknowledge in the context of its dark history. As Enrique Dussel remarked, "from the deepest reaches of the ostensible good (or goodness claim) of the dominant social order there appears a face, many faces, who clamor for life at the very edge of death. These are the faces of the unintentional victims of the dominant system that makes this goodness claim. Now, suddenly, from the standpoint of these victims, truth begins to reveal itself as nontruth."[37]

Make no mistake, true to its communist-leaning politics, Badiou's thought expresses solidarity with the oppressed on several occasions and shows itself sensitive to their conditions. However, the very architecture of his philosophy, with its naïve paralipsis of the negative, prevents him from genuinely acknowledging the history of the oppressed or their ongoing struggles. The embodied philosophy of revolutionary dignity, which runs through Black theology discourse and where it is made manifest in the well-known slogan "freedom or death," offers a possible way out of this alternative between two symmetrical positions of innocence (that of the state and that of "communist" philosophers). But it is also at play in some critical theory, as attested to by Adorno: "The need to lend a voice to suffering is a condition of all truth."[38] This echoes Cugoano's obscure prophecy which boldly affirms the power of the negative. His words are spoken by someone who, forced into the hold of a slave ship, came to know death intimately before even becoming a man.

> I must yet say, although it is not for me to determine the manner, that the voice of our complaint implies a vengeance, because of the great iniquity that you have done, and because of the cruel injustice done

THE UNIVERSAL BY ACCIDENT

unto us Africans; and it ought to sound in your ears as the rolling waves around your circumambient shores; and if it is not hearkened unto, it may yet arise with a louder voice, as the rolling thunder, and it may encrease in the force of its volubility, not only to shake the leaves of the most stout in heart, but to rend the mountains before them, and to cleave in pieces the rocks under them, and to go on with fury to smite the stoutest oaks in the forest; and even to make that which is strong, and wherein you think that your strength lieth, to become as stubble, and as the fibres of rotten wood, that will do you no good, and your trust in it will become a snare of infatuation to you![39]

Compared to a Black uprising over a worthy cause, the neglect of death reveals what it truly is: the casual disregard of masters, unaccustomed to death's haunting presence, strangers to its regular visits. This indifference, elevated to an ontology, is without doubt a defining feature of Prospero's political theology. Along with this is the holy belief in the possibility of freedom granted without the negative journey through *liberation*, which is to say, the bitter and cruel struggle for freedom by precisely those who have been deprived of it. The aristocratic desire to ignore death fails to recognize that it is death itself, in the form of indignity, that intrudes into the lives of the oppressed and plagues their entire life experience. The common point between the Eurocentric "communist" logic and that of the secular state lies in this universalist voluntarism. Both positions consider themselves as purely affirmative manifestations of a modern sensibility.

Down with Prospero! Long live Caliban!

Politics of the Particular

Philosophers such as Žižek or Badiou repeatedly point out the importance of the universal and the derisory or asphyxiating character of the particular. Yet such insistence may be more baseless than its constant litany suggests. The assumption that a politics of the particular is impossible, or the hasty reduction of this politics to some kind of avatar of chauvinism, must be questioned. To unthinkingly accept this assumption is to demean any politicization of the Black condition as fascist. Although rarely expressed so baldly, the ideological mistrust of politicizing the particularity of Black lives has plagued thinking on this matter. So much Black political thinking has been made acceptable by framing it as universal that one begins to

103

doubt there is any other way of thinking about it. To be sure, as the example of Negritude has shown, the notion of universalism is by no means absent from Aimé Césaire's or Léopold Senghor's thinking, where it finds a compelling expression worthy of careful consideration. But the disproportionate attention given to this notion—taken as the point of entry into the thought of these writers—poses its own problems.[40]

This skewed view forgets that Black movements such as Negritude or the Harlem Renaissance are born of the historical necessity to reassert the value of Black specificity and reaffirm the dignity of this singular existence which, throughout its history, modernity has held as abject. Of course, focusing on the universal is above all a strategy to give credibility to Black philosophies, ethics, aesthetics, and political thinking. But it is worth asking why the universal represents such a high standard in the first place. What is lost—or avoided—with this focus? The very pervasiveness of universalism makes one wonder if the *condition of readability* of Afro-descendant authors depends on its affirmation. Would the absence of universalism open the Black text to ridicule or accusations of ethnic chauvinism? Harping on about the universal reach of Negritude or of other Black movements implies in effect that Black particularity remains "unpresentable" in Western culture. Never demanded from European thinkers, this pronounced universalism stands as the necessary condition for the reception of Afro-descendant writing.

Devaluing the notion of the particular while inflating that of the universal isn't a problem unique to Black thought. It is a much vaster problem. Judith Butler has argued persuasively that "social movements may well constitute communities that operate with notions of universality which bear only a family resemblance to other discursive articulations of universality. In these cases, the problem is not to render the particular as representative of the universal, but to adjudicate among competing notions of universality."[41] In other terms, universality can find distinct political articulations; it need not represent an ahistorical ideal. Drawing on Hegel, Étienne Balibar has taken up and expanded Butler's theory.[42] He contends that any utterance of universality bears within it a fundamental contradiction: any political action or expression that lays claim to universality by necessity particularizes the universal. The very nature of political action demands that claims for universality be named. These claims are always represented by a specific group, made to comply with new laws, and so on. Thus, there is no utterance of the universal that doesn't announce at the same time its particularity.

104

Conversely, any political claim to particularity, insofar as it aims to be recognized by those who do not belong to the group in question and makes demands on others, presupposes the possibility of its own universalization.

This logic should have led Balibar to declare that the universal and the particular are but two names of the same tactic adopted in many political struggles. They represent two discursive registers or actions, whose value is measured solely by its impact, its effectiveness, and its ability to adapt to a given context and to the questions of life and death at stake. But, quite unexpectedly, he maintains that "debates about the opposition between the universal and the particular, and *a fortiori* between universalism and particularism, are much less interesting and decisive than debates opposing different conceptions of the universal or different universalities."[43] Balibar thus unambiguously trivializes the concept of the "particular." It is so clear to him that the particular is *less interesting* and *less decisive* than the universal that he doesn't bother justifying his position.

This positive framing of the universal is the default position of contemporary social critique. Adorno had already warned against the assumption—central to the philosophy of identity—that "nothing particular is true,"[44] and he criticized the tendency to make Truth manifest through the violent eradication of all singularity. But his warning went unheeded by contemporary philosophy and social critique. In practice, this tendency is expressed by what I'm calling a *universalist voluntarism*: an unrelenting desire to bring about or embody universality. Here too the work of Žižek and Badiou on Saint Paul are representative. Indeed, Badiou goes so far as to denounce the "catastrophic pronouncements of the sort: only a homosexual can 'understand' what a homosexual is, only an Arab can understand what an Arab is, and so forth. If, as we believe, only truths (thought) allow man to be distinguished from the human animal that underlies him, it is no exaggeration to say that such minoritarian pronouncements are genuinely *barbaric*."[45] But these so-called minority pronouncements, which are in fact efforts to politicize the singularity of the oppressed, are claiming that there are negative social experiences, qualitatively different from other experiences. As such, they cannot be adequately described or captured by metaphor in a language that is shared and understood equally by all. An extreme, but telling, example of this structural impossibility of making negative social experiences sufficiently intelligible is found in Jean Améry's reflections on torture. A Jew who was part of the resistance in World War Two, he himself was tortured by the SS. In his work *At the Mind's Limits: Contemplations by a Survivor on Auschwitz and Its Realities*, he gives an account of this unspeakable experience:

> It would be totally senseless to try and describe here the pain that was inflicted on me. [...] One comparison would only stand for the other, and in the end we would be hoaxed by a turn on the hopeless merry-go-round of figurative speech. The pain was what it was. Beyond that there is nothing to say. Qualities of feeling are as incomparable as they are indescribable. They mark the limit of the capacity of language to communicate. If someone wanted to impart his physical pain, he would be forced to inflict it and thereby become a torturer himself.[46]

It bears repeating that this is an extreme example. But it shows what is at stake in what Badiou calls "minority pronouncements," and what Badiou fails to grasp.[47] The lived experience of torture resists communication. To consider the examples Badiou treats, the same can be said of experiences of homophobia or racism, even if, fortunately, these rarely reach the degree of intensity of the torture Améry describes. They can be grasped conceptually on a general level, but a clear and distinct understanding of their full range of meaning can only be attained through physical, bodily, and personal experience. But according to Badiou, when homosexuals or Arabs refuse to concede to the universalist that he knows as much as they do about the dehumanization they routinely face, they are immediately on the side of barbarism. In this sense, barbarism is that which perpetually stands in the way of universalist voluntarism, which is to say, the desire, typical of the Western world, to appropriate everything, to become anything one chooses. In essence, this is the colonial logic of conquest in its purest form, which deems anything that resists its control barbaric. Although Badiou calls for *"an indifference that tolerates differences,"*[48] his goodwill fades immediately in the face of any serious effort to politicize the dignity of these differences. Slavoj Žižek expresses as much in no uncertain terms: "every politics that grounds itself in the reference to some substantial (ethnic, religious, sexual, lifestyle...) particularity is by definition reactionary."[49] Following this reasoning, the only way to think politically about singularity is by subtraction or omission. Otherwise, one risks appearing reactionary or barbaric—which are but two sides of the same enemy. The first lacks a fully developed political consciousness; the second is just plain stupid and unaware.

However, the failure to fully comprehend these experiences, as well as the seeming unbridgeable chasm that separates disparate politico-historical positions, do not in any way stand in the way of forming a coalition assembled from a diverse set of alliances, communities, and political organizations. This can be accomplished provided their distinct problems are fully accounted for. Neglecting singularities doesn't lead to the sublime realization of the universal. Rather, it is the surest sign of a lazy and self-centered politics. This wasn't lost on Steve Biko, who denounced what he called the "myth of diversity" which, in the context of apartheid, held that equality is achieved through the equal participation of white and Black people in the same political organizations. This myth misses the point that "no matter what a white man does, the colour of his skin—his passport to privilege—will always put him miles ahead of the black man. Thus in the ultimate analysis no white person can escape being part of the oppressor camp."[50] Black people needed to reaffirm their own dignity before there could be collective action between different South African racial groups. To be sure, Black people and white people can and should understand each other on equal terms. But to accomplish this, white people must admit that they will never know racial violence as intimately and deeply as Black people whose bodies have been shaped by it. Such an understanding doesn't depend on penetrating the inner workings of the Black soul. White people can strive to understand Black experience through this very impossibility. This can function as an ethical acceptance of an alterity that can never entirely be grasped conceptually. Understanding the other, in this sense, means accepting the unknowability of this deep historicity, of this singular embodiment of dignity. In other words, it means acknowledging that knowing the other will not amount to erasing his or her untamable alterity.

The emergence of two competing slogans in 2013 speak to the urgency of rethinking a politics of the particular. The first is "Black Lives Matter." With these three words, Black activists affirm their dignity in face of the constant threat of death posed by state-sponsored racism. If a small racist group formed under the banner "White Lives Matter," its impact is marginal compared to the more strategic response of white supremacists. This response rallies under the slogan "All Lives Matter." It is impossible to argue against its claim: declaring some lives have more value than others is deplorable. The slogan "All Lives Matter" is indeed more *universal* than "Black Lives Matter," which is why white supremacists have taken it up. The hegemonic group need not name itself. Articulated thus, this slogan's abstract universality obviates the need to grapple with the historically specific conditions of indignity under which Black populations have lived—and continue to live—in North America. There is no denying that all lives matter. But for half a millennium it is above all Black lives that have been singularly held as marketable, killable, expendable. Dissolving the specificity of Black experience into an ill-considered universalism makes it impossible to grasp the deep historicity of the Black condition, and, with it, the legitimacy of the struggle for Black dignity and the purpose of its political motives.

The history of Black dignity and thought is in large part that of the effort to politicize the particular. This simple fact doesn't justify deeming it barbaric, reactionary, unimpactful, or even unworthy of consideration. But it would be equally misguided to adopt the opposite position by delegitimizing the universal as intrinsically Eurocentric. This has been the approach of some decolonial thinkers, who, pointing to the role the concept of universalism has played in colonial history, caution against its use, which they equate with rationalism.[51] Although this approach is on strong ethical ground, it overlooks a key matter. The strength of Balibar's argument is its contention that one's own potential universalism cannot be completely contained. We can never be sure if our discursive position will have universal reach or, *a minima*, will be universalizable. Universalism exists of its own accord, governed as though *by chance*. The question of universalism isn't right or wrong, but it is a question not in need of posing. It arises on its own and poses *itself* as a question.

Universalization is an accident of political circumstances, not a cause. Hence, it is neither possible nor desirable to deny the universal. Rather, we must guard ourselves against universal voluntarism. For it is the voracious and vicious desire to impose universality, and not the concept of universality itself, that is behind colonial plundering and the division of the world into two camps: the civilized and the barbaric. Striving for universalism, taking care to couch one's discourse in universalist terms when a radical transformation of the social order is called for as a matter of survival, is, to paraphrase the old village leader from Kurosawa's "Seven Samurai," akin to worrying about your beard when your head is hanging by a thread. Worse still, setting universality as a goal or explicit condition of politics is to fall victim to a colonial logic whose primary ambition is to abolish alterity. Whereas the universal arises from the struggle for dignity and liberation, the *mission civilisatrice* arises from the struggle for the universal.

Dignity and Universality

In the previous chapter, I sketched the historical development of Black dignity, which was used to combat different forms of imperialism, colonialism, and racism that shaped modernity. In so doing, I didn't mean to imply that only Africans and Afro-descendants are capable of understanding dignity. Throughout modernity, dignity was deemed universal, defined as inherently human, as the basis of the human condition. I have no qualms with this basic definition, but will strive to clarify it and develop it further. Kant's moral philosophy cast itself as a secularization of Christian ethics,[52] but his bourgeois and benevolent vision of ethics excluded the oppressed from its purview. In the following chapters, the discussion will be reframed in the terms outlined by Black liberation theology. For now, though, it bears clarifying how the universal relates to the particular in an Afro-decolonial conception of dignity.

What is truly universal, in the ordinary sense of "valid for all," is never a political point, but only human neoteny—that is, the "immature" condition human beings display at birth.[53] Surprisingly, for some philosophers, neoteny indicates that human beings have the capacity to develop independently, and this self-development is an expression of a radical freedom owing to the species's very lack of deterministic assignations.[54] This ignores the fact that neoteny implies first and foremost what Judith Butler calls *precarity*, defined by one's vulnerability in the face of violence and deprivation and the inability to survive without the help of others: "precariousness is coextensive with birth itself (birth is, by definition, precarious), which means that it matters whether or not this infant being survives, and that its survival is dependent on what we might call a social network of hands. Precisely because a living being may die, it is necessary to care for that being so that it may live."[55] However, although it implies at its core human finitude and the original dependence on the helping hands of others, neoteny often connotes omnipotence: the human ability to strive toward perfection, to gain ever more control over one's surroundings and over oneself. This overlooks the fact that before being the architect of one's own fate, before fashioning one's physical and intellectual characteristics, the infant is a being whose dependence is absolute and whose subsistence is radically impossible without the help of the community within which it is born. Most acutely felt at birth, this innate dependency never really leaves human beings. The notion of the self-made man is a myth of modernity. The language we speak doesn't belong to us; the knowledge we depend on daily was handed down to us by others; we are incapable of producing and transforming the totality of goods we consume. Neoteny—the anthropological feature that best highlights our vulnerability in the face of chance and arbitrary circumstances—has been dressed up as a mark of human omnipotence, displaying the bad faith typical of European moral philosophy described in the first chapter. Thus, the real implications of defining dignity in relation to neoteny remain to be explored. If there is one thing neoteny makes clear, it is the perpetual risk of death that threatens the powerless child. This is what gives rise to dignity, which can be understood as the will and power to keep death at bay.

It should be recalled that dignity has no predetermined content. As established in the second chapter, it is first and foremost a rejection of indignity, such as when one refuses to abandon an infant who can't survive on its own. But it also refers to the indignation felt in the face of violence or humiliation, and to the belief that those who endure this are not reduced to this existence. Just as the dependency of childhood doesn't just disappear once and for all in adulthood, dependency, vulnerability, and the risk of death plague the oppressed at all stages of life and, therefore, their fight for dignity is never over. "The dignity of persons is their ability to contradict what is, to change and be changed, and to act in the light of that which is not yet,"[56] Cornel West writes. Such is the conceptual core of dignity: it is brought to light by social negativity and is itself a form of negativity, which is to say, it is an active refusal, destroying or transforming that which it rejects. Parents who acknowledge the dignity of their newborns *refuse* to abandon them, which would be tantamount to letting them die; slaves convinced of their dignity *refuse* to let racial terror get the better of them. Dignity manifests itself when one no longer accepts the normal order of things. But the negative underpinning of dignity, as an immediate refusal or rejection of death or oppression, remains, strictly speaking, without any content. It is initially devoid of meaning for any collective group. It is only through history, when cultural forms develop from this original negativity and begin to take shape, that dignity comes to have a positive, shared value. The most powerful manifestations of dignity—those that are capable of greatly impacting the lives of the oppressed—spring historically from collective formations founded on a refusal of the form-of-death (several examples from the history of Afro-descendants were taken up in the third chapter).

THE UNIVERSAL BY ACCIDENT

In no way am I suggesting that dignity belongs uniquely to particular groups. Rather, recognizing the historicity of dignity entails rejecting its abstract understanding à la Kant, according to which dignity belongs to all rational beings without distinction. In Black history, the term *dignity* denotes the power of survival, the ability to endure suffering and humiliation by turning death itself into a resource. If this understanding isn't reflected in modern European philosophy, it is because there was no need for it. What it needed, instead, was the leveling out implied by the notion of "human person," which blinded this philosophy to extreme inequality and stark differences in social conditions. "Indignity" is absent from European philosophy. It preferred a different type of dignity, such as Prospero's undifferentiated dignity which offers nothing to the oppressed and fails to recognize the confinement of the enslaved. There is no question that dignity is the basis of all humanity. But it doesn't follow that dignity means the same thing for different groups. The notion of dignity, which at its core refers to the effort to make life "livable," is the stage of ethical conflict. It has taken on distinct, conflictual meanings depending on its material context. These historical accretions should not be dismissed as aberrations, nor understood as opinions built up over time that mask a pure or original meaning of dignity. These "aberrations" and "opinions," these conflicts and disagreements, make up the history of life and the very concept of dignity. Any response given to the question "what is life worth living for?" constitutes part of this history. Dignity can thus no longer be viewed as an unchanging and eternal part of human nature. It is formed, rather, through a network of relationships situated at a specific time and space, through living relationships with people, with hardships, and with the memory of these hardships and the assurance that there will be more.

My goal here is not to establish an opposition—inevitably reductionist—between a primordial dignity which, at its origin, would be universal, and the forms it would subsequently assume as it took on specific meanings through particular histories, losing its neutrality and indiscriminate applicability along the way. In reality, the particular ways the notion of dignity has been put to use are no less universal than the primary rejection of indignity. The psychiatrist Bernard Doray is right to claim that "dignity appears like an internal cultural production, clearly determined by nature (the dependency of children and the vital obligation to cooperate on a social level), but which is constantly recreated in a singular form in each person."[57] Frantz Fanon's thinking also proved itself universal in hindsight

111

when his analysis, developed specifically as a response to the unique revolutionary power he saw in Algeria, was taken up and translated by the Shiite liberation theologian Ali Shariati, the Bolivian revolutionary Ernesto Guevara, or the South African activist Steve Biko. His thinking had an impact in places, languages, and contexts outside of its specific field of reference. Thus, it is when thought diligently tends to the specificity of a case of oppression and the power that allows it to be confronted and conquered that one witnesses how dignity becomes universalizable. In other words, what is behind this struggle is revealed in this way. Paradoxically, universality derives from the effort to grasp in precise and rigorous terms an irreducibly specific situation. To put this another way: political and ethical thinking isn't achieved by shaping a current situation to fit a so-called universal norm or ideal. It is achieved by bringing one singularity to bear on another, thereby seeing the latter in an unexpected, revealing light. Marx's works on the revolutions and counterrevolutions of nineteenth-century France, just like Fanon's writings on the Algerian revolution, are cases in point. They capture specific moments of engagement, which then allows these moments to be connected to other future ones. Universalization is the name we give to these kinds of productive connections and fruitful juxtapositions. Any thought born of a specific context of liberation is potentially universalizable insofar as it can be adopted and adapted by other oppressed peoples. Universality is achieved when the oppressed fighting for their own dignity recognize their fight in other oppressed peoples waging the same battle. It never exists *a priori*, but always *a posteriori*. Political discourse or action that can be replicated in countless other situations is universal.

The following two chapters share this aim of thinking through the most singular circumstances in the hope of applying their lessons to future struggles. To do so, attention will be given to important historical expressions of dignity whose specificity lies in their unique intermixing of ethical demands, theological meditations, and political thought. The first of these will focus on Black liberation theology developed in North America, which will be viewed principally through the prism of James H. Cone's work. The second will look at how a Bantu conception of dignity was taken up in the latter half of the twentieth century in the philosophical and religious discourse of the Ubuntu. Black political theology offers fertile ground for a reflection on dignity since, rather than being confined to the immanent presence of a restricted political space, it explores the consequential territory beyond life.

— 5 —

A THEOLOGY OF BLACK DIGNITY IN NORTH AMERICA

This chapter offers a closer look at the original conception of Black dignity as it was articulated in the context of North America, with its history of slavery, the slave trade, segregation, and the enduring "afterlives" of these practices.[1] This concept took shape notably in a religious context, where a political consciousness formed in conjunction with a dignity empowered in the face of oppression. Decisive in combatting imperialism and white supremacy, African American religion is thus deserving of more critical attention. And there is perhaps no figure more radical in the tradition of Black liberation theology than James Cone, who came to prominence in the 1970s. Black churches fought struggles that were costly and not without risk, invented theologies and philosophies, and developed a cultural imagination centered on devotion, which disproves the idea that faith is a form of alienation. They showed, too, that the Bible can be read to support a radical and revolutionary transformation of the social order.

Black religious practices in North America fit uncomfortably within the categories most often associated with the "matter of religion." They bring together theology and politics while drawing on ancestral and modern traditions. If, as Jacob Taubes contends in his challenge to the assumed division between monotheism and polytheism, the primary form of all devotion presupposes a living presence of God within the community, then Christianity as reinterpreted by slaves shares some essential features with this ancestral conception of devotion. This god may be singular, but he isn't infinite: the community he speaks to and through represents the limits of his finitude. Only when this bond is broken and the unity of God is no longer felt as actively and intensely present in "my"

113

life does an omnipresent, universal, and homogenous figure arise in abstract terms: "the God of world religions (when 'authentic' peoples no longer exist) doesn't represent a reality, but an abstract idea. The god of a concrete people doesn't have infinite power, but what he can do, he does it powerfully. In contrast, the God of world religions is a God who can do anything, who possesses infinite power—and is only, for this reason, an empty formula, an ideological façade that can be filled by anything. In world religions, the relation between God and man is a mere fiction."[2] By assimilating the abstract world religion of white people, Black people reactivated, in a way, what remained of their African religious imagination, reigniting a fervor for devotion. From the homogenous universality of modern Christianity, slaves fashioned a novel religion specific to their world, where a Black God or Black Christ helped them confront unspeakable violence. As this chapter sets out to show, this explains why the relation between slaves—and the descendants of slaves—and God is no fiction. Instead, an oppressed people found an ally in a divine power to confront adversity.

It seems fitting to begin this discussion with music, since it stands as slavery's most significant contribution to modern world culture. Paul Gilroy has been particularly emphatic on this point: "The power of music in developing black struggles by communicating information, organizing consciousness, and testing out or deploying the forms of subjectivity which are required by political agency, whether individual or collective, defensive or transformational, demands attention to both the formal attributes of this expressive culture and its distinctive *moral* basis."[3] But we must also grapple with the dark side of this history of music. Cone provides a manner of broaching its fundamental ambiguity. Black music isn't only a practice. It is also a way of thinking. And this thinking is prophetic. Indeed, it is part and parcel of the development of a Black consciousness, which finds expression in an institution that is at once political, ethical, and religious: the Black church. Its prophetic character is meant to awaken Afro-descendants to their own dignity, to inspire confidence in their individual being as they combat oppression collectively.

The Spirit of the Blues

Music was, and remains, a privileged site for expressing the deep historicity of Black culture. For James Cone, the rigorous study of Black music necessarily entails a politics of the particular: "I am

A THEOLOGY OF BLACK DIGNITY

therefore convinced that it is not possible to render an authentic interpretation of black music without having shared and participated in the experience that created it. Black music must *be lived* before it can be understood."[4] Clearly, this doesn't mean that imprisonment on a chain gang is a prerequisite for feeling the resentment in work songs or living in a township is needed to appreciate South African music. But, on a more general level, this means that only those who have experienced indignity, racist dehumanization, or colonial violence can grasp the essence of Black music. Cone adds that academic studies and the objective approach of the social sciences fail to address the most pressing matter of Black music: namely, its unflagging desire for survival. In other words, Black experience is expressed through music in the new form of a cursed subjectivity, one that is born from modernity as "an artistic rebellion against the humiliating deadness of western culture."[5]

There are numerous studies on the sociophilosophical and ethical dimensions of African American music. Spirituals and blues figure prominently in these studies, with the African slave and the newly emancipated serving as the protagonists. These studies are driven by the seeming paradox that bodies deprived of freedom, the cursed bodies of the most wretched of the wretched of the earth, could, against all odds, demonstrate such boundless artistic creativity and limitless imagination. As the writer and African American musicologist Amiri Baraka (also known as LeRoi Jones) claims, in the United States the "notable fact is that the only so-called popular music [...] of any real value is of African derivation,"[6] which is all the more surprising given that it emerges in a context so hostile to artistic expression. This startling fact, first observed by W.E.B. Du Bois, cannot be ignored in any attempt to understand the dignity of the oppressed.

A widespread reading views this music optimistically as a testament to the unwavering resilience of slaves, as a message to the world, as an expression of positivity defined against a backdrop of violence and death. "The Negro spirituals speak mental resistance and the permanence of God on the side of the oppressed. The blues are a form of existentialism where personal irony resists the tragic. Jazz is the passion of syncopated or antiphonal polyrhythms in which life passes through fire without ever being reduced to ash. [...] To face the disaster is to overcome it. To submit to it is to die."[7] The philosopher Cornel West is perhaps the most prominent defender of this view. As he strikingly puts it in a 2011 interview, "I think that for me the deepest existential source of coming to terms with

115

the white supremacist bombardment was music. And I think, in some ways, that this is true for black America as a whole, from spirituals and blues through jazz, rhythm and blues, and even up to hip-hop."[8] West speaks of the heuristic potential of Black music, which carries, at the same time, an emancipatory charge. He likens it to a performance of παιδεία (*paideia*). In other words, it serves as an education for listeners, arousing in them an intellectual and affective awakening. The musician embodies a higher message that disrupts the mournful monotony of daily life, re-enchanting the grisly reality of the plantation or the misery of the ghetto through an affective register. Black song is thus described as what *conquers* indignity, like a ray of light beating back darkness. It will always be stronger than the dehumanization and the despair it endures.

The critic Saidiya Hartman argues from a sociophilosophical perspective that this interpretation of the power of Black music downplays, if not outright omits, the violence Blacks have been subjected to throughout their history. She rejects the simplistic claim that Black music thrived *in spite* of racial violence, or that it offered some kind of escape from it. On the contrary, regimes of violence and exploitation repeatedly made use of Black music to their own advantage. Black music's ambiguous role during the slave trade begins on the deck of the slave ships where the ships' crew would periodically line up the "cargo," making them sing and dance to keep their bodies loose and their minds occupied.[9] Henceforth, rhythm and song would accompany the most unbearable moments of the slave trade, making a bitter pill, so to speak, easier to swallow. According to plantation doctors, "music was the antidote to black sloth and torpidity."[10] But it was above all an instrumental strategy in the marketing of bodies: slave traders forced slaves to look like willing and joyful participants in this process. Vigor and ebullience were put on display to entice potential buyers. Song and dance were, then, indispensable tools for dressing up the most sordid subjugation as a form of lively entertainment.

A key, underexamined, moment of the economic cycle of modern slavery is found in the specific desire to purchase Africans. It is the desire for an "erotic body—substrate for the exchanged signs of desire,"[11] to borrow the description Baudrillard gives to late twentieth-century consumer society. Indeed, consumption, in its most current understanding, is exactly what is at stake here. Contemporary depictions of the slave trade highlight its unspeakable brutality. Films such as *12 Years a Slave* or *Birth of a Nation* show the institution of slavery from the victim's point of view, exposing the cruelty of the

116

masters, the violence of the whip, cases of rape and humiliation—in short, living conditions marked by indignity. Showing all this from the slave's perspective faithfully and truthfully reveals the horrors of the institution of slavery. But this appalling reality should not obscure the counter-view—that of the slaveholder—which allows us to understand to no lesser extent slavery's conditions of possibility. For all their exactitude, most representations of slavery only show one side of the story, neglecting the lure of acquiring, as a consumer, a Black body (a notable exception to this is Jordan Peele's *Get Out*, which brilliantly dramatizes this ghastly theme).

From the perspective of white masters, the institution of slavery was to be celebrated. Taking pleasure in depriving a humiliated and degraded African of his or her freedom does not, of course, come naturally. This pleasure depended on a whole system designed to transform distraught human beings into desirable goods. As Marcus Rediker makes clear, this transformation began in the hold of the slave ship as part of the preparations for arrival: "[This process] entailed taking the constraints off the wrists and ankles of the men about ten days before arrival, in order to let the chafing heal. It also included careful cleaning, shaving the men (beard and sometimes head), and using a lunar caustic to hide sores. Gray hair would be picked out or dyed black. Finally, sailors would rub down the African bodies with palm oil. The whole process was one of value creation and enhancement. Thanks to the sailors' labor, a shipload of expensive commodities would soon be available for sale."[12] The music performed by slaves fueled this economy of desire. It responded to the slave traders' demand to be beautiful, joyous, brimming with verve and vigor. Everything was staged so that acquiring another human being could not only be a pleasurable activity, but also a rapturous experience of ownership. The act of possession was designed to elicit a natural exuberance. Slavery wasn't defined solely by beatings, misery, and harsh discipline. It was also driven by the awe and desire provoked by a Black body one was free to possess without guilt or shame. This shameless desire was made possible by a nascent capitalism. The erotics of slavery still persist today in vestigial form (the aestheticization of toned and muscular Black bodies, seen for example in the work of the once politically oriented Alvin Ailey Dance Theater, is a case in point).[13]

Throughout modernity, the music of slaves was used to disguise suffering as joy in a deliberate attempt to entice future buyers. This is a blatant distortion of Aristotle's κάθαρσις (*katharsis*), which famously functions by purging suffering. Or to borrow Philippe

Lacoue-Labarthe's more precise formulation, "the very strange 'alchemy' of *katharsis*: the transmutation of pain (*lupè*) into pleasure. Or, to put it more brutally (and in anticipation), of *negative* and *positive*."[14] Setting the Black condition to music and putting it on exhibit foregrounds suffering at the same time that it hides it, giving rise to a desire to possess not a body beaten into submission but a vigorous workhorse that is immune to pain. Hence the countless representations of Blacks as naturally upbeat regardless of their condition. And the aesthetic and erotic effect of this staging isn't all that is to be gained. It also helps legitimize, and even encourage, the overexploitation of slaves. Hartman thus reveals the unfortunate flipside to the argument that Black music speaks to the vital endurance of Africans: it unintentionally reinforces the idea that it was the solid build of Black slaves that led to their enslavement at the beginning of the sixteenth century, rather than that of Native Americans, who were considered to be weak, frail, and morally suspect.[15] The belief in the strength and endurance of slaves is shared by their masters, who have every interest in drawing as much work out of them on a daily basis as possible.

Lest there be any doubt about the persistence of these slave-era beliefs concerning the Black body, allow me to share a personal story. I had just given a talk about, of all things, the condition of Black slaves, at a conference. As I was getting up from my seat to leave the room, a presenter at an earlier session (a professor emeritus, which is to say, an old white man), clearly impressed by my size and stature, said to me, with a disarming casualness which he tried to inflect with humor, "Wow, you sure are huge! I get why the slavers chose *you*!" Whether or not he found my talk unconvincing is beside the point. All it took was for me to stand up for the old man to want me as his servant rather than his colleague. Reasoning from this firsthand experience, he was able to see the logic of slavery as legitimate in this respect.

But what does the performance of Black music actually perform? According to Hartman, certainly not *paideia* or the sort of lesson about community Cornel West found in it. It doesn't negate racial violence, nor is it an antidote to the suffering in the Black condition. As Jared Sexton has expressed, "black social life does not negate black social death by inhabiting it and vitalizing it."[16] In short, according to this interpretation, music in a slave context serves to make the unacceptable acceptable. First of all for the slaves themselves: it helps them survive. But also for their buyers, who hope to see the considerable violence involved in possessing a human body

A THEOLOGY OF BLACK DIGNITY

in a gentler light. There is, however, a downside to this otherwise radical and lucid argument. Following it to its logical conclusion, Black culture becomes in essence pathological, or a pure product of oppression. As such, it can be readily and unapologetically dismissed in favor of assimilation and modernity.

The position of Black liberation theology offers an alternative to West's "optimism" and to Hartman's "pessimism." It invites a different approach from that generally adopted in regard to this matter. Indeed, we speak reductively of Black music as a *practice* or a *performance*, which confines it to a sort of micropolitics. But it is also possible to imagine it as a form of *thought*. For Hartman, slave practices couldn't be qualified strictly speaking as political since, as chattel, they lacked the rights of citizens. This assumes that the arena of politics is defined by the norms established and reinforced by state and legal institutions, rather than seeing political action as a sort of collective mobilization designed to bring about fundamental social change. Black liberation theology has been for the most part driven by this second understanding of political action. Steve Biko, for instance, has called attention to the social function of African music: "with Africans, music and rhythm were not luxuries but part and parcel of our way of communication. Any suffering we experienced was made much more real by song and rhythm. There is no doubt that the so-called 'Negro spirituals' sung by Black slaves in the States as they toiled under oppression were indicative of their African heritage."[17] The system of slavery could only co-opt African practices of music if it succeeded in shifting its primary function. James Cone shares this view: "In Africa and America, black music was not an artistic creation for its own sake; it was directly related to daily life, work and play."[18] But in addition to this functional level, which provides the basis of Hartman's reading, Black music also works on a speculative level, which is to say, as a form of thought that continues to resonate beyond its temporal performance.

Rather than perform and amplify the slave's condition of submission, Negro spirituals and even the blues are inconspicuously propelled by a new form of thinking, a form that is foreign to white Christianity and is at once religious, ethical, and political. According to Cone, Black music is at its core a vehicle for a Black eschatology, secretly bearing the prophetic message of liberation. This prophetic vision shines a new light on Hartman's reading while supporting its principal claims: Black music and indignity are interrelated. Nor does it contradict West's claims. Far from it. In their enigmatic, eschatological thinking, spirituals and blues envision the empowerment of

Afro-descendants. *Strange Fruit*, perhaps the most emblematic song in the history of African American music, attests to these paradoxes. Written and composed by Abel Meeropol, its darkly poetic depiction of lynchings taking place across the south reached a new level of intensity when Billie Holiday began performing it in 1939. Some have even viewed this occasion as the beginning of the civil rights movement. For James Cone, *Strange Fruit* was "a prophetic call for blacks to take up the cross of black freedom because nobody was going [to] carry it for them."[19] Unlike any other song in the history of North American music, with its daring and radical approach, it didn't so much move its listeners as provoke in them a desire and passion that couldn't be disentangled from a deep and unsettling unease. Its brutal and natural imagery challenge listeners to take a position on the matter, even if their first reaction is an emotional one. Through a deft use of hypotyposis, the extreme violence endured by African Americans is held in tension with the haunting image of hanging corpses, the peaceful innocence of the South, and the untroubled conscience of the white world.

The Church of Revolt

If Black music thinks, and thinks prophetically, it is because it emerged mainly within a context and a tradition that made this possible. I am speaking about the tradition of the Black church in North America, which positioned itself against slavery. Indeed, as the theologian Bruno Chenu writes, "this history of men and women fighting for their dignity makes little sense outside of its religious framing."[20] It was paradoxically in the terms of the slaveholders' religion that some of the most trenchant critiques of slavery were made and uprisings were led. The argument that Christianity and Black identity politics are fundamentally at odds thus demands reconsideration. To see oneself as Afro-descendant and Christian is not necessarily an instance of *alienation*, of contamination by the lifestyle of the master or the colonizer. The history of the Black church in North America, at the very least, shows that this is far from the case when slaves and their descendants appropriate this religion as a matter of survival—which wasn't an infrequent occurrence.

Black slaves were not converted to Christianity upon arrival in North America: the plantation owners, who were divided over this issue, had no shared policy of mass conversion. In fact, some 150

A THEOLOGY OF BLACK DIGNITY

years separate the beginning of slavery in the sixteenth century and the major undertakings of conversion in the eighteenth. This means that during a century and a half, against all odds, slaves kept alive a religious imagination rooted in African traditions. Christian faith wasn't foisted on a religious and cultural blank slate, nor was it adopted as a result of brainwashing Black workers. It developed, instead, from African practices and rites, which had themselves undergone significant changes under conditions of life characterized by secrecy, servitude, and contact with other ethnically and linguistically diverse Africans from different regions. To be sure, in North America, in contrast to the West Indies or South America, the practice of traditional religions was severely punished. But this wasn't enough to suppress them, especially since medicine-men were often seen as a necessary evil and thus escaped being repressed by their masters who might have to solicit their services one day. These respected figures, feared by the masters, commanded a certain authority on the plantation. Reputed by many as capable of curing snake bites or poisonings, one was loath to question them. According to W.E.B. Du Bois, these medicine-men, more than white pastors, were the real ancestors of Black preachers.[21]

The conversion of slaves is often represented as a violent act of coercion and deculturation. This might very well have been the case if Africans, their bodies bound by the chains of servitude, lacked spiritual endurance in their souls. However, as Bruno Chenu argues, "it is first and foremost Christianity's affinity with African religion that led to the conversion of black Americans."[22] In other words, their reception of Christianity wasn't one of blind acceptance; they took up and reimagined only certain aspects of it. Far from passively accepting any teaching as the true word of God, slaves countered religious discourse that put them in a subordinate position, even contesting the theological grounds of such a position. To say this is in no way to absolve the church of its complicity with the slave trade, which it undeniably tolerated, or to downplay its deliberate use of racial terror. White theology clearly sought to legitimize Black servitude. The wild fantasies and distorted representations of Africa that figure throughout modernity and which were particularly pronounced during the eighteenth and nineteenth centuries speak to this. White religion had to prove that, for all its flaws, for all the ill-feelings it provoked, the condition of slavery was better than life in Africa, which was "driven to the edge of reality."[23] The blanket demonization of Africa dignified to a certain extent a life of servitude and helped to appease the white conscience. But, by placing God

121

on the side of white people, European theology opened the door to merciless violence.[24]

The conversion of slaves was a contentious matter. Many plantation owners feared that the Gospel would engender a spirit of sedition in the slaves. The Anglican Church believed just the opposite: the divine spirit would render them docile. This idea was naturally welcomed by owners but met with staunch resistance by the Black masses. A third, minority, position was offered by the Quakers, who fought for abolition in the name of the Bible—while taking care to keep their distance from Blacks. The first conversion of slaves took place during what has been called "the First Great Awakening" of 1740. This was brought about by a new form of Protestantism which valued the living experience of conversion over the adherence to doctrine.[25] But the real turning point came with the evangelical "Second Great Awakening" at the end of the eighteenth century. White and Black people jointly partook in impassioned sermons staged outdoors, with the latter greatly moved by the inspiring and imagistic teachings. Not only did this expression of religion resonate with what remained of African traditions, but its influence throughout the South convinced more plantocrats to convert their slaves.

At the beginning of the nineteenth century, as Bruno Chenu explains, a division had formed between a white church imposing a catechism of submission on slaves and a Black Christianity preaching independence and stirring up a revolt:

> In truth, black religion is more than just the mirror of white Christianity. It is a unique reality rooted in an African past, forged in the fire of slavery, which came into its own during the religious "awakenings" of the eighteenth and nineteenth centuries. It is a unique creation, fundamentally African *and* American. It surged onto the stage of North American Christianity as a new religious identity with an independent and critical spirit. Black people had built from within a movement based on an experience of faith and a coherent religious vision.[26]

Black people were thus not deceived into embracing Christianity. They saw clearly the hypocrisy and false piety of their masters. Their conversion, then, presents a paradox: although their new religion originated with white people, Black people saw themselves from the outset as more authentic disciples. This is in line with Cornel West's Christian pragmatism, for, in their legitimate and theologically precise interpretation, neither science, art, nor even religion can claim to possess eternal truth. Indeed, human finitude and the limits of knowledge are central tenets of Christianity. Beliefs—be

A THEOLOGY OF BLACK DIGNITY

they religious, scientific, or artistic—are thus judged true only within a specific community of believers. As mortals, even Christians can never be assured of the truth of Christ's message. They must experience it on an existential level within a finite community.[27] Slaves were put through this test of experience, and for this reason were able to recognize the finitude and vanity of their master's aspirations to omnipotence. The latter's longer history with the Bible does not make them the keepers of its truth. On the contrary, it is this illusion that makes truth an appropriable good, one that can easily be confused with the legal truth of the state and the actions of its police force. It is also the surest proof of the masters' moral depravity and intellectual folly.

African American Christianity found its most authentic expression in remote pockets of the plantation and surrounding forests where Blacks were protected from the white man's gaze. Later, these expressions would become codified in independent Black churches. These churches tended to bring together the poorest segments of the community whereas the few who were well off sought to become part of the white churches and remained scornful of the African heritage found within the Black church. As "religion is not for them a separate sphere but a vital dimension of the life of the community,"[28] Black Christianity took on various and unexpected social functions. For example, as Black people tended to receive a poor education, the church strove to make up for this educational lack and redress the injustices of a segregated system. Following the teachings of the Gospel, some believers drew their strength from their faith. This is what allowed them to survive the hardships of a merciless world, or what gave them a reason to live. But faith also inspired rebellion. This last point is more specific to Black religion than to other, more common, expressions of Christianity. Key figures in the slaves' rebellion such as Gabriel Prosser, Denmark Vesey, or Nat Turner were religious, even prophetic figures. But "the black Church provided the base for all this insurrectional activity,"[29] much more so than a handful of illustrious leaders. The Black church, resistant by design to a social order founded on white supremacy, harbored revolutionary ambitions.

The beginning of the twentieth century saw the exodus of Black Americans, who fled the rural South in favor of the great cities of the North, which is to say, in fact, their ghettos. Initially, this demographic upheaval posed a major setback for a Christianity of liberation, which emerged out of the fight for the abolition of slavery. "Urban churches [...] abandoned their previous political engagements once they moved out of the countryside...For the most part they adopted a conservative attitude: they preached more about the afterlife than the social struggles of the present as they sought to integrate into the existing society. The model of the white middle class was far too enticing to resist. This led to the birth of a black *petit bourgeois* Christianity that was quick to turn its back on the masses of proletariats."[30] Pentecostalism, which spread throughout Latin America and sub-Saharan Africa over the next three decades,[31] is also representative of this historical moment. Liberation theology, hostile to the white world, slowly gave way to a theology of prosperity, which preached personal enrichment and painted Christ and his apostles as part of the bourgeoisie and their lives of luxury. With an increasingly whitewashed Church that showed little interest in their plight, Black proletarians began abandoning religion, even growing resentful of it. Newly rich pastors became the targets of the same kind of criticism that Kierkegaard had leveled at Bishop Mynster of Copenhagen a century earlier: they were accused of having transformed the word of God into a gospel of profit, and of leading comfortable and privileged lives that couldn't be more opposed to Christ's example. In short, their interests in Christianity were solely financial. Yet it was an illusion for the oppressed to believe they could simply ignore social and political matters, and the newly arrived Black people in the North would soon be reminded of their inescapable condition.

As previously mentioned, *Strange Fruit* offered a glimpse of the radical critique of American society that would later be taken up by the Black masses in the civil rights movement. But it would be wrong to see this song as inaugurating the movement. While, as described in the third chapter, racial violence operates primarily in the silence of daily life, there are certain events that rock the collective conscious with unprecedented violence. The lynching of Emmett Till on August 28, 1955, in Money, Mississippi, was such an event. It shaped the prophetic fate of the African American conscious in the mid-twentieth century. More than Billie Holiday's voice, the collective grief suffered after this crime provided the impetus, according to James Cone, for the civil rights movement. It wasn't by chance that three months after this Rosa Parks refused to give up her seat to a white man on a bus in Montgomery, Alabama. The murder of Emmett Till created an acute need for the impassioned discourse of Black liberation theology. In this respect, Black liberation theology stands apart from white theology which, in line with Western science, is more concerned with carefully respecting norms and tradition than devoting itself—body and soul—to human suffering.[32] In Cone's eyes,

A THEOLOGY OF BLACK DIGNITY

"theology arises out of life and thus reflects a people's struggle to create meaning in life."[33] In light of the appalling reality of lynchings, these words should be heard with the full weight they bear. Giving meaning to such an event is not, as the cliché of a spiritual mission would have it, to imbue it with a higher purpose. Nor does it suggest that one should keep carrying on, but with purpose. The desire to give meaning to something derives from a revolt against the injustice of the social order, not from a legal concern over its possible illegitimacy. But neither does giving meaning to an event suggest, as a more elaborate theological approach would have it, making it part of a larger historical narrative or fitting it into a providential succession of events that unfolds in accordance with a plan ordained by God. On the contrary, it is a question of bringing everyone face to face with the absurdity and offense of the matter. Rather than seeing lynchings in the elevated space of God's unknowable plan, Black prophetism holds them before the oppressed to see with their own eyes, telling them: "you see this hanged man, *that's you!*"

In 1969, soon after the civil rights movement became radicalized, James Cone articulated his vision of a Black theology: "There is a need for a theology of revolution, a theology which radically encounters the problems of the disinherited black people in America in particular and the oppressed people of color throughout the world in general."[34] Reframing the history of the Black church, Cone was not only trying to give theoretical legitimacy to the struggle of Black power, but also to recover the memory of past struggles for his community. By recovering and re-establishing the oppositional position of Black religion throughout its history, Cone galvanized the current protest movement by situating it within a much longer tradition. Rather than a set of disparate struggles that fade once they fall out of relevance, these struggles are shown to belong to a longer history of the oppressed. This is accomplished by interrogating the meaning of God, Christ, truth, in *the very consciousness of slaves.* Such an effort isn't aiming to articulate a "slave's theology," but rather a theology of survival and the courage of existing in the face of extreme adversity. These particular historical roots distinguish Black theology from the liberation theology of Latin America, which sprang from the syncretism of Catholic theology and Marxist social philosophy.[35] For Cone, African American theology is by definition a critical theology. Equipped with its own historical resources, it has no need to draw on the Marxist archive to think through oppression and deliverance (which Cornel West would lament beginning in the 1980s). The history of the Black church and the radical politics of

125

African Americans are almost impossible to disentangle. From this perspective, Black Power is not a "new social movement," but the legacy of several centuries of struggle. It is propelled by a notion evoked several times in this work: that of *prophetism*. A clearer understanding of this term is now in order.

Afro-Prophetism

Black liberation theology considers its own discourse as a prophetic one: "Black suffering needs radical and creative voices, prophetic advocates who can tell brutal and beautiful stories of how oppressed black people survived with a measure of dignity when they were not meant to."[36] Indeed, the prophet is defined by his or her word: φημί (*phēmi*) in ancient Greek. The verb πρόφημι (*próphēmi*), which is derived from this, means *to speak before*, with *before* (*pro*) capable of holding a spatial or temporal meaning. The prophet is neither a god or an oracle, but rather the person who "always directly addresses the community to share matters of import."[37] Prophetism is an intellectual intervention and a form of social critique. It gives voice to the dignity of the oppressed in situations where this voice is ignored or undermined. This is why Cone deems Martin Luther King and Malcolm X—those towering martyrs of justice—the two most important prophetic voices in the modern history of the United States. Prophetism requires being physically and vitally present in one's discourse, as well as assuming the risks this presents: "Prophets take risks and speak out in righteous indignation against society's treatment of the poor, even risking their lives, as we see in the martyrdom of Jesus and Martin King."[38] This prophetic discourse can be recognized throughout the history of the Black church through three defining features, which are particularly pronounced in contemporary writing on liberation theology.

The first of these is its *minority position*. Gilles Deleuze and Félix Guattari gave this concept a rich definition in their book on Kafka. Their contention that "a minor literature doesn't come from a minor language; it is rather that which a minority constructs within a major language"[39] is especially useful in understanding Black religion. What they say about literature equally applies to religion and theology. In other terms, what is at stake here is the invention of an illegitimate or refractory language, not outside of, but within, a legitimate language. Black religion invented its own language, one that was still haunted by Africa and fueled by revolt. This language took shape within the eminently legitimate language of the evangelical Christianity of North America. As Jacob Taubes has shown, prophecy is a discourse of exile born of the absence of geographical roots; it is a stateless discourse that maintains a certain foreignness to itself. "To be alien means: to come from elsewhere, not to be at home in this world. The here and now is the state of alienation and the un-canny. Life spent here is a life of exile and we are subject to the fate of exiles."[40] This description of the life of ancient Jews is also an apt one of the life of Black slaves. But the hardships of exile do not speak only to transporting bodies through the "middle passage." This experience coincides with the emergence of a modern world where being Black becomes synonymous with illegitimacy and exile. This was further reinforced in 1885 as colonial powers divvied up Africa: even in their own ancestral land, *Africans are forced to live in a world of exile.* And prophetism gives voice to this being of exile.

The second feature of prophetic discourse is its *community-centered position.* The study of prophetism is often beset by clichés that stem from a sociological approach established by Max Weber. He describes the prophet as "a purely individual bearer of charisma, who by virtue of his mission proclaims a religious doctrine or divine commandment."[41] This emphasis on the individual is in stark contrast to the concept of prophecy, which relies in no small part on self-erasure[42] (this is what distinguishes it from that of a messiah, who can speak in his own name: "In truth, I tell you..."). Paradoxically, the supposed charisma of the prophet is not "purely personal" as Weber argues. Instead, it depends on the fact that the prophet's speech and discourse do not belong to him, but rather to God or some celestial messenger. Thus, to be perceived as a prophet is not to be recognized for one's personality, but for one's absence of self, one's status as living spokesperson. For the prophet's word to spread and represent a larger collectivity, it cannot entirely be *his* or *her* word. Ultimately, more than any single charismatic figure, regardless of his or her importance and influence, it is the Black church itself that is prophetic.

Finally, there is its *dialectical position.* As Cornel West writes: "To prophesy is not to predict an outcome but rather to identify concrete evils."[43] Prophecy delivers a critical truth, one that possesses at the same time negativity and the power to inspire the faith needed to confront the challenges implied by this negativity. Hegel's interpretation of dialectics and negativity—although he wasn't the first to articulate it—has without doubt had the greatest impact on how these concepts are understood.[44] In the preface to his *Phenomenology of the Spirit*, he outlines a distinction that is at the philosophical core of his thought.

He argues that there are two ways of refuting a principle, which is to say, the foundation of a philosophical system. The first is nondialectical. The nondialectical way claims that the principle is false, and the very fact of this falseness quite simply disqualifies it. Refuted in this nondialectical way, the principle is cast aside, deemed impractical, uninteresting, and unworthy of philosophical reflection. The second approach, the one embraced and advanced by Hegel, is dialectical. The dialectical way believes refutation, which is to say *negativity*, is invited by the flawed principle itself. It considers the flaw as that which invites correction, and, therefore, improvement. You can only negate that which is negatable. Flaws, errors, dysfunction thus play a positive role, too. They encourage rectification via negation. The flaw pulls negation toward it like a vacuum. For dialectical thought, imperfection has the benefit of instigating improvement, driving history forward and allowing for change. Hegel calls this action of negation, serving as a response and facilitating progress, *determinate negation*. According to him, there are two ways of conceiving reason. The first is a vulgar and mechanized view of the functioning of reality. The second, derived from a determinate negation, is more than a simple option: it describes real historical progress in thought. Of course, Black prophetism is not, strictly speaking, Hegelian. But it, too, is part of the dialectical history of Christian thought. Although this prophetism bears no trace of modernity's unwarranted optimism or its reckless faith in progress—both of which are inspired by Hegel's thought—it recognizes the power of negation. "Black theologians have either consciously or unconsciously employed a dialectical methodology in approaching their respective subject matter and arriving at conclusions," West reminds us.[45] This dialectical method helped Black theologians understand that the indignity they endured doesn't represent their fate; rather, it calls for rectification and allows for the emergence of a new humanity: "divine truth is not an idea but an event breaking into the brokenness of history, bestowing wholeness in wretched places. Only one who has experienced and is experiencing the truth of divine liberation can tell the story of how God's people shall overcome."[46] Driven by their faith in God, Black people are called upon to refute and negate that which dehumanizes them. And what emerges from these ruins isn't an African humanity that predates the slave trade and colonialism, but rather something entirely unprecedented.

These three positions of prophetic discourse—minority, community-centered, and dialectical—are clearly illustrated in the way Black liberation theology treats the figure of Jesus Christ. This treatment brings together two aspects that are often held apart in philosophy and critical theory centered on Christianity: incarnation and resurrection. James Cone combines these to create what I'm calling, with full awareness of the apparent contradiction it presents, a *materialist Christology*.

In recent times, the subject of incarnation has animated critical thinking around the notion of forms of life. Critical theorists view it from a perspective that foregrounds the imitation of Jesus Christ. Such is the case with Bernard Aspe: "if Jesus came to incarnate God's word, this incarnation must be taken as a model of life [...]. It isn't a question, then, of extending his teachings, but of 'duplicating' them on an existential level. With this duplication, existence itself is transformed on the most fundamental, and the most mundane, level."[47] In a similar vein, Giorgio Agamben identifies within Franciscan theology a quasi-anarchist effort to flout laws, rules, and norms, by following the model set by Jesus. Monastic life becomes the life of Nazareth and, henceforth, "the form is not a norm imposed on life, but a living that in following the life of Christ gives itself and makes itself a form."[48] Imitation allows a singular life to embrace and re-enact the singular life of Christ. For both Aspe and Agamben, it provides a *model* for escaping the norms of the dominant society and imagining a new form of community.

Cone's Black liberation theology shares some of these concerns. For him, too, the figure of Christ has perhaps more political than religious significance. But his position differs from theirs in two ways. First, according to Cone, "any interpretation of the gospel in any historical period that fails to see Jesus as the Liberator of the oppressed is heretical."[49] From the church's very beginning, Christology has failed, in his view, to appreciate the historical dimension of Jesus, whose unwavering commitment to the poor, the marginalized, and the oppressed is what most defines him. In contrast to the conventional image given him by a Christianity more obsessed with power than justice, Jesus makes his political allegiance clear: his prophetic spirit is driven by a concern for the life of the oppressed. Which leads to the second point. Whereas Agamben or Aspe invite readers to emulate and identify with the life of Christ, Cone calls attention to the striking parallels between the inhumane suffering endured by Christ and that endured by Black people. The cross becomes the lynching tree. In other words, Jesus isn't a model to emulate. Like Justice or Truth, God is the name of the universal. But he works through and is embodied by a particular group (for example, the Jewish slaves of the Old Testament) or a particular human (such as the Christ of the New Testament). And, in every case, he sides with the oppressed, who are the true elected people. Today, Jesus "*is* black because he *was* a Jew."[50]

"When blacks sang about the 'blood,' they were wrestling not only with the blood of the crucified carpenter from Nazareth but also with the blood of raped and castrated black bodies in America—innocent, often nameless, burning and hanging bodies, images of hurt so deep that only God's 'amazing grace' could offer consolation."[51] The mutilated body of the lynching victim unfailingly recalls Christ's battered body. Ordinary people are not called upon to imitate Christ since it is God who, through his incarnation in Jesus, imitated the poor and the voiceless. Or, more accurately, he sided with the oppressed by lending them his words and sharing their Calvary. To those who would retort that Christ has no race, that he represents all of humanity, Cone reminds us that throughout the world, this raceless Christ is always depicted as a white man, often with blond hair and blue eyes.[52] Needless to say, this ignores Jesus's Palestinian roots, and it hardly evokes today's poor, oppressed, and persecuted masses. The Christian notion of incarnation places Christ directly among the oppressed of a given period and society. In North America, this is primarily the Black population.

Almost thirty years before Cone developed his Black liberation theology, Aimé Césaire gave a precise and impassioned description of this aspect of African American religion. He drew a sharp distinction between the European tradition of mysticism—such as that of Meister Eckhart, for example—and Black materialism. Whereas the former is founded on the ideal of detachment (a matter of letting go and abandoning everything that binds us to the world), which allows one to experience God's very nature,[53] in the latter it is God himself who invites himself into the world, expressing his full significance through a literal incarnation. "In other words, when mystical thinking dehumanizes man; when it requires man, in order to contemplate God, to die to hope, to fear, to time and space, to the world, to himself, it is then God who enters into the limits of space and time, who takes up the life of the body, who assumes a place in the world and truly becomes a part of our humility."[54] Black liberation theology doesn't ask Afro-descendants to find God through asceticism and mortification, but rather to think dialectically and recognize in their own dignity the divine power within them. And this they do, in spite of the indignity of being consigned to the zone of nonbeing, in spite of the indignity of being nailed, day after day, to the cross of imperialism and white supremacy.

A THEOLOGY OF BLACK DIGNITY

In the previous chapter, we saw how Žižek and Badiou—as well as much of contemporary critical theory—have embraced Paul of Tarsus, viewing his teachings of resurrection as a path to immortality. Jesus plays for the most part no role in this theory. In contrast, Cornel West draws a sharp distinction between the Greek notion of the immortality of the soul and the notion of resurrection. Death is far from insignificant in the latter, but neither does it represent a sort of release, as in Epicurean thought.[55] To suffer the trial of death, to free oneself from its grip, one must first feel its weight and observe the horror it provokes. But this also teaches that it can indeed be confronted. As Nathalie Etoke observes, slaves and their descendants call this understanding of resurrection "survival." "To survive is to resist the conditions of a sinister, tragic, and catastrophic existence. [...] To survive is somehow to go beyond death without entering eternity."[56] For Black liberation theology, resurrection proves to Black people that the suffering they endure is illegitimate, unjustifiable, unwarranted. Above all, this suffering will not have the final word. Resurrection reveals the vanity of those in power here on earth and provides assurance that they can be overthrown. This kind of suffering can be faced knowing that "there is a dimension to life beyond the reach of the oppressor."[57] Suffering becomes political once its motivation is called into question by those who endure it, once the oppressed know they can triumph over their oppressors. Such is the message of resurrection.

Christ's incarnation serves as a reminder that resurrection follows death, just as Rosa Parks's insurrection followed Emmett Till's burial. In Cone's materialist Christology, Jesus provides an existential diagnosis: he allows one to identify and map out cases of social suffering. But he is also a messenger sent to remind the poor and the humiliated of their dignity and their ability to confront and conquer the evil assailing them. In the end, Black prophetism has a single goal: to awaken in the oppressed their sense of dignity and to urge them to confront with all their strength the challenges of survival. For "the dignity of man is a self-evident religious, philosophical, and political *truth*, without which human community is impossible."[58]

The Call of Dignity

Louis Althusser's well-known description of ideology—"ideology interpellates individuals as subjects"[59]—is useful for understanding how prophetic speech awakens the dignity of slaves and their

131

descendants. Except that for prophetism, it works the other way around: prophetism interpellates subjects as individuals. Slaves are subjects only insofar as they are subjected to their masters, and, even then, only insofar as, according to Althusser's theory, this subjection is accompanied by the illusion of free will (at the beginning of this chapter, we saw how music helped slaves accept their servile condition). Similarly, young Black people are subjects today only insofar as they are at all times subjected to the violence of police harassment [*la violence de l'interpellation policière*]. In "Ideology and Ideological State Apparatuses," Althusser focuses on religious ideology, whose universal formula he claims to reveal in the following terms: "I address myself to you, a human individual called Peter (every individual is called by his name, in the passive sense, it is never he who provides his own name), in order to tell you that God exists and that you are answerable to Him."[60] In Black liberation theology, this is far from the case. To be sure, transcendence isn't absent from prophetic discourse, but it isn't addressed to individuals in order to make them answerable. On the contrary, it calls on them to make their own voice heard and to demand justice—even from God himself, the white God, the racist God who, for some inscrutable purpose, allows an iniquitous social order to prevail: "We cannot accept a God who inflicts or tolerates black suffering."[61] Individuals shaped by prophetic interpellation are put in a position to choose their God, to make their own decision pertaining to God. This individuality, in other words, is a function of dignity, that is, the power to reject the present social order.

We can deepen our understanding of this reformulation of Althusser by turning to the work of another great theologian, Søren Kierkegaard, an immensely important theorist of both interpellation and individuality. In *Fear and Trembling*, Kierkegaard describes divine interpellation in terms that allow for an understanding of a "prophetic interpellation" that goes beyond Althusser. This work presents itself as a reading of a specific passage of the Old Testament, namely, that of Abraham's sacrifice in Genesis 22:1–19, which tells of Abraham's interpellation by God. In this story, God demands that Abraham sacrifice his only son Isaac. For Abraham, committing infanticide will not only destroy his lineage, but also, and above all, this means that he will be committing one of the most serious crimes, one of the most incomprehensible and terrible transgressions that exists. The next morning at dawn, without saying a word, Abraham leaves with his son. After a three-day journey to the sacrificial site, he builds an altar upon which he places his son. As he unsheathes his knife and

A THEOLOGY OF BLACK DIGNITY

gets ready to kill his son, the angel of God intervenes and prevents the infanticidal act. God's demand was a test of Abraham's faith, which he proved was unshakable. A ram takes the place of Isaac, and God gives his blessing to the patriarch and his descendants. Taking as his point of departure this existential test of Abraham, and, more specifically, the faith behind it, Kierkegaard's *Fear and Trembling* offers a compelling interpretation of this biblical story. The Danish thinker begins with the contradiction between the seeming abjection of the patriarch's willingness to kill and the sublime feeling this arouses in the believer. This paradox, at the basis of all religion, is explained by Abraham's "teleological suspension of the ethical itself."[62]

Ethics (in Kierkegaard, this refers to Hegel's legal philosophy) designates that which gives an individual a purpose within the universal or larger whole—that is, in a civil society founded on a set of agreed-upon norms. Individuals are a part of an organic community, whose rules they recognize and whose rules recognize them. They are part of the machinery of civil society, whose laws they respect. And this civil society elicits desires that reinforce its own cohesion. But faith poses a paradox, since "the single individual is higher than the universal" and the individual "relates himself as the single individual absolutely to the absolute."[63] Though formed by the larger universal, the individual rises above it. The only relation Abraham's action has to the larger whole, which is to say, to the moral standards of civil society, is one of violation. Unlike the tragic hero who, like Antigone, lays claim to a higher ethical standard than that shared by everyone else, Abraham suspends ethics in favor of another teleology, of another purpose that has nothing to do with ethics. The meaning of his action is internal and private, and, since common language is, in essence, the expression of the larger whole, Abraham remains silent. During this teleological suspension of ethics, when Abraham must resolve to carry out an act condemned by the whole community, an act universally held to be abject, he can only count on his own authority: there are certainties that must come from within, certainties that can't be conveyed like the opinions of others. Abraham is driven by a certainty that is fundamentally individual—it depends on no higher ethical standard.

There are two ways to read this story. The first is a conventional reading à la Althusser: God *forced* Abraham, he made him answerable to him and compelled him, by his sovereignty alone, to commit a reprehensible act. The other is a prophetic reading: God *gave Abraham the power* to act as an individual, which is to say to carry out an impossible act, contrary to all accepted norms, moral

133

standards, and the prevailing order. This recalls the lyrics of the spiritual "Go Down Moses," immortalized by Louis Armstrong, in which God calls upon [*interpelle*] Moses to awaken his dignity within, which is to say, to awaken the strength needed to confront Pharaoh and free the slaves. This is not the God who issues arbitrary commandments, but the one who legitimizes the liberation of the oppressed in direct defiance of sovereign and institutional authority.

Kierkegaard's enigmatic formulation—"a teleological suspension of the ethical"—might be better understood as an interruption of moral standards or common decency. In the history of European moral philosophy, dignity is often viewed as a universal quality possessed by all. To use Kierkegaard's terms, it is an ethical matter. But in anti-Black societies, Black dignity is unheard of. This dignity conflicts with the most widespread forms of life, the most unconscious habits: "Violence is embedded in American law, and it is blessed by the keepers of moral sanctity. [...] If we take seriously the idea of human dignity, then we know that the annihilation of Indians, the enslavement of Africans, and (Reinhold Niebuhr notwithstanding) the making of heroes out of slaveholders, like George Washington and Thomas Jefferson, were America's first crimes against humankind."[64] Black dignity begins where Orwell's ordinary decency—the "instinctive ability to perceive good and bad"[65] belonging to ordinary people—ends. The two young men who lynched Emmett Till were themselves ordinary people who carried out a sentence they felt was proportionate to the teenager's wrongdoing; an act deemed ordinary, at any rate, by an all-white, eminently ordinary jury, who pardoned them. Black dignity must affirm itself against the ordinary decency of slavery, against the ordinary decency of lynchings, against the ordinary decency of segregation, against the ordinary decency of police killings and public humiliation. The moral standards of the United States, like those of all slaveholding nations, are founded on the negation of Black dignity, which is to say, the capability of Black people to affirm their status as individuals. And affirming one's dignity as an individual, as Kierkegaard and Cone both show, entails turning one's back courageously on society. "To be black is to be committed to destroying everything this country loves and adores."[66] Affirming Black dignity means daring to act in one's own name, in one's own interest, to take oneself as an end in itself in a society where this name, this interest, and this end are systematically relegated to nonbeing.[67]

Through prophetic interpellation, Black people hear the stifled voice of their own dignity rising up from within. For Cone, divine grace is synonymous with the "art of survival." In other words, it is a "way of remaining physically alive in a situation of oppression without losing one's dignity."[68] This suggests that for Cone survival has a twofold meaning. The first is physical. It is simply a matter of persevering, of resisting death in the biological sense of the term. But dignity also represents the spiritual side of survival. This is its second meaning. Without this, even with a heartbeat and cerebral activity, there is no life. In this sense, dignity represents the existential dimension of survival. And this dimension takes precedence over mere physical survival: between "death with dignity or life with humiliation, we will choose the former."[69] The Christian notion of life's endurance is expressed through dignity rather than through biological subsistence. "The struggle to *survive* in a white supremacist society was a full-time occupation for black people. But how to survive with one's *dignity* intact—that was the challenge."[70] Without dignity, the hope of survival gives way to a sort of zombification. "Because black families were brutalized and broken by slavery and oppression, God became the stabilizing and liberating force in their lives. [...] God becomes everything that the people need in order to sustain their lives with dignity."[71] In Black liberation theology, God is intimately bound up with dignity, to such an extent, in fact, that Cone almost equates them. Dignity is like a divine spark within the oppressed, who are urged by prophetic interpellation to never abandon the territory of history.

We are living today in a period that philosophers such as Jacques Rancière or Chantal Mouffe have called "post-political." In other words, in the Global North (but not exclusively), electoral politics gives the illusion that there are starkly different positions between political formations that are, in reality, almost fundamentally the same. This neoliberal leveling of political positions—shaped according to the interests of international finance—doesn't however signify that forms of radical political engagement have disappeared. They simply shifted, in part, to the religious sphere. In numerous contexts, religious discourse leads the opposition against the reigning order—a position currently impossible to adopt in the political sphere. In progressive political theory, it is thus customary to diagnose the collapse or perversion of the political sphere, in which case there is "the danger that this democratic confrontation will be replaced by a confrontation among other forms of collective identification, as is the case with identity politics."[72] But another option can be conceived: that of recognizing the politicization of the religious sphere, and, following the example of James Cone, viewing this as an opportunity.

Secularism, though proudly held up as a model by many, hardly exists outside of western Europe. In most other places, religion hasn't faded in the face of secularism. This is as much the case in the United States as it is in Latin America, where Christianity thrives; in Africa where religious practices overlap, intertwine, and inform one another; even in socialist China where popular religions, Taoism, and Buddhism (among others), continue to be practiced. The arrogance of those who tout the virtues of modernism and secularism and see themselves as rationally superior as they are no longer held down by religious dogma, derives in fact from an experiment extremely limited in time and space, an experiment whose real contributions have yet to be determined. The example offered by Cone's Black liberation theology shows that no radical political or social project can ignore, in the near future, political theology. Placing dignity at the center of his political project, Cone identified the driving force of radical Black politics.

— 6 —

UBUNTU: PHILOSOPHY, RELIGION, AND COMMUNITY IN BLACK AFRICA

That there exists an African perspective on Africa—one that accounts for the social interests of Africans—shouldn't be taken as self-evident.[1] This chapter focuses on the emergence of an ethical thought in Africa that is tied to the context of modernity and attuned both to the painful reality of the continent's current political situation as well as to the dignity of its history. The mid–twentieth century debate over African philosophy will serve as the point of departure, not because it was particularly influential (although its influence should not be underestimated), but because the questions it raised were later repeatedly posed in other fields of knowledge (theology, politics, law). These questions all point to the same problem: that of the legitimacy of Africans to conceptually grasp their situation through the use of their own conceptual tools. In other words, to ensure that their thinking reflects the lives they live. Such a problem is likely to arise in any context shaped by the "epistemic violence" of coloniality, given its delegitimization or even erasure of vernacular knowledge.

Thus, once outside of Europe, the "geophilosophical" problem brought to light by Deleuze and Guattari becomes less clear-cut. This is because it is no longer simply a matter of accepting that thinking "takes place in the relationship of territory and the earth." [2] Now it is the very philosophical nature of thinking, which is to say, its value, that is called into question. And when dealing with African philosophy in particular, the ordinary suspicion of illegitimacy is plagued by a deeper doubt. At issue here is a geopolitics of knowledge. As the Cameroonian philosopher Marcien Towa has written in his *Essai sur la problématique philosophique dans l'Afrique actuelle*, African philosophy was primarily evoked in studies on the prelogical mentality of Negros.[3] A product of modern European colonialism,

137

this question gave rise to attempts in intellectual circles to affirm an African specificity throughout the latter half of the twentieth century. These attempts were not always well received. The French anthropologist Jean-Loup Amselle, for example, argued that there could be no authentic African philosophy or social science. He outright rejected any claims to the contrary, dismissing them as hyperbolic.[4]

The very notion of "African philosophy" is thus generally treated with mistrust, either because it evokes a racist narrative, or because it serves as a Trojan horse for a self-indulgent, identity-based fundamentalism. In both cases, it becomes a hollow and pernicious ideology. The seemingly inarguable point that it makes no more sense to talk about *an* African philosophy in the singular than it does to speak of *a* Western philosophy overlooks a key matter: Western philosophy has already been widely accepted as a singular phenomenon. Or, more accurately, it has assumed this singular status after a long process of selection and revision, of "fitting" works and ideas into a historical narrative that conforms to preconceived notions. This is how the raw material of philosophical thought gets processed and packaged in recognizable form. From Hegel to Heidegger, Derrida, or Schürmann, Western philosophy can be said to have assumed a recognizable form. But the conditions of its recognition depend on the concurrent construction and writing—philosophical in their own right—of its own narrative. There is no reason to doubt that an African philosophy can emerge from a similar process of assemblage and revision to give rise to a unified narrative.

Philosophies of history such as those of Hegel or Heidegger were explicitly developed within determined geographico-racial borders, which also respected the global boundaries of the social violence of their times. Hegel deliberately excluded Africans from his account while Heidegger consigned Jews to a ghetto of the history of being.[5] African philosophers knew they were prohibited from doing the same. This is why Giorgio Agamben's claim—that Europe's recourse to an archaeology of knowledge to better understand itself is specific to that continent—is untenable.[6] Once again, this claim views the innumerable victims of the West as set adrift with no past or thought while forever bound to a simian immediacy. What is called the Global South today would take exception to this European position, since its own account doesn't have the luxury of excluding alterity. Alterity has made itself impossible to ignore. Beginning with the work of Paulin Hountondji, we will see the forces of delegitimization at work as a European definition of philosophy is applied abroad. Turning then to the work of Fabien

Eboussi Boulaga will further highlight the limits of this approach while calling attention to a generative site for thought that has been neglected by a Western philosophy obsessed with the purity of its own principles: the site of disaster. Finally, we will see that this thought must be accompanied by a meditation on ethical reparations—on the Ubuntu—which also serves as a theory of the social order. The life and work of the South African Archbishop Desmond Tutu will provide the prism through which we will read the contemporary reinvention of Bantu thought.

Paulin Hountondji: An Epistemological Critique of Ethnophilosophy

One cannot speak about contemporary African philosophy without speaking about what has been called, since Towa and Hountondji (although the Ghanaian Kwame Nkrumah was the first to use the term), "ethnophilosophy." "*Bantu Philosophy*, the 1945 work by the Belgian missionary Placide Tempels, is probably the first text where 'philosophy' was applied to an African reality."[7] The term "ethnophilosophy," often proudly used, has been deemed problematic by many. The Beninese philosopher Paulin Hountondji uses it to classify Tempels's work, which sought to identify a sort of spontaneous African ontology through the study of proverbs, linguistic etymologies, and formal structures. Hountondji defines it as a discourse arrived at through three interrelated arguments. The first claims that Black Africans share a worldview, or a restricted set of worldviews. The second posits that these worldviews can be understood as philosophies. Finally, the third argues that these philosophies should be reconsidered today and taught throughout Africa.[8] Whereas the explicit goal of Tempels's work was to facilitate colonization and the conversion of the Black continent by helping Europeans to understand the complexity of the indigenous way of thinking and, above all, by showing its compatibility with Christian revelation, the ethnophilosophical project is taken up in a more or less critical spirit by many African intellectuals. Some of the most noteworthy works coming out of this movement were penned by another man of faith who combined meticulous linguistic analysis with traditional scholasticism: the Rwandan Alexis Kagame.

Although Kagame undeniably shared the evangelical impulse of his white predecessors, ethnophilosophy takes a turn once Black people, who up until then were excluded from the Republic of Letters, were at the helm. The Beninese philosopher Stanislas Adotevi has thus called attention to the influence Tempels's thinking had on the Negritude movement and on Léopold Senghor, who fought to give Africans a seat at the table of world culture.[9] According to Hountondji, what Tempels gave to these thinkers was a renewed faith in their own humanity. He allowed them to recover their dignity. But at the same time they overlooked the imperialist impulse at the heart of Tempels's work. This was expressed in the Belgian philosopher's work by the exoticization of Africans' "spiritual outpourings," which the spiritless and technologically obsessed Westerner, who has forgotten his connection to the earth, would do well to embrace. Tempels also was driven by a *mission civilisatrice* that imposes the supposed universal values of this same Western civilization on Africa. Drawn to one aspect of Tempels's thought, African intellectuals turned a blind eye to the colonial ideals it represented.[10]

In light of these arguments, it is perhaps unsurprising that the debate perceived to be at the origin of African philosophy took place between two opposing camps: the ethnophilosophers and their critics. But in reality the so-called representatives of the "critical camp" had very little in common. More than an adversary in its own right (although there is an effort to reclaim this title today), ethno-philosophy saw itself as laying the groundwork for new theoretical approaches, creating a space for intellectual inquiry that exceeded its own scope. Hountondji's 1976 work, *African Philosophy*, probably attained the greatest notoriety during the course of this debate. However, for all its staggering erudition, it was hardly the most original or rigorous work to come out of this debate.

In the 1970s, Hountondji's main argument (which he would later refine) challenged what he called the "unanimity" of the ethno-philosophical approach. The approach he challenged viewed many distinct African languages as being in harmony on intellectual and cultural matters. In Hountondji's view, this promulgates "the myth of primitive unanimity, with its suggestion that in 'primitive' societies—that is to say, non-Western societies—everybody always agrees with everybody else."[11] The unanimous hypothesis thus lends credence to the argument, popularized by colonial psychiatry, that African collectivities are incapable of allowing for individuality. Or if they do allow this, it would stand as a major challenge to collective life.[12] Hountondji points out the irony that, although ethnophilosophers have naturally taken the philosophical lives of pre-colonial Africa as their objects of study, they fail to achieve in their respective works the very unanimity they claim for them.

The Beninese philosopher's strategy is thus to expose the weakness of the unanimity thesis by highlighting points of divergence in the works of ethnophilosophers and in their objects of study. In so doing, he rewrites the mission of the ethnophilosophers: rather than accept their own vision of their research (namely, to restore modes of thought of traditional Africa), he claims that they, far from being mere interpreters of an existing reality, have fabricated their own, using the raw material of African languages to invent their own doctrines. And this is what prevents them from conforming to the contradiction-less unanimity they praise. They are not exempt from the laws of the history of philosophy. In Hountondji's eyes, every philosophical doctrine emerges both by bracketing that which preceded it, and by positioning itself in relation to its philosophical heritage (thus Kantian critique, which casts itself as a radical break from the *Kampfplatz* of the history of metaphysics, can only position itself within the space traced by Wolff, Hume, Rousseau). This history is a succession of radical ruptures, fully aware of what they are breaking away from.[13]

If Hountondji thus shatters the illusion of harmony in ethnophilosophical discourse, he does it in favor of the civilized eristic driven by a quest for truth. This stems from a certain idealization of scientific research. Hountondji likely inherited this idealization from the tradition of French historical epistemology (represented by Bachelard, Canguilhem, the young Althusser), which he learned at the École Normale Supérieure in Paris and the Sorbonne. Hountondji detaches philosophy from its social conditions, which is to say, its context. According to him, the history of thought forms part of a broader history of society in a Marxian sense, but it remains governed by its own set of rules and order. It occupies its own gnoseological sphere amid the empire of class relations. "The only fruitful prospect for our philosophy today," he claims, "is to attach itself closely to the destiny of science by integrating itself with the immense movement towards the acquisition of scientific knowledge that is now developing on the continent."[14] This defines the normative position he assigns to the history of thought, sealing its fate.

At this level of generalization, Hountondji isn't capable of grasping the singularity of African history, and therefore he fails to understand the role philosophy should play in the formulation of a history that depends on its singular point of view. The idea that philosophy should serve science is contradicted by the very aim of *African Philosophy*, which set out to counter the most overblown attempts to reassert the historical conditions of Black people. Hountondji is free to assume, as did Plato, that philosophy springs from the contemplation of science's eternal truths. But this ignores what, in the southern Mediterranean, gave rise to philosophical questioning itself: a vital concern for the dignity of Black human beings. In Africa, modeling philosophy after science precludes the possibility of reflexivity, which is to say, the act of *thinking oneself*. As Towa reminds us, ethnophilosophical discourse derived from the belief that philosophy is an expression of human authenticity. Works on Bantu philosophy sought to prove the authenticity of African humanity.[15] Indeed, more than any philosopheme, the theoretical matter at the heart of African philosophy springs from the need to prove itself.

There is no African, no Black person of the diaspora, who isn't a descendant of the colonized or of the slaves taken from their land. Now *that* is a "question of being" worth pondering. It has nothing to do with science. One cannot criticize ethnophilosophy, or its contemporary iterations such as Afrocentrism, by merely denouncing the therapeutic rather than the theoretical ambition of its writings.[16] On the contrary, the question is how to make the deeply felt and constantly considered need for therapy the very object of study. Such a project is driven by the desire to heal the wound of dehumanization, but it does so without recourse to the abstractions of science or without inventing fantasies of the past, which only divert attention away from the main question or offer cheap consolation. The question at hand is still deserving of an answer. Hountondji avoided this question, which is at the origin of African ethnophilosophy: namely, what are the epistemic and existential consequences of unchecked racist violence? He dodged the question and focused on what interested him, producing a rather conventional argument on the origin and function of European philosophy, which he arbitrarily applied to the African continent. And he did this in defiance of what he himself called "philosophies" in direct reference to ethnophilosophies as well as their critiques. But what they had in common was their need to address the "original exclusion of the African from humanity"[17] underlying modern colonialism.

Ironically, Hountondji ended up falling under the sway of "the powerful mimetic fascination with Western thought"[18] that characterizes the work of Kagame. Led by the best intentions and equipped with a keen intellect, the Beninese philosopher ended up suppressing African historicity in favor of a mode of reasoning directly derived from a certain European epistemology. This arbitrary and unnecessary calque is in line with his desire to detach philosophy from social matters: "Our own contention [...] asserts the autonomy of the political as a level of discourse, and we think it unnecessary to try to base this on any other discursive authority."[19] Striving to keep philosophy independent from politics, Hountondji's purism only served to isolate it from the social world. He was probably right to reject the idea of a metaphysical foundation of politics, but he failed to consider what stands in direct opposition to this: the decidedly political origins of African philosophy.

Addressing the problem raised by contemporary African philosophy entails both abandoning the illusion of European positivism and confronting the question of the disaster, which is to say, colonial dehumanization. This is why, as Lewis R. Gordon explains, Africans whose humanity had been negated for so long turned primarily to anthropological philosophy.[20] And behind this turn, too, was the pull of politics, which was waiting, so to speak, in the wings of philosophy to rectify matters.

Fabien Eboussi Boulaga and the Hermeneutics of Muntu

Kwame Anthony Appiah has argued that solving the problems of Africa requires understanding the cultural world of its inhabitants. The shortcomings of ethnophilosophy were due to its failure to reach this stage of cultural sympathy, which is only the first step.[21] It should be noted that the driving force behind ethnophilosophy is not the traditional past it seeks to restore, but, unbeknownst to its practitioners, the disaster of colonialism, the memory of which compelled these philosophers to rediscover their origins. The Cameroonian philosopher Fabien Eboussi Boulaga clearly understood that the troubled past of Africa could not just be brushed aside in favor of an essentially contemplative and science-oriented philosophical approach. The chiastic title of the work where he treats this matter speaks volumes: *Muntu in Crisis: African Authenticity and Philosophy*. The "features" of European thought (crisis, or *Krisis*, and philosophy) are placed on an equal footing to those of African thought (Muntu, the relational human of the Bantu languages, authenticity). This blurs the strict boundary between ethnophilosophy and colonial thought.

This framing is in no way meant to show deference to ethnophilosophy. In fact, Eboussi Boulaga is an outspoken critic of it. According to him, the routine confusion between customs, or cultures, and theory in which this thinking remains mired, precludes this philosophy from engaging in any form of *Bildung*, of fashioning an individual or collective self. Indeed, the agent is stripped of agency and becomes incapable of self-scrutiny and self-reflection. This criticism aligns in many respects with that of Towa and Hountondji, but Eboussi Boulaga goes one step further by analyzing the rhetorical position of ethnophilosophical discourse. In his view, this discourse strives to convince a cultivated European public of the quality of African cultural works. In other words, the authors of these works are held up as worthy interlocutors. But the search for recognition is bound to end in disappointment if the inequality of the playing field isn't taken into account. Those who are benefitting from this structurally unequal relationship won't put an end to it out of goodwill and concern for others. Their authority to assign value is a fundamental part of their power and domination. For Eboussi Boulaga, this aporia doesn't mean one must give up on a context-based approach. On the contrary, it signals the return of the repressed. "The repressed includes the 'non-philosophical,' the concrete situation that is the driving force behind the yearning for philosophy, warping it, whichever it is, displacing imperceptibly its perspectives and causing its concepts to be shaky."[22]

This diagnosis of a philosophical thought beset by heteronomy stands in stark contrast to Paulin Hountondji's widely embraced plea for pluralism. The implications of this term are twofold. First, it suggests that Black people were well aware of the multiplicity of thought and cultural expression within their continent before Europe's involvement, and, secondly, that this multiplicity must be reaffirmed today. In sum, in direct opposition to the unanimity he had decried, Hountondji pushes for Africa to become an "open system of options."[23] Rather than strive toward an impossible ideal characterized by unanimity, one should adopt a pluralistic approach. It is hard to ignore the conflict this term-by-term opposition seemingly presents. It is bound to remain unresolved unless the importance of history is emphasized. This is just what Eboussi Boulaga does:

> to one who lives the destruction of one's own "world" due to the violence dealt by other worlds and who witnesses the making of cultural hierarchies after the criterion of force, it is permitted, to say the least, not to be satisfied with either the relativism which relishes the equal taste of the various cultures that be or with the pluralism that calls on everyone to tend to the beautiful form of one's original culture, nothing withstanding.[24]

In short, unanimity, relativism, and pluralism are equally meaningless propositions when thought is compelled to accept the morbid relativism imposed by colonial domination. By this measure, a position like Hountondji's can be accused of being objectively complicit with the dominant order. "Pluralism is the conservative ideology of those who are in a position of strength and power, who can alter the balance of forces in their favor."[25] Pluralism isn't the adversary of unanimity; it is the sum of local unanimities, held under the control of those who administer them. Those in power retain the right, like the other cultures they govern, to remain what they are: namely, the governing power.

If Hountondji's conception of philosophy falls in line with the tradition of French historical epistemology, Eboussi Boulaga's conception is closer to that of Antonio Gramsci's. For the Italian theorist, far from designating a coherent system or the perfect crystallization of the knowledge of a given period, philosophy designates a set of values and concepts of the world defined on the level of the group or individual. The specific contribution of intellectuals or professional philosophers is thus not explained by a natural difference. Rather, it is the time their profession as intellectuals affords them to study different worldviews that allows them to probe the historical depths of these views, to discover their idiosyncrasies, but also to propose new ones and point new ways forward.[26] Like Gramsci, Eboussi Boulaga views philosophy as an integral part of the intellectual production of a community, even if it serves at times as a tool to navigate one's way through it. On this point, he is more in line with his compatriot Marcien Towa. Towa advances an avowedly "revolutionary" conception of African philosophy, denouncing the desire among ethnophilosophers to rescue or revive traditional ideologies that led to Africa's collapse under European colonization. To bring about change in Africa, he calls for a revolution of the self and criticizes the nostalgia for weakness. "The history of our thought shouldn't seek to exhume a philosophy that would exempt us from philosophizing, but rather determine what in us should be subverted so that a subversion of the world and our present condition be made possible."[27]

Although he isn't opposed to Towa's progressive stance, Eboussi Boulaga does not agree with the voluntarism Towa promotes by inviting Africans to imitate the strongest aspects of the colonizer. Eboussi Boulaga is aware that it is the shared experience of colonial violence that first gives rise to the idea of a common African tradition. This tradition is at its outset synonymous with "colonizable."[28] But, he argues, there is something that can be done with the-being-in-common born from this negative foundation, a being who is also the bearer of ancient modes of life. He does not accept the idea that reviving the cultural, scientific, and political creativity of Africans entails abandoning the very notion of an African tradition. Nor does this entail imitating Europe in a servile manner. It is harder to let tradition thrive inside oneself while robbing it of its legitimizing power than to amputate a part of oneself. It is harder to be certain that the old rules need not be followed, that one is, in fact, entitled to break them or transform them for the better, than to jump into the arms of new masters in whose world these rules don't apply.

Rather than simply abandon any reference to African tradition and replace it with idealizations of hegemonic referents such as science or Europe, Eboussi Boulaga argues for a revolutionary and more compelling conception of tradition. The understanding offered by ethnophilosophy, which sees tradition as harmonious and imbued with pure positivity, stood in the way of a more existential, forward-looking conception. "Tradition as it must function to be true to its concept implies the imperative of fulfillment, in the future, in the form of a community of destiny. The past is always poised in relation to action or to a project."[29] This is how the Muntu—the Bantu-speaking human being who, in Eboussi Boulaga's writing, is at once the oppressed and the person who feels and experiences tradition and who carries it forward—rediscovers dignity, which is to say, his or her profound historicity. Eboussi Boulaga identifies three existential aspects of this rethinking of tradition, respectively tied to the past, the present, and the future.

The first is what he calls "vigilant memory." This entails grappling with those limiting experiences—colonization and slavery—which open tradition up to its own finitude and vulnerability. These underlie tradition's historicity and self-awareness. The negative pull of vigilance must be countered by an "identification," which is produced by the community, a non-abstract self-affirmation from the being-of-the-whole. This may find expression through religion, culture, or knowledge, or derive directly from the world of African life. Finally, tradition must be driven by a "utopian" impulse. It must offer countermodels that push back against current norms while respecting local realities: "Tradition is an ethical relationship with those of the past, as hope is an ethical relationship with those to come, of the future, those for whom my actions will appear as a given to be transformed, to turn into meaningful destiny, and who will recognize in us their own anticipation."[30] In this way, Eboussi Boulaga is advancing an existential conception of tradition: it should not be seen as imposing conformity or any consensus-seeking norm, but simply as that which one inherits, the fact of having a past and of being free to repeat it or betray it, insofar as one is guided by an ethics. This relationship to tradition, understood as the ability to position oneself critically in time, distinguishes the Muntu from a unanimity that negates individuality, and also from a Eurocentric, science-based epistemology founded on the illusion of the sovereign self, which is wholly autonomous and independent. Instead, Eboussi Boulaga describes the Muntu as a relational being: "The individual I am is an empirical segment of the world, a momentary figure of relations, a provisional knot of attributes and roles in a determinate context, in a location."[31] Generating a renewed interest in Bantu languages—through a hermeneutic and existential approach rather than an ethnophilosophical one—Fabien Eboussi Boulaga allowed the continent to display its intellectual depth, which it did in the succeeding decades.

Ubuntu and Loving Thy Neighbor

The Bantu word *Muntu* is the root of a term that would take on considerable political significance in South Africa in the 1990s with Desmond Tutu, Nelson Mandela, and their search for a peaceful end to the apartheid regime. That term is *ubuntu*. I am linking this term, which refers to both the essence of humans, or that which characterizes them, and to their value, or the reason why they matter, to the notion of dignity. Some scholars, such as the North American philosopher of law Drucilla Cornell, draw a clear distinction between ubuntu and dignity. "Dignity is usually associated with individual human rights, with a strong emphasis on autonomy and personhood, while uBuntu is associated with communalism and such virtues as loyalty and generosity."[32] But this is only true if one uncritically accepts a Eurocentric definition of dignity. The aim of this book has been to show how this understanding of dignity has been, time and time again, called into question and redefined to account for the social interests of Africans and Afro-descendants.

As Eboussi Boulaga has indicated, this African conception of dignity is unique in that it is centered on the community rather than the individual person. Or, to be more precise, the being-in-community, the individual as a relational being. The Anglican Archbishop and Nobel Peace Prize winner Desmond Tutu has placed the concept of ubuntu at the core of his liberation theology,[33] and it is no accident that this theology resembles that of James H. Cone.

His thinking stands in my reading as a major contribution to the Black history of dignity which, as opposed to what Drucilla Cornell suggests, is not centered on notions of autonomy and the individual. Tutu defines *ubuntu* in the following way:

> In our African idiom we say: "A person is a person through other persons." None of us comes into the world fully formed. We would not know how to think, or walk, or speak, or behave as human beings unless we learned it from other human beings. We need other human beings in order to be human. I am because other people are. [...] Our humanity we know is caught up in one another's. The solitary, isolated human being is really a contradiction in terms. [...] The quality of *ubuntu* gives people resilience, enabling them to survive and emerge still human despite all efforts to dehumanize them.[34]

Ubuntu thus refers to the dignity of the individual and, at the same time, to the dignity of the wider community of life. From this perspective, the Kantian notion of "the dignity of the person" appears contradictory since, strictly speaking, the abstraction of the "person," which is to say, the subject perceived to be absolute, sovereign, and detached from the network of human relations, is by definition without dignity. Indeed, dignity depends on one's ability to form relations with others, to maintain these relations, and to receive the support of others. The European tradition of ethics sees the solitary and isolated human as representative of dignity—this is its major flaw. As I argued in Chapter 4 with the notion of neoteny, there is no such being. It is hard to overstate the consequences of this pervasive fiction. It can be seen most notably in the tendency to view social relations within a paradigm of competition, where the strength of the individual is in direct correlation to the weakness of another. "According to ubuntu, it is not a great good to be successful through being aggressively competitive and succeeding at the expense of others."[35] There are thus two types of success: the first is egotistical, socially destructive, and for this reason often related to cannibalism or witchcraft in the popular imaginations of Central and Southern Africa; the other is collective, seeking what is best for the entire community.

The most striking expression of Tutu's rejection of the principle of competition and the survival of the fittest can be seen in his iconoclastic view that "God is not a Christian"[36]—no more than he is Jewish, Muslim, or Buddhist. In saying this, Tutu aims to counter the conventional conception of salvation—belonging to the chosen people alone—which places the devout above the sinful, the faithful above the unfaithful, and the godly above the ungodly. Such a view of the world infects the daily life of believers with rivalry, forcing them to police others and obsessively compare themselves to others. But in Tutu's view, heaven isn't governed by *numerus clausus*. Instead, all of humanity collectively participates in the salvation of each individual. In the idiom of Christianity, such a collaborative effort among a larger collectivity, which puts aside rancor and rivalry, goes by the name of *love*.

Binding a theological understanding of love to the notion of dignity flies in the face of one of the founding arguments of Kant's moral philosophy. To establish a moral system without recourse to the figure of God, Kant sought to turn the notion of love into a simple metaphor for moral law. Indeed, Kant contends, love cannot be the basis of any universal ethics since "love as an inclination cannot be commanded."[37] There are individuals whom we love and others we cannot bear. Excluding love in favor of obedience to the law, Kant's entire ethical system is rooted in a misunderstanding of the Christian conception of love, as he fails to see how it allows one to perceive and experience the dignity of others (while also being able to dispense with the need to lean on a positive conception of God).

Despite Kant's efforts, the empirical fact that we each like some people and dislike others doesn't by itself invalidate a theological conception of love. This is because its contribution lies in its insistence on the possibility, and necessity, of *creating* this love. "God didn't say 'Like your enemy.' It's very difficult to like your enemy. But to love your enemies is different. Love is an act of the will, where you act lovingly even if you do not always feel loving."[38] Christian love isn't a feeling, but an ability to act that no law can elicit or control. And, above all, love isn't detached from history, but takes shape within it. As Fabien Eboussi Boulaga writes, "love is the name of the driving force that invents organizations and institutions with a view to making new life possible."[39] But for this to happen, there must be an encounter between beings. Love that derives, as Kant believed, from the respect for an abstract person isn't sufficient for ubuntu. But nor is it enough to *love* thy neighbor *in God*, as many Christians would have it. One might argue that theological love is a matter of loving all humans *as God's creations*, since each of us is a recipient of the creator's infinite grace. But this, too, fails to explain theological love. First of all, if human understanding is finite, it would be in vain to try to emulate God's infinite love. Additionally, this conception runs up against the same problem that plagues Kant's: it erases the empirical individual in order to hold up, as an object of love, "God's creation" in the most generic sense. Thus, we "love" the other like we love anyone, or anything, since the Creator is at the origin of all things here on earth. With indistinction as its condition of possibility, such a "love" costs nothing.

To understand the importance of Christian love in the context of an African ethics of dignity, the concept of God must be stripped of adornments. Paradoxically, theological love is in essence an empirical and immanent love on the most basic level. The search for community requires loving the features of humanity as they are stubbornly expressed in a particular individual. To love thy enemies—as violent, spiteful, exploitative, and oppressive as they may be towards you—is not to love them in God. It is to seek out what is lovable in them beyond the abjection of their actions and the enmity that will always be there. It is to discover, here and now, the ability to sympathize. Theological love is defined by this search, regardless of its success. It ensures that the dignity of others will be taken into account. Indeed, it entails grappling with a tremendous difficulty: that of accepting the depth, complexity, and historicity of the other, of following the signs of a singular, self-driven individuality. For the nonbeliever, this serves as a reminder that the other is always both commensurable and incommensurable to oneself. But for the clergyman like Tutu, it is a matter of seeing with the eyes of God: "as you begin to see with the eyes of God, you start to realize that people's anger and hatred and cruelty come from their own pain and suffering."[40]

To understand others in their dignity, which is to say, in their historicity and relationality, does not require downplaying their hostility toward us or giving them a free pass. But it is the surest guarantee to curb the desire to eradicate others, the desire to reduce our neighbors to nothing, which is made possible by dehumanizing them. And this, in turn, is made possible by an even more profound dehumanization of oneself. As James H. Cone writes, "to love the white man means that the black man *confronts* him as a Thou without any intention of giving ground and becoming an It."[41] Love is not the opposite of struggle; it is one of its driving forces. Conflict isn't necessarily propelled by a sort of blind violence. As Frantz Fanon made clear, in the struggle for liberation, you have to risk—with potentially disastrous consequences—re-humanizing your enemies at the same time that you fight them. This is why Cone takes issue with the argument that nonviolence is the only legitimate manifestation of Christian love. He sees this as an attack on other Black movements and their capacity for revolutionary love.

150

Love is thus the ethical act of recognizing the dignity of others: their personal and collective histories, their situation, their sense of belonging or attachments. This is what makes it fundamental to ubuntu and why it is an indispensable prerequisite of any community—and especially a community defined by a common struggle. To find something lovable in the other means accepting the relative opacity of each singular being. It is a matter of accommodating the history and personality of *someone* rather than imagining an abstract "person" or generic "creation of God." As Cone writes: "Christians fight not for humanity in general but for themselves and out of their love for concrete human beings."[42] Having the awareness that your neighbor is an individual with a history is already a sign of love. Of course, this isn't a strong love, nor does it need be. It is enough to make the dignity of others visible. Acting in full awareness of the singularity of others isn't without significant political risk. For the oppressed, they run the risk of quelling the furor fueling their revolt, of developing a certain tolerance for injustice—but these are only true if love and dignity are poorly understood. For the oppressor, the risk is even greater, since acknowledging the dignity of one's neighbors amounts to forfeiting one's domination over them or, at the very least, foreclosing the recourse to ignorance that enables domination.

If dignity, understood as ubuntu, is not an abstract trait shared by every "person" or "creation," but is located in a network of relations and the web of history, then it is no longer possible to determine in advance what it consists of and who can lay claim to it, since these are forever negotiable. Hence the capital importance of love as the key to understanding singularity. Besides, the evil and violence that ubuntu is combating are always signs of a relation suspended or terminated. Tutu offers a compelling critique of secularism in this respect. If he questions the separation of religion from other spheres of existence in the West, it isn't with the aim of establishing or restoring a society built on a foundation of Christian morality, but rather to call attention to the pathology of a compartmentalized life. For the devout, religion has already been separated from the whole of existence, reduced to a fixed schedule of actions such as going to church or practicing charity. Faith has been patently reified and consigned to a specific set of institutions. In this way, the various aspects of one's existence no longer complement each other, but wither in isolation inside their respective institutions. Ubuntu, for its part, emphasizes the interdependence of the various spheres of existence and the interconnection of all human beings.

Both in its concern over the fragmentation of life among supposedly independent spheres and in its development of a new relational ethics of love, ubuntu is driven by the recognition of the fundamental precariousness of the human condition. However, seen from Desmond Tutu's vantage point, this precarity ceases to be the purely negative trait attributed to a modernity born of domination, power, and rivalry. Rather, it is what allows every human being to love and be loved: "It is through this weakness and vulnerability that most of us learn empathy and compassion and discover our soul."[43] Precarity forces humans to leave the icy confines of their solitude. Without precarity, there is no community, no society, there is not even a human world, just an anonymous quantity of invulnerable entities aimlessly adrift, with no sense of belonging and no purpose in life.

A Humanism Born from the Disaster

The most significant and striking demonstration of the concept of ubuntu in modern politics was its use by the Truth and Reconciliation Commission (TRC). Chaired by Desmond Tutu himself, the TRC played a fundamental role in peacefully dismantling the apartheid regime. Established in July 1995, its role was to hear from both victims and perpetrators of human rights abuses, with the TRC having jurisdiction to grant amnesty to the latter:

> The commission began its work in December 1995 and most of its hearings were completed by 1998. The TRC submitted its final report—consisting of five volumes and 3,500 pages—to President Mandela in October of that year. A total of 20,000 people came forward to offer their testimony to the TRC. Of these, 1,800 victims were "selected" to testify in public, lending their voice to the suffering of an entire population. The TRC was mandated by law to rehabilitate these victims, to restore their moral and financial dignity, and to make recommendations to the government for how such violations could be prevented in the future. It was also given the difficult task of granting amnesties. More than 7,000 former fighters belonging to the security force, the liberation movements, and the extreme right applied for it.[44]

The question of amnesty arose in fact as a response to a very concrete political need: the pardoning of its own people was a condition set by the white National Party, which had no intention of ceding power to Nelson Mandela's African National Congress if it was going to lead to a Nuremberg-style trial. It is very likely that without this monumental concession, the white party would have fought to stay in power. The goal was therefore to avoid a civil war. However, despite these difficult conditions, which have at times given the impression that the TRC was tacitly on the side of the beneficiaries of apartheid, and despite the many aporias inherent in its approach, the TRC demonstrated a remarkable philosophical consistency, a fact that is too often overlooked. Under the neoliberal pressure stemming from the deadly structural adjustment programs imposed by international institutions, the reparations promised to the victims were far from equal to the harm suffered. Nevertheless, despite the undeniable shortcomings of its implementation, the TRC's unflagging commitment to the spirit of ubuntu makes it an unparalleled example of what an African philosophy of dignity looks like in action.

Indeed, the TRC wasn't conceived as a vehicle of criminal justice—that is, as a punitive apparatus—but as a process of reconciliation in the strongest sense of the term.[45] As Desmond Tutu explains: "Reconciliation meant that those who had committed serious abuses of human rights should have a chance to become humane once again."[46] In the ethical framework of ubuntu, such a restitution of humanity entails re-establishing relationships and reintegrating those harmed as well as the perpetrators of appalling crimes into the same social body. If, as we've seen, human dignity as envisioned by Tutu takes shape within relationships, a justice founded on dignity can never operate by casting individuals out of society, whether this be by sentencing them to death or by imprisoning them. Thus, the specificity of TRC's practice of justice lies in its focus on the relationships formed between citizens, which is to say, between the different members of the community.

In a penal system, this is a moot point. Exchanges between legal subjects are narrowly viewed according to their respect or violation of the law. The TRC is more concerned with the character of the relationships maintained between individuals, with the affective register of their interactions, and with the shared memory that binds them together. Tutu's core argument is that the South African nation as a whole is in need of moral healing, which can only be achieved through a perilous process of reconciliation, while being mindful of the fact that there can be no true reconciliation without conflict: "True reconciliation is based on forgiveness, and forgiveness is based on true confession, and confession is based on penitence, on contrition, on sorrow for what you have done."[47] This is why it was important for the criminals to speak about the crimes they committed, to tell the true story of their wrongdoing. Not to provide the court with a confession, but to confess, in theological terms, to the larger community. The court confession is bound up with interrogations, accusations, the weighing of evidence, and the search for a motive. The theological confession, for its part, with its assurance of forgiveness, encourages one to speak freely. This is why, in Tutu's view, the TRC could only take the form of nonpunitive justice, or a "restorative justice" where the "central concern is not retribution or punishment," but rather "the healing of breaches, the redressing of imbalances, the restoration of broken relationships, a seeking to rehabilitate both the victim and the perpetrator."[48] If the immediate political stakes entailed avoiding a civil war, there were no less decisive moral consequences at stake if they failed to address South Africans' isolation, resentment, and unconscious desire for revenge. Not only to create the conditions for social harmony, but above all because this kind of social fragmentation, according to ubuntu, signals a full-scale dehumanization. In this respect, the idea of a society where the wounds of the past discourage people from contributing to the common good is unacceptable.

Restoring the dignity of human beings—re-establishing them in ubuntu, allowing them to regain their Muntu quality—invites them to rebuild all the relationships that the considerable violence they suffered or committed had made impossible. In this sense, and in line with the notion of dignity advanced by North American Black liberation theology, Desmond Tutu's ubuntu theology arises out of a refusal of indignity. Indeed, as Drucilla Cornell rightly shows, it is defined by its intrinsic political ambition: "uBuntu is not just an ethical ontology of a purportedly shared world, but an ethical demand to bring about a shared world."[49] In this respect, Tutu's thinking is emblematic of a much broader trend that could be described as an African community-based humanism. Throughout the history of the entire continent, there have been many ethical approaches that bear a strong resemblance to the South African ubuntu of the 1990s. There is significant overlap in its ambitions with the Manden Charter of the thirteenth-century Malian empire[50] as well as with the concept of Ujamaa developed by Julius Nyerere while serving as President of Tanzania in the 1960s.[51] Pointing out these commonalities isn't meant to recuperate the old idea of unanimity refuted by Hountondji. African community-based humanism is a conceptual framework that contains a variety of viewpoints, just as liberal individualism, from Hobbes to Habermas to the constitutions of most Western countries, presents itself as a flexible notion that finds expression in a variety of ways as it adapts to new contexts.

It is important to consider the cultural context of Desmond Tutu's effort to put an end to apartheid to grasp the urgency that an ethics of African community-based humanism presents today. Indeed, understanding dignity as ubuntu responds to a concrete need: that of creating a cohesive political community with which most citizens can identify. And this is achieved without recourse to the kind of triumphant origin stories that Western nations gushingly recite, especially the most imperialist among them. As Fabien Eboussi Boulaga perceived, contemporary African philosophy—which is to say, the *need* to philosophize—is born from disaster, extreme violence, and evil, just as are today's sub-Saharan nations. "What comes first, for Muntu, is neither astonishment nor wonder but just stupor caused by an overall defeat."[52] The notions of Muntu and ubuntu show how African traditions can be called upon without ceding to the illusions of unanimity or a "superior" Eurocentric position. The relationality underlying these notions is closely tied to disaster. Desmond Tutu was well aware of this as he developed the key principles of his ubuntu theology. A being-in-relation allows an individual ethics to be defined, despite one's troubled, violent, and dehumanizing past. The value of "tradition" lies in its invitation to establish an ethics oriented toward the present—not by subserviently adhering to the memory of the past. In this respect, the use of a Bantu vocabulary isn't harking back to an idealized, precolonial past, a past from which one has been forever severed after so much suffering and violence. Instead, this use represents an effort to reinvigorate philosophical, ethical, and political thinking. It is meant to animate living cultures and to imagine a common world beyond the catastrophe. African philosophy was born from disaster, rather than from the spirit of conquest, which is bent on destruction. This is its primary virtue.

Postscript on an Irreconciled South Africa

In 2014, the South African rap group Dookoom recorded a song called "Larney jou poes"—which, to give a frank translation, means "Fuck you boss." Laying down a verse in Afrikaans filled with rage, followed by a verse in English with no less fervor, over a throbbing electro beat that screams urgency, the rapper Isaac Mutant gives voice to the unbearable conditions of agricultural labor in his country. The song begins like a nursery rhyme, sending a clear message: "Farmer

Abraham had many farms, I work one of them, and so would you, so let's go burn them down!" This is followed by a first-person account in Afrikaans of utter exhaustion, misery, and, above all, anger among workers. Mutant shifts to English in a second verse which, moving from a personal level to a theoretical one, tells the story of the founding of South Africa as an essentially criminal act, blending together seventeenth-century history and a present plagued by racism and alienation. The music video shows a small group of Black agricultural laborers who become armed, practice shooting, and then set out to attack a farm.

The NGO AfriForum, which represents a white South African minority and serves as a PR firm for wealthy landowners, immediately filed a complaint against the song and its music video, claiming that it incites murder. The lyrics of the song are, in fact, dramatizing a social reality that haunts the country. Since 1994, 3,000 white farmers were reported killed and, since 2010, there has been a significant rise in attacks on farms.[53] This is a clear indication of the (at least partial) failure of the TRC to ensure both a just and peaceful transition. This doesn't so much point to the shortcomings of the ubuntu spirit, or even to those of nonviolence as a strategy, but rather to the failures of a superficial approach to justice and equality, which has been overly focused on public apologies for past crimes without tending to the consequences of those crimes. In other terms, despite claims to the contrary, the process of reconciliation has had zero impact on inequality.[54] A political system defined by racial capitalism has, by necessity, lacked the courage to take on a profoundly unequal economic structure and has thus reached an impasse. The consequences of forgoing justice in the name of security, as nation states tend to do, are being played out in South Africa. The extremely unequal distribution of land between whites and nonwhites on which apartheid was built has gone for the most part unchallenged. What's more, Black workers continue to earn miserable wages. They are also at times still subject to the deplorable "Dop system," which allows them to be paid in part in cheap wine, with obvious public health consequences.[55]

Dookoom's song thrusts us into the same ambiguous ethical space as Nat Turner's revolt. This is a reminder of the unavoidable aporias that plague the notion of dignity in Afro-descendant thought. In societies historically marked by anti-Blackness, Black violence is only visible in the uneasy space where self-defense, revolutionary action, and crime become almost indistinguishable.

Part Three

Forms-of-death in the European Necropolis

Leur haine envers nous est omniprésente
Comment oublier tout ce qu'on représente ?
[...]
Je suis le bébé de ma mère, un oubli de mon père
Un enfant issu de l'immigration
Je ne suis pas communautaire
Mais autour de moi tout est sombre,
des tours de béton à la population
Ça vend la mort juste en bas de la maison
des fantômes hantent le tiekson
La hass prend le dessus sur ma vision
Les représentants de la nation parlent de nous
qu'en période d'élection
Iblis est en constante érection
Je vis la mélodie de cette malediction

Their hate towards us is omnipresent
How can anyone forget what we represent?
[...]
I'm my mama's baby, my father's neglect
A child of immigrants
The social enclave I reject
But everything is dark around me
Concrete towers is all we got
Right outside the door death is bought
Ghosts haunt the block
It's misery around the clock
Politicians only talk about us
During an election
Iblis has a constant erection
I live the melody of this infection

Jok'air, "La voix du bloc" (3'20), Album: *Jok'Rambo*,
La Dictature, 2018.[1]

— 7 —

RECOGNITION AND DIGNITY IN THE ERA OF GLOBAL APARTHEID

On Friday, November 10, 2017, the German newspaper *Der Tagesspiegel* published a list of 33,293 migrants who died between 1992 and 2017 while trying to reach Europe. Many of them remain unidentified, with the circumstances of their death being the only details known about them. This interminable article, literally unreadable, whose estimates are by necessity conservative, offers a glimpse into the immense necropolis that the Mediterranean Sea has become in the last few decades. Despite the constant display of ethical concern from European heads of state and government officials, at the time when coastguards cause more shipwrecks than they prevent, the idea that international law is dedicated to establishing the conditions of human dignity[1] seems increasingly in doubt. Each day international law appears more and more like an instrument of white supremacy and racial capitalism. As Bruno Latour has compellingly argued, our current moment is characterized by the conviction, which is increasingly winning over the ruling classes of the West, that "the earth no longer had room enough for them and for everyone else."[2] This sentiment is all the more pronounced when dealing with the issue of migration. This is no accident. The seemingly neutral term *migrant*, in fact, conceals the obvious: once taken out of the context of the existential experience of forced removal and exodus, or the impact of migration felt across generations, the "issue of migration" or the figure of the "immigrant" are mere euphemisms for speaking in broad sociological terms about the question of race. Their use points to the lack of courage to tackle this issue head on or to speak openly about the imperial system that sustains it.[3] Those dying at Europe's borders are former victims of colonization, former victims of forced labor, former slaves.

159

The coloniality of power, a central concept of contemporary Latin American critical theory, sheds light on the geopolitical order that is at the root of the situation. This concept calls attention to the structural continuities of the North/South colonial power relations that have persisted in spite of independence.[4] The South African political scientist Sebelo Ndlovu-Gatsheni applies the term to the situation in Africa. He defines it as "a global neo-colonial hegemonic model of power that articulates race and labour, as well as space and people in accordance with the needs of capital and the benefit of white European people."[5] As we will see, the belief that the populations of the Third World can be displaced and disposed of according to the needs of capital is central to understanding the contemporary conditions of migration. As borders throughout the world continue to tighten, the present era of global apartheid signals the inevitable decline of multiculturism and the politics of recognition. But their decline is not to be lamented. In fact, the politics of recognition and multiculturalism laid the groundwork for our current crisis by reinforcing the hegemony of an imperial and narcissistic West. As Fanon has shown, an ethics equipped to challenge this status quo must begin by rethinking the relationship between dignity and sovereignty.

Recycling Disposable Lives

Today's growing number of disposable lives—a clear consequence of Europe's botched handling of the migrant problem—has deeper roots in French colonialism. Under colonial rule, a distinction was drawn between an *Afrique utile* or "useful Africa" and an *Afrique inutile* or "useless Africa." As the political scientist William Reno has argued, the persistence of this distinction demonstrates the continuity between colonial and postcolonial regimes. "Whereas the contemporary version of *Afrique utile* is delineated in terms of controlling salable resources rather than of colonial concerns with labor, its *inutile* counterpart still denotes regions and people that are best governed lightly, if at all, rather than waste scarce revenues in attempts to control them."[6] *Useless Africa* refers to the growing clusters of nonplaces on the continent forsaken by globalization. Understanding Africa's place in a globalized context entails not only taking into account an ever-increasing interconnection of different regions of the world, but also the "selectivity" of the network.[7] The hyper-connected points—capitals or mineral extraction zones controlled by multinationals from the Global North—stand in stark contrast to entire territories, and their people, that suffer from complete neglect. Neither states, dispossessed of their resources and ravaged and extorted by multinational firms and international financial institutions, nor even NGOs, have the slightest concern for these places and their people.

Contrary to the official discourse of the IMF and the World Bank on "good governance," it is not the "stable" and "democratic" states that attract the most foreign capital, but rather the quasi-states, deemed "bankrupt" or ravaged by civil war and plagued by corruption. In other words, puppet states where neither concern for social rights nor strong claims of territorial sovereignty are at stake. Angola is a case in point. Despite a long civil war (1975–2003), almost no threat has been posed to its offshore drilling operation. When it was threatened in 1993, the government called on the South African private security outfit Executive Outcomes to protect it. The reliance on mercenary work is becoming widespread.[8] This model of privatizing African resources perfected by Western multinational offshore operations can also be found on land where territories, guarded and policed, are materially and symbolically cut off from their own country despite being fully integrated into the world economy.[9] These neocolonial land enclosures constitute the bulk of "useful Africa." Zoning, enclosure, extraction and other "processes of dispossession spawn reactions of resistance that are relatively autonomous in the form of global migratory patterns that pose a threat to the North and its 'imperial mode of life', for they call into question the stability of the border between the Global North and the Global South."[10]

As theorists of the coloniality of power have shown, world borders are in essence symbolic, creating a false division between civilization and savagery, white and Black, the *métropole* and the colony. Frontex, the European Border and Coast Guard Agency, which was reorganized in 2016, ensures that migrants from these *arbitrarily* disqualified areas are kept out of Europe. "In 2009, [Frontex] already possessed 25 helicopters, 21 planes, 113 boats and 427 security units. Since October 2016, it is the official European body of coast and border protection, one of whose primary mandates is to physically prevent Mediterranean crossings."[11] As Judith Butler has written: "These regulations seek to ensure the racial hegemony of whiteness, but also national ideals of purity, evidencing a resistance to the cultural heterogeneity of Europe that is already irreversible, and importantly so."[12] Migration policies in Europe, especially in the former colonial *métropoles*, are historically founded on the false assumption that these countries' economic and social privileges derive from their domestic development, not from their predatory position in the world economy. In reality, the peaceful, normalized lifestyle of the Western middle class derives from the exploitation and pillaging of the resources of the Third World, without which this lifestyle couldn't exist.

If the discourse of the media depicts Western countries as besieged fortresses, it omits the fact that the principal source of wealth they are defending is located far outside the walls of the nation-states themselves. These sources of wealth are protected under military or paramilitary guard within neocolonial enclaves of the Global South. This reality is masked by the logic Étienne Balibar has described as that of "the social-nation state," which makes many social and public benefits conditional on national belonging, or at least on the racial purgatory of a *situation régulière*, or "permanent residency." Thus, it is made to seem as though basic needs can't be met for everyone, but rather must be fought over between citizens—the elite class in this situation—and the rest of the world. And this competition, which has dealt a major blow to the international workers' movement in Europe, is made possible by ignoring the ongoing pursuit of colonial plunder by other means.[13] This state of affairs belies the political commonplace, widely diffused by the media, that pits a legitimate form of migration— that of so-called political refugees—against an opportunistic, even comfortable form, which is deemed "economic" migration. The difference between the two—codified by the Geneva Convention—is of course illusory. Pillaging the resources of "useful Africa" and demolishing sovereign states with Western armies or the tools of international finance are driving millions of African and Middle Eastern lives toward extinction. Under these imperialistic conditions, there can be no form of migration other than a political one.

Under a selective globalization, the traditional opposition inherited from political liberalism between citizens and foreigners is increasingly seen in tandem with the distinction between useful and useless lives. Bertrand Ogilvie rightly points out that contemporary capitalism is fueled by "a logic of indirect and delegated extermination" by creating surplus lives, an excess of beings for which capitalism has no use. "In Latin America, these populations that don't fit into national and international schemes of production and exchange are provocatively called '*poblacion chatarra*', a population of trash, waste, refuse [...]. This is the modern production of the disposable man."[14] One NGO estimates that in the European Union and its border countries, there are 360 migrant camps designed to accommodate, in theory,

47,000 migrants.[15] The nature of these camps is extremely varied, from the state-sponsored to the improvised and the privately run. Indeed, as Angela Davis has remarked, "the most profitable sector of the prison-industrial complex is immigrant detention and deportation."[16] In Europe, no country has gone further in this direction than the United Kingdom with its multinational security force G4S. Camps are run, both structurally and conceptually, like prisons, but without individual confinement: the migrants are allowed to walk freely within the confines of the center, and even use cellphones provided they have no cameras. As we'll see, this isn't to protect the camps from being exposed, but rather to prevent at all costs the conditions of detention from being shown from the perspective of the detainees themselves. Those in power seek to maintain a monopoly of representation over these camps.

The camps that have had the greatest negative impact are those found at the entry points to Europe, known as "hotspots," such as the Moria camp on the Greek island of Lesbos. The tight clusters of prefabs and containers surrounded by barbed wire are plagued by sanitary conditions that Doctors Without Borders have deemed inhumane. Exiles are crammed together, often waiting up to several months before their applications are even considered. The growing number of camps like these is a symptom of a much larger problem. For the anthropologist Ghassan Hage, the end of France's *trente glorieuses* (thirty years of economic prosperity) marked the beginning of a new era in the treatment of migrants, who were henceforth judged according to their use value. He described this shift in an interview:

> Historically, refugees have always been conceived as waste originating from elsewhere. But in the 1940s, refugees appeared to be "recyclable." But now, people look at them and think they aren't recyclable. [...] Today we're in a situation where people who see themselves in the position of the white domesticator, whether this concerns nature or humans, feel overwhelmed by the arrival of unmanageable waste, both in the form of refugees and natural waste.[17]

This representation of the disposable lives of migrants as non-recyclable, that is, as utterly useless to capital, is meant to be seen as a sign of decline. But even this idea seems to me like wishful thinking. Indeed, to insist on the Global North's inability to "recycle" refugees is to point to a powerlessness that would be cause for celebration if it were to herald a real decline. In other terms, Hage is diagnosing "a colonizing power that remains powerful enough to colonize, but that is nonetheless in a state of decline, fearing that it is losing its grip over what it has historically dominated."[18] Although the diagnosis of such a feeling of fear is indisputable, Hage seems to neglect the fact that the state is busy inventing new modes of recycling in response to this situation. A camp like Moria is proof of this. It is too soon to declare these places telltale signs of a looming collapse, as though the problem is too big to handle. This forgets the fact that as human lives lose value, new and inhumane ways of assigning value are invented. Modern slavery is a striking case in point: stripped of all value, dehumanized, and reduced to abjection, Africans have been the main victims of this since the dawn of modernity. This is precisely what made it possible for them to enter the world economy as commodities. It displays a form of negative revaluation.[19]

Today's migrant camps are not covert operations, as was occasionally the case in the mid-twentieth century.[20] The Greek and Italian hotspots are exploited by Europe as a strategy of deterrence.[21] This means that the abject living conditions that prevail there are designed to attach a negative symbolic value to migration. For this to work, extensive media coverage is required. It is thus misguided to see the spectacle of refugees amassed in camps as useless waste. In fact, these masses of frail and fatigued bodies are themselves already a perverse form of recycling. In their very indistinguishability, these bodies serve as a campaign of dissuasion aimed at potential migrants, with the corollary of attracting well-meaning investors to flood the coffers of NGOs in Paris, London, Washington, D.C., or New York. Through their ostensible destitution, refugees are embodiments of the border, or worse: embodied borders. The collective and persistent memory of a prosperous and cosmopolitical Europe inherited from Kant must be challenged. Instead, we have a European necropolis where the possibility of living a decent life is dependent upon a racialized understanding of nationality. Once viewed as a haven of peace for its own citizens, Europe now shows itself to be a vast morgue for the citizens of the Global South, a representation it not only accepts but cultivates in the hope of reducing the operating costs of its necropolis.

Rightfully fearing these new modes of human recycling, one may think a return to the Europe of yesteryear appears tempting. But even those halcyon days have lost credibility in European political discourse. The pervasive dialectic of the useful and the useless makes a return to what went by the terms *integration, inclusion*, or *multiculturalism* seem like a viable option. With these, there is an ostensible concern for the dignity of each individual. But the underlying ethics of these policies, which considered together are often called the ethics of recognition,[22] are themselves cause for concern.

164

Inspired by the philosophy of a young Hegel, the theory of recognition is a principal trend of contemporary social philosophy. An overview of this philosophy must begin with its three main tenets. First, its insistence on the moral dimension of social life: action is not only guided by interests but also by ethical values. Second, the idea that individuals only exist as part of a larger human collective to which they belong. And finally, the belief that social conflicts stem from the expectations of inferior social groups, whose moral experience of being the target of contempt drives them to demand inclusion within society. The theory of recognition has leaned on these three tenets to sketch a general theory of social exclusion and to propose targeted solutions. Recognition is a means of integrating those excluded from legal protections, from the benefits of citizenship, or from participating in the political community. But in a context defined by imperialism and coloniality—the ravages of which have been evoked above—it is imperative to adopt a more critical perspective, such as that advanced by Frantz Fanon. Such a perspective doesn't deny the importance of recognition. Rather, it places it alongside the more pressing matter of dignity. In what follows, I'll take this as my point of departure and interrogate its implications and consequences. In so doing, I'll follow the lead of the Canadian First Nations theorist Glen Sean Coulthard, who, in his work *Red Skin, White Masks*, argues that "in Fanon recognition is not posited as a source of freedom or dignity for the colonized, *but rather as the field of power through which colonial relations are produced and maintained.*"[23] However, despite both of us taking Fanon as our starting point, my argument departs from Coulthard's important work in two significant ways. To begin, my angle of attack is different. Whereas Coulthard focuses his critique on the approach to recognition adopted by Anglo-Saxon liberal political philosophy—especially in the work of Charles Taylor and Will Kymlicka—I will turn my attention to continental social philosophy, whose leading figure is the German philosopher Axel Honneth. Second, Coulthard is primarily making his case on behalf of indigenous people. My argument is designed to serve exiles and, more generally, the dehumanized populations of the Global South, especially Africans.

Fixation

Citing Fanon on this matter has become de rigueur. The Canadian Charles Taylor, for instance, describes how Fanon led the charge against the "lack of recognition" by insisting on the need for minorities to free themselves from "a depreciatory image of themselves."[24] But this strikes me as a superficial reading of Fanon. Fanon's contribution to this debate lies in his shift from questioning the various forms of denial of recognition to interrogating the very nature of the act of recognition. Fanon examines what makes recognition possible in the first place and the relationship it establishes among "the recognized." He is less interested in the existence or absence of recognition than in what gets qualified as recognition. Taylor's binary frames recognition as necessarily *beneficial* in itself. Fanon would take issue with this characterization.[25] It is thus worth dwelling on three interpretations of recognition found in Fanon. These are, respectively, fixation, asymmetric recognition, and full recognition.

To take what Fanon calls "fixation" not as an obstacle to recognition but a display of it constitutes a critique in itself of the dominant forms of an ethics of recognition. Indeed, the dominant line of thinking contends that there are originally two distinct entities, which need to be brought together peacefully. But this makes two problematic assumptions. African and Middle Eastern exiles who flee to Europe are not simply "foreigners." They have always been bound to the West by a powerful tie: that of dispossession. Refugees in Europe are hardly newsworthy. Their motivations are not enigmatic, nor are they themselves unfamiliar. They are not unrecognizable to state agents or to the media shaping public opinion. They are on the contrary always recognized, received with a whole series of pre-established judgments inherited from a colonial and imperial past. This is one of the reasons why it makes little sense to see recognition as a uniform welcoming or valuing of the other. Instead, a wide range of emotional responses is bound up in the process of recognition, including hate, desire, paternalism, love, genuine respect, among many others.

For Fanon, fixation represents the most pathological, the most unequal and asymmetrical form of recognition. It serves to classify others in nonnegotiable terms. It is closely related to verbal abuse: "Look, a Negro!" heard on a street corner, the effects of which Fanon closely examines in *Black Skin, White Masks*. He describes this experience in the following way: "I stumble, and the Other *fixes* me with his gaze, his gestures and attitude, the same way you fix a preparation with a dye. I lose my temper, demand an explanation... Nothing doing. I explode. Here are the broken pieces of myself reassembled by the other."[26] It is a pre-established understanding, a way of judging the actions of Black people before they even take place. Even revolt, evoked here through a metaphor of explosion, has no effect. It is the observer who sets the scene and establishes its meaning, cutting it to fit a pre-determined pattern. Black people are imprisoned within a narrow representation seen through the sole lens of race.

> As long as the black man remains on his home territory, except for petty internal quarrels, he will not have to experience his being for others. There is in fact a "being for other," as described by Hegel, but any ontology is made impossible by a colonized and acculturated society. [...] Ontology does not allow us to understand the being of the black man, since it ignores the lived experience. For it is no longer a question of just being black, but being black before the white man.[27]

The ontological erasure under coloniality has little in common with Sartre's existentialism or Derrida's deconstruction. It is neither a matter of liberty prevailing over the inertia of being, or the unlimited play of substitutions. Rather, it is the establishment of a morbid relationism. A hierarchical relation, with one party forcing the other to recoil and retreat, denying the very existence of the unbreakable connection they share. This fixation, this orientation of existence by an exterior definition, gives rise to a split consciousness. Fixation thus explains how self-perception takes place through the hostile gaze of the other. This is what Black people are forced to confront before the white gaze.

Fixation is the process by which white people recognize Black people as "Negroes," which in the mind of the former implies a fixed set of derogatory, and fitting, characteristics: "deafened by cannibalism, backwardness, fetishism, racial stigmas, slave traders, and above all, yes, above all, the grinning *Y a bon Banania*."[28] Fixation is experienced as violence, as the inability to live and to give meaning to one's actions, which Fanon describes through the use of another metaphor: "I sit down next to the fire and discover my livery for the first time. It is in fact ugly."[29] The livery of Black people is their skin. Skin which, in the eyes of white people, gives them the name "Negroes" and indicates subservience. Fixation encourages Black people to maintain the same kind of relationship to their skin as a server does to his work outfit. Their social role escapes them. The white world dresses them up only in slave's rags. Fixation precludes any "emergence,"[30] in both a literal and a figurative sense. It demands a tautological self-immanence in its purest form by erecting a barrier around the existence of the other. Worse than cultural misrepresentation, racist fixation leads to the troubles that are part and parcel of necropolitics. Fixation is what confines Black people to a space where life and death become indistinguishable. It is the moment when the gaze of the other already spells death.

The Asymmetry of Recognition

The difference between fixation and asymmetric recognition is that between an unlivable world and a world that is hardly bearable. Black people remain confined by fixation and, although racist societies now seek to treat the effects of this, they dare not deal with the root cause. This shift represents the path that colonialism itself offers to Black people as a way out. But the terms and conditions of this path are determined by a dehumanizing society, making its promise of liberation a hollow one. Most critiques of the notion of recognition argue that its main proponents—most notably Axel Honneth—minimize its dark side. This is a fair point, but it only addresses one of its problems. Emmanuel Renault has called attention to a shift in Honneth's philosophy, as the "theory of recognition was recast as a theory of promises inscribed in the fundamental institutions of modernity."[31] Thus, a "young" Honneth, under the sway of Adorno's and Horkheimer's social critique, gave way to a liberal thinker attached in older age to the values of Western institutions. Honneth abandoned a critical phenomenology centered on the negative experiences of modernity. But this was taken up fruitfully by Renault, who gives careful attention to the liberation efforts of the oppressed. However, the turning point Renault identifies in the theory of recognition seems to me to have already been present as far back as Honneth's *magnum opus*, *The Struggle for Recognition*. Despite the relevance of some of its core ideas, this book isn't just an imperfect expression of critical theory. It is an outline of the principles of alienation and social violence that underly the logic of liberal identity politics.

From a Black point of view, the ethics of recognition, an emblem of a tolerant and socially democratic multiculturalism, isn't blind to the dark side of democratic societies. It is itself, *in itself*, a part of this dark side. On this point, the Puerto Rican philosopher Nelson Maldonado-Torres rightly points out the major difference between Fanon's interpretation of Hegel and that of Axel Honneth. The former sees the struggle for recognition as one divided between masters and slaves.[32] The social order is scarred by the fixation of slavery, which is to say, racial dehumanization. To be sure, just like

RECOGNITION AND DIGNITY

Hegel in Honneth's reading, Fanon must begin with "the perception of a deficiency or 'suffering' in the lifeworld of the present,"[33] but he handles it differently.

Honneth's interpretation of the phenomenon of racism illustrates this difference. Drawing on Ralph Ellison's *Invisible Man*, he speaks about the paradigm of invisibility, or the "non-existence in the social sense [of the term]" targeting black people.[34] While this approach allows him to recognize that non-perception is a willful act and thus comes from a position of power that produces the invisibility of subaltern groups, it also repeats Charles Taylor's mistake by believing the only harm associated with recognition is its absence. In this view, social violence stems from an *absence* of recognition rather than from the *institutional structures and practices that govern* recognition. What's more, unlike Fanon who emphasizes the racism of segregationist and colonial societies, Honneth sees social invisibility as an intersubjective problem, as though only concerning the domain of the personal. The conclusion he draws exposes the shortcomings of this approach:

> the social invisibility from which the protagonist of Ralph Ellison's novel suffers is the result of a *deformation* of the human capacity for perception with which recognition is connected—or, as the author put it, "a matter of the construction of their inner eyes, those eyes with which they look through their physical eyes upon reality."[35]

Why one's perception is distorted is never addressed. Moreover, Honneth's lexical framing leaves no room at all to question how individuals are *taught to see* race in the first place. Honneth suggests that racism modifies the modes of perception of alterity. But not only does he fail to support this claim, he never even indicates the origins of such an argument. This neglect is a product of the social immanentism at the heart of Axel Honneth's theory. Indeed, his philosophy is based on the idea that there is a conflict between two opposing traditions.[36] The first is a Machiavellian or Hobbesian philosophy that sees interpersonal opposition and conflicts of interest as constituting the governing forces of society. The other, which he embraces, places a strong emphasis on the moral interdependence of subjects. His irenic vision of the struggle for recognition explains why Honneth prefers the Hegel of *Elements of the Philosophy of Right*, or the Jena Lectures, rather than *Phenomenology of the Spirit*. In these works the concept of *Sittlichkeit*, or "ethnicity," figures prominently. This notion allows Hegel to emphasize, against Kant's formalism,

169

the importance of shared social values, which alone give meaning to abstract moral injunctions. Inspired by idealized Greek cities, Hegel and Honneth both appeal to a model of organic sociality. Individuals have their place in the larger society like organs in the body. Individual desires that reinforce collective cohesion should mirror social desires and be actively encouraged. As Kierkegaard had already noted, according to this view, "the single individual is the particular that has its telos in the universal, and it is his ethical task constantly to express himself in this, to annul his particularity in order to become the universal."[37] Stressing the interdependence of individuals, Honneth's philosophy seeks to repair all forms of social division through an ideal of homogeneity.

It is in the name of this immanentism—bolstered by Hegel's idea that the social body functions according to its own moral metabolism and is controlled by a rational structure that cannot be altered without negative consequences[38]—that Honneth argues that "the social integration of a political community can only fully succeed to the degree to which it is supported, on the part of members of society, by cultural customs that have to do with the way in which they deal with each other reciprocally."[39] This argument underscores the incompatibility between the theory of recognition and an Afro-decolonial philosophy: Honneth accepts that there are groups and individuals excluded from the community while arguing that the solution to this rejection is proposed by the very community responsible for it. The same assumption he makes in his interpretation of racism and social invisibility is repeated here: the principal foundations of society are *by their very nature* beyond reproach, and thus remain unexamined. If the three conditions of recognition are lived experience, the voluntary limitation of freedoms that this implies, and, finally, reciprocity,[40] then the substantialism of "tradition," which stands in for a no less violent Hegelian state, functionally precludes the third condition.

For his part, Fanon demonstrated how the conferral of recognition was asymmetrical. If Honneth allows for certain critiques of the recognition paradigm, he does so by pitting a so-called ideology of recognition against authentic recognition, which can only be distinguished through the test of time.[41] He is quick to point to the recognition of Uncle Toms by white masters as proof that every era is defined by different, though universally shared, norms, while passing over the negative judgment held of Uncle Toms by their Black contemporaries who, as "runaway slaves," fought against the system of slavery and were propelled by a prophetic faith in equality. It is worth recalling Caliban's reproach of the mulatto Ariel in Césaire's *A Tempest*: "What good has your obedience done you, your Uncle Tom patience and your sucking up to him. The man's just getting more demanding and despotic day by day."[42]

It isn't, as Axel Honneth naively claims, changing times that make it possible to criticize Uncle Tom. It is the anger he inspires in all the Calibans of the Black world that shakes up history and rewrites time. Besides, the problem with recognition has no more to do with its truth value than it does with its presence or absence. Fanon reminds us that inequality is potentially at play in any instantiation of recognition. Asymmetrical recognition isn't made racist by purveying some chance belief or ideology. It is racist in its very structure, in its primary impulse. This is what Fanon calls "indifference or paternalistic curiosity"[43] which is at work in any recognition that seeks to maintain the status quo.

Honneth accepts the premise that the social world is the direct reflection of its composition of individuals, and that these individuals exist there in the same manner. But Black and white people do not "reflect" the same world. The objects and obstacles they encounter are not of the same nature. White people are greeted respectfully while Black people are met with disdain and neglect. In this respect, the fact that society creates its own norms of individuality in order to reproduce and perpetuate itself is in fact part of the problem. And yet, for Honneth, social critique is always carried out in the name of society's "ultimate values."[44] But as James Cone noted, it may well be that the violent exclusion of a group doesn't contradict these ultimate values. The destruction of certain bodies may be the most conspicuous, the most truthful, test of the fundamental values of a given social system. Honneth subscribes to the widespread assumption that a society's core values can be found in the discourse it holds about itself rather than in its actual structural organization—to wit, the racial abjection that pervades it. If some must fight to obtain the equality that a nation prides itself on, it is because, ultimately, keeping some people in a state of indignity is more crucial to society's functioning than the false promise of equality.

Hegel's concept of objective spirit, which emphasizes the existence of an irreducible social rationality, informs Honneth's approach at every step. This foundation of social rationality fuels the fight for recognition. But this neglects the fact that a human group can be kept out of the sphere of legitimacy and citizenship in the name of eminently rational principles, which may rely on an economic rationale, or appeal to traditional practices or national culture. The *doxa* which posits that severe political violence is a result of irrationality is belied by the history of fascism.[45] This doesn't mean we should re-embrace the relativist idea that what is rational for one group is not necessarily so for another. Rather, it is a matter of identifying the Eurocentric push for rationality itself, which, to attain universality, must define its own limits. This often entails judging human groups as backwards, and no one has been targeted more in this respect than sub-Saharan Africans. Relativism always serves as a much-needed straw man for an imperialist universalism. The social rationality of former imperial capitals is guided in part by the opposition between the savages and the civilized, which justifies the need to educate the intellectually inferior races, prohibit Muslim women from wearing the veil, and abolish traditional family structures. It is part and parcel of a colonial logic.

The asymmetrical model of recognition raises, then, two related problems that correspond to two opposing perspectives on the matter: that of the oppressed, and that of the society that imposes the norms of recognition for the other. Note that the colonized seeking recognition exemplifies what Achille Mbembe calls "the subjection of the native by way of desire."[46] Indeed, such a desire for recognition, one that unwittingly reinforces the colonial enterprise, is in essence the desire for the very thing that excludes, brutalizes, abuses. It is a desire for that which banishes entire populations from society. There is a masochistic impulse behind any desire for recognition. Fanon argued convincingly that seeking this kind of recognition from colonizers amounts to taking them as a *de facto* model of humanity.[47] Fighting to gain recognition from this kind of society serves to legitimize it. No liberation can come from monopolizing the desire of the oppressed through violence and exclusion. However, while the colonized's alienated desire deserves attention, the most pressing problems are still found on the side of the oppressor.

The kind of recognition being sought is not a recognition of alterity. It is a sort of self-recognition in the false appearance of the other. One finds oneself in the other. In this model, a racist society recognizes itself in the oppressed, contemplates in them its own best qualities, inflates its self-worth. Asymmetrical recognition is assimilation: major differences give way to only minor ones, with the aim of preserving the "original" identity of the community. Assuming a position of authority that can sanction recognition is among the attributes of an imperialist society. Just because it recognizes some of the oppressed, or rather recognizes *itself in* them, does not mean it ceases to be imperial. Asymmetric recognition functions like a dialectical reversal of fixation: the whole society becomes fixed in its position and Black people are called upon to move in the direction of this fixed point.

When the state acts according to its own principles, one might argue, in the manner of Honneth, we are witnessing the beneficial march of history toward a rational universal accepted by all. But a more compelling counterargument can be made too, which sees this as the morbid immobility of a necrotic society, condemned to repeat itself and legitimize itself, rendering itself incapable of accommodating momentous change and alterity. Fanon had identified this tendency, which he deemed a product of "bourgeois society":

> Intellectual alienation is a creation of bourgeois society. And for me bourgeois society is any society that becomes ossified in a predetermined mold, stifling any development, progress, or discovery. For me bourgeois society is a closed society where it is not good to be alive, where the air is rotten and ideas and people are putrefying. And I believe that a man who takes a stand against this living death is in a way a revolutionary.[48]

Lewis Gordon has perhaps given one of the most precise descriptions of the danger of this sociopathological immanentism as outlined by Fanon.[49] He has shown how social structures, as well as intellectual disciplines, tend to view themselves as ends in themselves. Any political or social community that, as a community, realizes its founding truths or ultimate values, is not in a state of continuous progress but rather in a state of decline. Progress—a problematic notion in itself—implies reinvention and novel strategies. But bourgeois society as described by Fanon prefers to collect the steady return on its initial investment. As such, nothing takes place that was not already foreseen or anticipated. In a model where a social system repeatedly follows the path paved by its principles and assumptions, existence becomes cyclical since one can only gain what is already presently available. Fanon thus allows us to understand Honneth's philosophy as an apology for a rotting bourgeois society. In so doing, he exposes the hollowness of the widespread xenophobic discourse that views the presence of immigrants in European cities as the cause of "social pathologies."[50] Indeed, it is the tendency of societies to see themselves as their own end, to see themselves as entirely self-sufficient, that represents a case study in pathology. This is what causes these societies to treat migrants as disposable. A consequence of this social decline, which accompanies any immanentist—read "tautological"—conception of the social order, is, according to Fanon, the collapse of recognition into *"comparaison."*[51]

> The black man is *comparaison*. That is the first truth. He is *comparaison* in the sense that he is constantly preoccupied with self-assertion and the ego ideal. Whenever he is in the presence of someone else, there is always the question of worth or merit. The Antillean does not possess a personal value of his own and is always dependent on the presence of the "Other."[52]

This impulse for comparison is only possible if there has been a reification of values in a given society, which Honneth naively equates to "a social realization of rational universalism."[53] At issue here is another aspect of reification as defined by Georg Lukacs, who described it as a total social phenomenon whereby "a man's own activity, his own labour becomes something objective and independent of him, something that controls him by virtue of an autonomy alien to man."[54] Allowing the "price" of human groups to be evaluated according to a standard set by a particular tradition, a standard that grants or refuses their recognition, is only possible when such a process of reification is at play. It isn't labor that is being reified here, but tradition itself. This means that tradition is no longer part of existence but detached from it, and held apart like a norm to which individuals must conform. Paradoxically, the metaphor of the organic society already implies that a set of normative values are imposed on individuals who embody them. Just as it would be detrimental to the organism if the heart or liver began to function abnormally, the traditional order forbids individuals from stepping out of their roles, from removing their tailor-made livery.

As dominant norms remain forever out of reach, the supremacy of supposedly rational and shared values prevents the oppressed from feeling they have intrinsic value. "The Martinican compares himself not to the white man, the father, the boss, God, but to his own counterpart under the patronage of the white man."[55] *Comparaison*, or comparison, is Black people asserting themselves to be better than others by the standard set by what they imagine, or even what they wish, to be the desire of white people. Black people assume the mode of recognition imposed by a white ethics without considering its criteria: these are tacitly accepted and reproduced. Fanon describes comparison as the dissolution of objectivity, after which only subjects remain. The refusal of the thing is a refusal of history, of self-development, of action. Hegel believed that "the bondsman, through working on the thing, embodies the principle of negation as an active and creative principle."[56] In other words, it is in their relationship to the thing that slaves exercise their liberty and begin to escape their state of servitude. It is in dialogue with matter, with the world, with nature that the transformative liberation of slaves takes place. The catastrophe of this breakdown of objectivity is that the criteria for liberation no longer reflect slaves' real conditions of existence, but rather their illusory value created by a reified system of valuation.

Fanon describes Martinicans as being inclined to believe that their human reality is absolutely independent of any objective fact. In fact, this reality is a product of their relation to the white gaze and their assimilation of its differential system of evaluating Blacks. It represents a competition for who will be the most "recognizable" by colonial society. In the absence of objectivity, all individuals, taking themselves as subjective totalities, turn to the imagined white gaze in search of recognition. The fewer criteria there are, the more they depend on comparison. Comparison is thus this process of isolating subjectivities, of divesting the world, and all *things* with it, of independent meaning. It goes hand in hand with a growing obsession with the gaze of the other and with seeking approval within the other's value system. Comparison is a social pathology where the value of individuals is indexed to their conformity to some self-referential cultural tradition. As a result, it is blind to any absolutes and to the singular value of each person. Comparison detaches individuals from their own diachronic dynamic, immobilizing them in a synchronous and limitless relativism.[57] Fanon clearly identified the fundamental flaw of the theory of the struggle for recognition, both when it promotes asymmetric recognition and when it devolves into comparison: "The black man stops behaving as an individual with *agency*. His actions are determined by 'the Other' (in the form of the white man), since only 'the Other' can validate him."[58] Recognition is another name for the way colonial society uses the Black man to establish its own value.

Of course, one may object to these critiques by pointing out that Fanon speaks to the bygone historical period of his own time, whereas Honneth is examining contemporary societies that have made clear progress on the issue of human rights.[59] But such an objection relies on the same faulty assumptions made by the theory of recognition. Taking social immanence as its point of departure and its end goal, it can only conceive of the oppressed, the excluded, and the "disposable" as humble and diligent applicants who, flooding the administrative centers of recognition, are patiently waiting for the

175

benevolent gaze of the other to kindly turn their way. This approach of treating social violence as though it were a matter of the past is doomed to fail. While colonization as described by Fanon may no longer exist, there is no denying that the contemporary societies Honneth examines are plagued by social divisions wrought by the coloniality of power. On a global scale, the North and the South are still divided by the imperial structures of inequality. This is why, rather than take comfort in the supposed progress made in colonial *métropoles*, one would do well to follow Fanon's lead and interrogate the social and political order from the periphery.

The Proposition of Sovereigndignity

"Who are they," Fanon asks in his first published text, "The North African Syndrome," "those creatures starving for humanity who stand buttressed against the impalpable frontiers (though I know them from experience to be terribly distinct) of complete recognition?"[60] Fanon continued to return to the notion of recognition, even after his withering critique of its inherent inequality, which was strikingly apparent during his time and remains unmistakable today. His renewed approach derived from the simple observation that recognizing alterity from a comfortable location of a tradition one hopes never changes is in fact a failure of recognition. Recognizing what already lies within one's affective, cognitive, and ethical grasp does not represent momentous change. To borrow from Derrida's insight that only the unforgivable can be forgiven,[61] we might say, for Fanon, *only the unrecognizable can be recognized*. The "light" alterity assumed in Honneth's approach represents in fact no alterity at all.

"Alterity of rupture, of struggle and combat"[62]—this is what alterity means in Fanon. To recognize an alterity of rupture entails abandoning one's own modes of recognition. This implies that the shared norms of the social order are themselves standing in the way of any full recognition. It is incumbent on the social order to acknowledge this. Such a *"re-cognition"* should be understood as a new beginning, a regenerative repetition, rather than a mere rehearsal: it is initiating a new form of *cognition*, of knowing. Fanon's argument—that recognition is only achieved by questioning the norms that govern recognition—is revolutionary. It requires rethinking the whole system of society's ultimate values. Of course, only a struggle in the strongest sense of the term, rather than the symbolic struggle described by Axel Honneth, can ultimately compel the social body to look outside its own limits to recognize what it *cannot* recognize. The upheaval this would entail would never be approved by an imperialist society. The West Indies colonized by France—a principal subject of Fanon's—clearly demonstrate this. With the exception of Haiti, they did not fight for their rights, but were granted them from on high thanks to the munificence of their former masters.[63] This is not liberation. It is permission.

What distinguishes Fanon's understanding of recognition from that of other contemporary approaches has been poorly understood. According to Fanon, "Man is human only to the extent to which he tries to impose himself on another man in order to be recognized by him."[64] Compare this argument to Alexandre Kojève's extremely influential contention: "It is only by being 'recognized' by another, by many others, or—in the extreme—by all others, that a human being is really human, for himself as well as for others."[65] For Fanon, recognition grants one no place among authentic humanity. Instead, engagement is what allows one to partake in a shared humanity: the will to repair the fissures caused by a dehumanizing present by *imposing oneself* as human. This is precisely what I am calling "dignity." Full recognition is achieved by establishing a new ethical order, a new manner of relating to others. And this is imposed by the oppressed, who reimage intersubjectivity to meet their own demands. Such a revolutionary imposition separates a recognition conditioned by the master's expectations from the full recognition that leads to liberation. This change in perspective provokes a shift from a theory of recognition to a theory of dignity. This entails moving from an act centered on the self-esteem of others or their place in society to a reflection on the oppositional self-affirmation of oppressed groups. Whereas conventional theories of recognition view the oppressed in the static position of claimant, for whom power is expressed through request, for Fanon, recognition is not the underlying foundation of ethics but rather a corollary of dignity. This has profound political implications.

This invites a re-evaluation of the politics of reception, not from the angle of recognition but from that of dignity. Or, more precisely, from the specific modes of recognition made available when the dignity of the oppressed is taken into account. Such a reconsideration calls into question the representation of "humanitarianism," including the display of sorrow and compassion generally expressed toward exiles. The anthropologist Michel Agier has paved the way for this approach: "the barrage of distressing images of death and suffering at the border accentuates the impression of sub-humanity associated with these precarious lives on the move, which is humiliating for them, as they see themselves as 'adventurers' or heroes for their own people, whose stories highlight the incredible courage and inner strength needed to embark on such a risky journey."[66] To understand the dignity of exiles, one must understand their strength and imagine the courage it takes to put one's life on the line. Their journey through Acheron illuminates by way of contrast the spineless and narcissistic mode of political existence currently offered to citizens of Western states. Any threat to the status quo of the majority population, to the safety and sanctity of their "way of life," is considered an unspeakable scandal. This shows the complacent ignorance of Western states of the perils faced on a daily basis by a large percentage of the world. The dignity of exile will have to be re-evaluated in these terms, but even then it still won't go far enough. Once again, we must turn to Fanon to point the way forward: certainly, the question of reception is of vital importance, but it is secondary to that of the sovereignty demanded by the people in the Global South, sovereignty of both their countries and their bodies.

Throughout his work—but most notably in *The Wretched of the Earth*—Fanon sketches an original definition of dignity. This definition finds expression in two distinct ways. The first is ethico-political: "The African peoples quickly realized that dignity and sovereignty were exact equivalents. In fact a free people living in dignity is a sovereign people. A people living in dignity is a responsible people."[67] In other words, for Fanon, there is no dignity without power, but there is also no sovereignty without ethics.

The second way this definition finds expression is through an ontological mode: "No leader, whatever his worth, can replace the will of the people, and the national government, before concerning itself with international prestige, must first restore dignity to all citizens, furnish their minds, fill their eyes with human things and develop a human landscape for the sake of its enlightened and sovereign inhabitants."[68] Let's call this the "proposition of sovereigndignity," with a deliberate nod to Étienne Balibar's "proposition equaliberty."[69] Dignity is indeed sovereignty—it is power. But, above all, it is the power to determine the essence of the human, and therefore to determine the boundaries of the human. Sovereignty is the power a political community assumes when it makes decisions about its being and its future. Fanon links this idea to that of dignity, as both concern what it means to be human. The impact of these decisions exceeds the limits of any single polity where dignity is at stake. Depending on how sovereignty is defined, and thus how the dignity of the members of a community is envisaged, foreigners will be either considered equals, enemies, or expendable beings. Traditionally, in law and political thought, sovereignty and dignity converge and crystallize in the notion of citizenship.

Defining human dignity always involves the risky endeavor of drawing a line between the human and the inhuman. Fanon makes this point clear: "During the colonial occupation the people were told they had to sacrifice their lives for the sake of dignity."[70] In the ethics of imperialism, dignity belongs to the colonizer, which makes the colonized beings those who can be sacrificed. This made it easy to send them to the frontlines of European conflicts, or even colonial wars, as their existence was without worth. In his *Discourse on Colonialism*, Césaire had already stressed that within colonial discourse, "compared to the cannibals, the dismemberers, and other lesser breeds, Europe and the West are the incarnation of respect for human dignity."[71] Equating citizenship within the colonial state and human dignity necessarily excludes the colonized from humanity. But, with a politics of resistance or revolution, sovereigndignity is made manifest by the willingness to put one's life on the line for the liberation of one's people. In these conditions, as Didier Fassin explains, taking one's life, the last possession remaining after having been deprived of everything else, can become a subversive act, a political statement, or simply a way of challenging state power. "Such challenge is unbearable for the state, to the point that, in the United States, even prisoners with a death sentence are subjected to special surveillance and extraordinary precautions to make sure they would not take their own life. They must live so as to be executed. Their suicide would be a formidable failure for the authorities, thus deprived of the sovereign act of killing."[72] From military sacrifice to the death penalty, the monopolization of dignity by the state—that is to say, of the sovereign power that vital existence can exercise over itself—dispossesses the oppressed of their own potential suicide.

Fanon responds directly to this ethical debate. Binding the question of dignity to the ontological definition of the human, he holds the conventional notions of political thought to a higher standard of responsibility. Dignity cannot be a feature or possession of citizenship, since that would imply that the noncitizen or the disenfranchised citizen is expendable. These problems, which are impossible to ignore at the level of individual existence, can only be properly addressed at the state or international level. The migrant problem plaguing contemporary society illustrates the pertinence of Fanon's concerns.

FORMS-OF-DEATH IN THE EUROPEAN NECROPOLIS

If African lives, especially (though not exclusively) the lives of exiles, are considered expendable or treated as commodities, it is because there is no African, or pan-African, sovereignty. Even national sovereignty is often an illusion. In Africa and the Middle East in particular, there are states that only exist in name. These states are incapable of ensuring even the minimum conditions of survival for their own citizens. Just as the ideal of recognition falls short as an ethical standard, so too does it fail within the realm of international relations.[73] In the mid-twentieth century, former African colonies gained independence and became states. Being recognized by well-established states and by international institutions is what allowed for this "transubstantiation." But the postcolonial state can have an autonomous legal status without having, as it is known in political science, "empirical statehood"[74] (the defining empirical features that characterize a state). The state is not reflected by its legal standing, which is underwritten by international relations of recognition. Its existence derives from its agency, which is reflected in the everyday life of its inhabitants. This doesn't just refer to its monopoly on sanctioned violence, but on its ability to collect taxes and use this revenue to provide public services, build infrastructure, and so on. The postcolonial nation may well be formally recognized, but, lacking agency and sovereignty, it remains at the whims of neo-imperialism. Such states, which share nothing with former colonial powers except in name, are proof that, in the European conception of sovereignty, the borders of the human are made to align with the borders of the Global North. Recognition may grant them their place among other nations, but without popular sovereignty, they have no agency.

In February 2017, through the "Joint Valleta Action Plan," the European Union provided Libya with 200 million euros to police its external borders. That July, an additional 43 million euros was added to this initial sum. But Libya is a state only in name. As a result of imperialist military intervention, it has lost all its sovereignty, all its monopoly of sanctioned violence, and any ability to give meaning to dignity. Clearly, this isn't lost on any European officials, but the objective of this kind of outsourcing doesn't depend on Libya belonging to what Fanon called a "human panorama." Libya represents above all a *border*. Little does it matter that beyond this border slavery, rape, and the social death of Black people rages on. The long history of Arab anti-Blackness explains in part why sub-Saharans are reduced to servitude and poor treatment in Libya. This has gone on for many years and no one seems to care. But this is what the conditions of indignity and endemic violence look like. Wherever popular sovereignty is demolished by imperialism, whether through military intervention or through the structural adjustment programs of the IMF and the World Bank, this is what results.

In the conclusion to *Black Skin, White Masks*, Fanon famously remarked: "Every time a man has brought victory to the dignity of the spirit, every time a man has said no to an attempt to enslave his fellow man, I have felt a sense of solidarity with his act."[75] Fanon is drawing on a Hegelian vocabulary here. In this vocabulary, spirit, in a word, refers to *transindividuality*: that which transcends the individual and thrusts him or her into a network of multiple relations. Spirit is the breath that animates the ethical life of a community. For Hegel, as shown in Honneth's interpretation, it takes the form of "the objective spirit," expressed by the immanent rationality of institutions. In other words, the state is an expression of human freedom. In contrast, Fanon calls for a radical engagement in the life of a community, in its dignity, which isn't contained by any institution. What's more, for Fanon, dignity doesn't belong to any one individual, but is a transindividual characteristic of a collective existence or sovereignty. Needless to say, spirit, in Fanon, is expressed through struggle rather than through the state.

But what does a "triumph" of the spirit and a "triumph" of dignity even mean in light of the distinct but overlapping histories of the Black diaspora? What meaning can be given to this when the lauded victories of the past consistently create unlivable and humiliating conditions? There is no shortage of examples to turn to. In the history of Black worlds, there is perhaps no greater symbol of the victory of dignity than that of the Haitian revolution led by Toussaint Louverture. It was a total revolution: political regime change, decolonization, abolition of slavery, complete transformation of a society founded on racial elitism. From Toussaint Louverture's perspective, as Aimé Césaire recounts, "it wasn't only a question of protecting a country from the enemy's attacks, but, more important still, of educating a people and forging a nation in the crucible of struggle. [...] For him, alongside a military war and those who deplore its violence, there was another war underlying it and dictating it: that of the education of the mind."[76] After defeating Napoleon's armies and sacrificing his life to establish a Black republic, Toussaint Louverture was succeeded by his lieutenant, Jean-Jacques Dessalines, in 1804. The establishment of the first Black republic stands as an undeniable victory which will never be forgotten. But it wasn't a triumph. In 1825, commanding a flotilla of fourteen warships, the King of France, Charles X, demanded that "the former colony pay the Deposits and Consignments Fund 'the sum of 150 million francs to compensate the former settlers for their losses'."[77] It would not be paid in full until 1972. For a century and a half, the "Haitian leaders were forced to borrow from French banks, such as Rothschild and Laffitte, which charged usurious rates. They implemented inflexible austerity measures, drastically raised taxes, imposed forced labor on peasants to increase state revenues and pay off the debt."[78] This history of Haiti shows the exorbitant, debilitating, enslaving price slaves must pay to escape servitude. And let's not forget the price that imperial violence demanded as the triumph of dignity, embodied by Toussaint Louverture, was laid to rest.

The assassinations of the pan-African revolutionaries Patrice Lumumba, Thomas Sankara, and Amílcar Cabral or the removal of Kwame Nkrumah from power attest to the persistence of coloniality. This is similar to how Jim Crow laws in the United States, which ratified segregation, arose as a backlash against the abolition of slavery. Or how police violence and mass incarceration surged once those discriminatory laws were repealed.[79] The political history of Black people is rich in victories; but it is also, in at least equal proportion, rife with counterattacks and thwarted prospects. In short, the real triumphs are few and far between. In this respect, Black political existence suffers the fate of Sisyphus: it is forced to endure a never-ending struggle where every effort ends in defeat. In this sense, this historical perspective elicits skepticism toward Black revolutionary political ambitions for the same reasons people have been skeptical of Black reformism, the politics of integration, and the dream of a "post-racial" society. But, in the end, no matter how hopeless it may at first appear or how fleeting its victories, doesn't the very effort embody Black dignity and the life of the spirit? Sovereigndignity is above all the ability to stay standing amid these setbacks. It was perhaps by defining dignity as the simple and resolute refusal to enslave one's neighbor that Fanon was able to reveal the precariousness inherent in Black ethical life.

— Conclusion —

BLACK POLITICAL ONTOLOGY AND BLACK DIGNITY

To be Black is to occupy a certain place in the world. *Negritude*, Césaire explains, doesn't necessarily refer to its adherents' "skin color" but rather to their sense of belonging "in one way or another to human groups that have been subjected to the most brutal violence of history, groups that have suffered and still suffer frequently from marginalization and oppression."[1] However, Black suffering does not constitute a historical exception, which would make it stand apart from other events in history and condemn Black people to eternal damnation with no way of sharing their otherworldly pain. Any experience of political violence is unique. It cannot be appropriated. But, for this same reason, it can point to other forms of political violence, calling attention to historical ruptures and continuities. In this respect, the particularity of Black history has nothing to do with any qualitatively singular relationship to violence. Rather, it concerns how the modalities of violence deployed by modernity have been repeatedly and deliberately used to undo Black bodies, which were to become, sooner or later, modernity's principal target. To claim that Black suffering has no analogue in history, as Frank Wilderson has argued, is inaccurate.[2] In fact, the opposite is true: Black life has had to endure each iteration of political violence, each refinement of the technologies of dehumanization, each new discovery of cruelty. Black life is the Rosetta Stone of social violence, a universal translator of negativity.

The Black condition belongs to the register of capitalist exploitation. As C.L.R. James has shown, the plantations in the Caribbean prefigured the factories of the industrial age. The historian Marcus Rediker goes even further, arguing that the slave ship was "central to a profound, interrelated set of economic changes essential to the

DIGNITY OR DEATH

rise of capitalism."[3] Indeed, the slave ship, linking accumulation and repression, was both a factory, which is to say, an itinerant commercial enterprise, and the first form of the modern prison at a time when this institution did not yet exist on land. Moreover, as the genocide of the Hereros and Namas committed by Prussian troops in Southwest Africa (the future Namibia) reminds us, mass extermination is also part of Black history. In 1904, general Lothar Von Trotha signed a *Vernichtungsbefehl* (extermination order, or, more literally, an annihilation order) targeting the inhabitants of the colony: "Any Herero found within German borders, whether man, woman, or child, with or without arms or cattle, will be executed. These are my words to the Herero people. Signed: the Great General of the All-Mighty Kaiser.—Von Trotha."[4] Black people who were not immediately hanged or gunned down were exiled to the Kalahari Desert, far from German colonial territories, with this message, translated into their local language, hanging around their necks. Some have viewed this colonial holocaust as prefiguring the European genocide carried out under the Third Reich. From 1905 to 1907, between one and three thousand Herero prisoners were also interned in the Shark Island *Konzentrationslager* (concentration camp). This is when this unforgettable word—*Konzentrationslager*—entered the German political lexicon. The doctor Eugen Fischer, a future National Socialist leader and mentor of Joseph Mengele, gathered skulls from there to establish, through his raciological experiments, Black abjection and Aryan superiority. Every scholar who studies the Black condition is criticized for being too focused on peripheral matters to the detriment of much more significant questions such as capitalist exploitation and genocide. But the unrelenting exploitation of Black people is what engendered capitalism. And the destruction of European Jews is not an unprecedented event: Blacks were exterminated for being Black, after having been kept in servitude for centuries for the same reason.

To Be Born: Black Political Ontology

The Franco-Cameroonian writer, Léonora Miano, has described the Black condition in the following terms: "capture, deportation, forced slavery, colonialism—these are all crimes against humanity, these are the constitutive forces that have produced today's black people. Racialization was the corollary of transatlantic human trafficking and one of its most pronounced particularities. [...] Wherever they are in the world, from East to West or in the southern hemisphere, today's

CONCLUSION

black people originate from the violence done to their forebears."[5] This diagnosis is shared by a certain trend in Black studies in the United States—beginning in the early 2000s and gaining prominence the following decade—that has given itself the controversial name of Afropessimism.[6] The two figureheads of this movement are Frank Wilderson and Jared Sexton. As Greg Thomas, a specialist in Panafricanism whose compelling work deserves more attention, has pointed out, this name evokes an indefensible history.[7] Indeed, until recently, "Afropessimism" referred only to the racist view that sub-Saharan societies were fundamentally incompatible with liberal modernity, democratic institutions, and a market economy. To avoid any confusion with this first understanding of the term, I will refer to Black political ontology rather than to Afropessimism.

Thomas rightly pointed out how theorists of this movement tend to ignore or obscure concepts and figures that are integral to a history of Black thought (such as the absence of Cheikh Anta Diop from their thought and, more generally, of African philosophy). He has also brought to light its tendency to perpetuate misinterpretations of canonical writers (Du Bois, Césaire, or Fanon, for example).[8] Add to this the tension between a constant focus on the North American context and the claim to speak of the Black condition on a global scale, which is to say, from a purported understanding of a totality that transcends local contexts. Despite these persuasive and pertinent critiques of Black political ontology, Thomas, in his ambition to counter pessimism, too readily discards one of the main insights of this paradigm. He believes he can identify in Afro-descendant traditions a pervasive vitalism characterized by an optimistic refusal of death.[9] But the work of Césaire, Fanon, Fabien Eboussi Boulaga, and several prominent figures of Black liberation theology discussed throughout this book belies this idea. The strength of Black political ontology lies precisely in its emphasis on the fact that, as Frank Wilderson writes, "there is a global consensus that Africa is the location of sentient beings who are outside of global community, who are socially dead."[10] My goal here is not only to push this argument further, but also to find a way of expressing it that avoids the American-centric position decried by Thomas. In other words, my aim is to depict in as true a light as possible what it means to be Black today. Aimé Césaire laid the groundwork for such an approach, describing the racism that plagued Haitian society as "more than a hierarchy, an ontology: on top, the white man—being in the fullest sense of the term—, below, the black man, with no legal personhood, a prop; an object, which is to say, nothing."[11]

185

DIGNITY OR DEATH

Political ontology deals with conflicts bearing on the very nature or structure of reality. It acknowledges that there are competing, even hostile, interpretations of what constitute human things and nonhuman things and that, therefore, this leads to incompatible behaviors toward them,[12] which is to say, to antagonistic ethical approaches. The question of birth is perhaps the most decisive matter for a politico-ontological understanding of humanity and its limits. As noted above, this is a matter of human neoteny: any newborn is bound to die unless it is cared for by a community for whom its life matters. Given the amount of time and energy this entails, it is a full-time commitment on the part of the community to see to its survival. This finitude, this original precarity inherent in the very act of being born, is the first point of reference for modern political ontologies. Such is the case with Judith Butler's discussion of the performative designation of gender at birth. And, as Giorgio Agamben has shown, in the modern state, to come into the world entails being seized by the law, which hands the body over to the nation from the start. Compulsory education, military service, taxes, controlling and tracking one's movement with passports—all of these are examples of the unique relationship to belonging that modern political ontology throws into relief.

And yet, these approaches fail to adequately describe what is unique about modern Black-being. This is because they view the relationship to violence as one of contingency. It may or may not happen: violence strikes only after birth, disrupting, like an alienating force, an individual's self-conception. The emblematic philosopher behind this line of thinking is none other than Jean-Jacques Rousseau. In the beginning of his *Social Contract* he famously declares: "Man is born free, and he is everywhere in chains." In other words, slavery isn't constitutive of humanity. There is a primordial freedom, intrinsically bound to birth, which allows one at all times to appeal to this natural right, the right to a primordial freedom that is a part of the human condition. But Rousseau's optimism is only possible—as is often the case in modern political history—because the chains of slavery are merely metaphorical. They allow him to dramatize the arbitrary power of the sovereign of the *Ancien Régime*. His aim is to convince his readers to challenge the monarch's despotism by envisioning a human constitution in accordance with popular sovereignty.

The philosopher Louis Sala-Molins offers a trenchant critique of Rousseau's metaphoric use of slavery: "The slave is the French from France, the white man of Christian whiteland, the Parisian from Paris; he is simply—and no one can deny the implied grandeur—the

186

CONCLUSION

citizen to whom Rousseau would like to restore dignity by elevating him to the level of the sovereign. The Black African isn't present. The Black West Indian even less so. It's clear: Rousseau has zero concern for the Black man of the *Code Noir* (*Black Code*). Let's face it: Rousseau could care less for the slave referred to in the legal sense in the French code of this time."[13] There were seemingly no words strong enough in the eighteenth-century vocabulary to describe a violent servitude targeting Europeans, leaving no choice but to evoke the figure of the slave, for no one else embodies the powerlessness and subjugation Rousseau wanted to convey. The slave alone makes the weight of oppression tangible; but, in the imaginary of the Enlightenment, the only slaves that really existed at the time were Black. From the vantage point of the slave, birth, then, is not synonymous with freedom.

In light of the notorious sorrow of the "Middle Passage" and the transubstantiation of Africans into Black people in the holds of slave ships, even the notion of birth cannot be conceived the same. As Christina Sharpe pointedly remarks, the vaginas of slaves who gave birth also served as a sort of middle passage. Plantations turned wombs into factories for producing Black slaves.[14] In Brazil, in the British colonies, and later in the independent states of the Americas, the doctrine governing the birth of Black children was based on a Latin phrase: *Partus sequitur ventrem*, or "offspring follow the womb." This is a brutal way of saying all newborns inherit the condition of slavery from their mothers. Racial slavery negates the very idea of a natural right by establishing a literal equivalence between birth and *social death*. Black political ontology in the United States has borrowed this concept from the sociologist Orlando Patterson, who defines it in the following terms: "The slave is violently uprooted from his milieu. He is desocialized and depersonalized. This process of social negation constitutes the first, essentially external, phase of enslavement. The next phase involves the introduction of the slave into the community of his master, but it involves the paradox of introducing him as a nonbeing."[15] Traditionally, slaves have always been foreigners, captives taken from elsewhere and thrust into a new context where they can only be recognized as subaltern.

Patterson has made clear that he himself borrowed the notion of social death from the French Marxist anthropologist Claude Meillassoux, but his anglophone readers have given little attention to this point. Meillassoux offers a more nuanced definition of the term. Focusing in particular on the African continent, he stresses the paradoxical relationship between slavery and birth: "In slave society the captive was put beyond social death and seen as *not-born*. Logically, since he had not been born, the captive could not make sacrifices to his ancestors; he had no access to the institutions which made possible the creation of ties of marriage, of affinity, even less of paternity, for how can a person who has never been brought into the world pass on 'life'?"[16] The slave is introduced into society like a foreign body. Captives are considered non-born because the rules and customs that presided over their birth are distinct from those of the society in which they now find themselves. Ties to their societies of origin have been deliberately severed. The corollary of equating social death and non-birth is that there can be no biological reproduction of slaves in traditional slave societies: "Since the slave class was reproduced through the plundering of alien societies and through purchase on the market, *the 'procreative' function was in the hands of men*, whether warriors or merchants: it was they who, by force of arms or by payment, 'procreated' the individuals who were to reconstitute the exploited class."[17] In other words, there is no procreation in the literal sense of the term in traditional slavery, since it is replaced by capture and trade, which serve to replenish the stock of an adult labor force.

In Meillassoux, social death is synonymous with capture. It is a matter of dying to one's society of origin, of losing one's affiliations. But this assumes affiliations existed in the first place. As Patterson himself explains, the high rate of reproduction of slaves in the southern United States stands apart from other contexts where reproduction was almost non-existent. In these contexts, only the constant influx of adult laborers made it possible to replenish the workforce.[18] It is thus surprising to see contemporary theorists such as Wilderson or Sexton elect social death as the distinctive feature linking racial slavery in the United States and the contemporary Black condition, given that this context is perhaps the most anomalous in regard to the first meaning of this term, a meaning that emerged out of debates between social scientists. Once a condition that was defined by capture, modern slavery becomes an innate state: being Black, infants are born slaves, and even sub-Saharan Africans are seen as destined for slavery before even being captured. But in Meillassoux and Patterson, there is no social death without capture. While being born Black may coincide exactly with the condition of servitude, strictly speaking there is no social death, even if both of these are equally impacted by conditions of indignity. By definition, newborns have known no *social* situation before slavery; they have no status they must symbolically renounce and become *dead to*. What Black political ontologists miss in their hasty approach is that social death is above all synonymous with rupture: you are only "dead" to a slave society because you are dead to the society where you grew up, lived, and socialized. But under the current conditions of Black life, it is no longer a question of a *social* death, strictly speaking, since this death preceded one's entry into society. The situation of Black newborns is defined by what I've called a form-of-death: a constant wavering between life and death, with the two ceaselessly becoming blurred.

For Frank Wilderson, framing the Black condition in terms of political ontology entails replacing Rousseau's idea of the subject's contingent relationship to the violence of subjugation with that of a subject constituted at its origins by violence.[19] Modern slaves—that is, Black people—are born from, into, and with violence. Indeed, in modern political institutions and thought, slavery is exclusively experienced by Black people. This is largely a product of the transatlantic slave trade. Not because it is seen as marking the beginning of the subjugation of Africans—this was preceded by what is commonly called the "trans-Saharan slave trade." But because it provoked an unprecedented "epistemological catastrophe"[20] by making the words "slave" and "Black person" interchangeable. Sub-Saharans became Black and, by this very fact, they became beings indiscriminately destined for slavery. The Black body was entirely subsumed by the being consigned to subjugation. In the Americas, *not being Black* was the only prerequisite for acquiring slaves. The African continent was thus transformed into a vast reservoir of beings-for-slavery, and, later, beings-for-colonization. With the slave trade, exile was all but foreordained for Blacks. With the second wave of colonialism, they then became exiles on their own land, where they were also declared illegitimate. This is how anti-Blackness imposed itself as the universal language of racism. Even the violence repeatedly targeting Congolese or Nigerian immigrants stems in part from this internalization of anti-Blackness among Black South Africans. It is expressed through a rejection of the "less evolved" or "less developed" group, in other words, of those more deeply ensconced in their own Blackness. When placed alongside white people, or Arabs, or Asians, or even other Black people, Blackness becomes *the safe-haven currency of xenophobia*. The argument made by Black political ontology, on which I am leaning here, is that Black people are still today confined to the institutional, scientific, and cultural position imposed on them by modernity. Their existence is structurally defined by indignity as they are maintained in a form-of-death. Black people, thrust into a dehumanized zone of non-being, are ceaselessly deprived of the ability to live a dignified life. This is taken almost to be a matter of fact.

Shades of Dignity

A politics of dignity—that is, a politics founded on the ethical affirmation of dignity—could be defined as a politics of the extreme. This is because the concept of dignity generally denotes the impossibility of expressing democratic demands. Either because to meet the demands made would require an upheaval—if not a collapse—of the reigning political system, or because direct action is taken to reclaim and impose a negated humanity without resorting to any demands. My argument here is that these two scenarios represent two particular historical modalities of translating the ethical demand for dignity into politics. The first has figured prominently in several significant social movements of the 2010s. A case in point is the Tunisian Revolution, also called the Jasmine Revolution, which succeeded in ousting President Zine el-Abidine Ben Ali. This was described by activists as a "revolution of dignity."[21]

It was around this same time that the Turkish economist and political thinker Ahmet Insel called the Occupy movement in Gezi Park and Istanbul's Taksim Square in 2013 "an uprising for dignity," a choice of words that was amplified by the media. He described this movement, which began as an effort to prevent the transformation of urban public space into a shopping mall, as a rejection of authoritarian rule over the lives of the Turkish people. The government's effort was seen as a way of standardizing daily life by official decree, of imposing top-down norms that clashed with the wishes and needs of the people. "The Gezi moment was thus an expression of the wounded civic dignity of those who did not recognize themselves in the standard of living imposed by the authorities and who demanded participation in public affairs. The term 'insurrection for dignity' was quickly adopted by some of the participants in the Gezi protests."[22] For Insel, this uprising of dignity is distinct from other forms of geopolitical rebellion in recent Turkish history. These other forms have resorted to extreme violence: armed struggle on the part of the Kurds and Armenians, hunger strikes that ended with the death of political prisoners (or rather imprisoned activists who claimed this title for themselves since it was generally denied them) of the Turkish far left. Despite their many differences, in all these cases, Insel argues, the protesters identify first and foremost as victims.

CONCLUSION

Having fetishized domination, these activists engage in fanatical behavior, free as they are of any moral concerns or consideration for alterity. In Insel's view, this victimized identity inevitably leads to the collapse of politics, since the self-righteousness of these activists puts in peril the ideal of deliberative negotiation. "The paradox of the victim's identity is that it largely cancels out the subjectivity of the subject, making him a prisoner of the identity of his real or imaginary oppressor. Consequently, recourse to violence is often perceived as the only means of reappropriating this alienated subjectivity within the enclosure of the One."[23]

What is egregiously lacking from this argument—as with any political argument wrapped up in questions of identity—is an understanding of the sort of political ontology outlined above. Contrary to what is implied by the above quote, there is a significant difference between real and imagined oppression. But Insel proceeds as though these were one and the same. Before attacking hypothetical people who supposedly see themselves as victims, wouldn't it be more prudent to identify and examine the living conditions of real victims of structural violence? This would likely show that the peaceful protesters occupying downtown Istanbul had the distinct luxury of not being the victims of anything significant. More than the soundness of their ethical position, this would explain the absence of any "victimization" rhetoric in their claims. This becomes all the more apparent when the Gezi movement is trumpeted as a model for having "learned that violent opposition, counter-violence using the means of violence to the extreme, is a masculine, paternalistic, patriarchal action."[24] There are two reasons we shouldn't rush to celebrate such a position. First, as the philosopher Elsa Dorlin has shown, the history of feminism demonstrates how the use of violence reflects a variety of strategies and tactics that don't reinforce or imitate patriarchal violence.[25] Viewing the recourse to violence exclusively as a symptom of the patriarchy normalizes male domination by presenting it as inexorable. Not only does this presuppose female passivity, but it also suggests that there is no proportionate response to structural male violence. To be clear, I am not defending "masculinity" against the accusation of violence, but rather defending the use of violence (on the part of the oppressed) against the accusation of masculinism. Second, equating violence with masculinity in racial terms has fueled the most violent forms of police anti-Blackness previously described. "In modernity, black life has always been the name for this scary thing, repeatedly projected onto the scrim, as it were, of white hatreds and fears."[26] This is why the mere fact of

Black male life is perceived as inherently violent and patriarchal, with some going so far as to seek to emasculate them and neutralize the "threat" of their virility through the act of rape.

Insel's position allows us to locate the ethical conflict between two possible interpretations of the concept of dignity evoked above. We can call his understanding of dignity "light dignity"—an unmistakable heir of the European traditions of Renaissance humanism, the Enlightenment, and deliberative democracy. His politics, then, is one of contingency. Political engagement is a display of power: opposing a commercial real estate project in the manner of the Gezi Park protest is driven by some absolute imperative. On the contrary, opposition represents a choice, one political option among others. It is even a contingent affirmation of contingency, since the very goal of the protest is to affirm the lack of necessity behind the project of urban renewal. Such an action seeks to restage the project as a matter for democratic debate. Judith Butler demonstrates this line of reasoning in her work on political movements formed in big city plazas, stating that "the collective assembling of bodies is an exercise of the popular will, and a way of asserting, in bodily form, one of the most basic presuppositions of democracy, namely that the political and public institutions are bound to represent the people."[27]

Another conception of dignity, which I am calling "black" or "dark" dignity, stands in stark contrast to this. It is driven by necessity rather than contingency. Fanon expresses it in blunt terms in the conclusion of *Black Skin, White Masks*: "For the Antillean working in the sugarcane plantations in Le Robert, to fight is the only solution. And he will undertake and carry out this struggle not as the result of a Marxist or idealistic analysis but because quite simply he cannot conceive his life otherwise than as a kind of combat against exploitation, poverty, and hunger."[28] This understanding arises in life-or-death situations. Conceiving of politics in this way has nothing in common with a politics based on the freedom of choice. This conception emerges from situations where existences, pushed to their limits, assert their power against a politics of powerlessness imposed by the state. Black dignity places necessity at the center of ethics and politics. In so doing, it brings people face to face with their own misery, their own suffering, and their own experience of the unlivable.

Viewed within this theoretical framework, the political singularity of the Tunisian Revolution seems to lie in its ability to effectively bring together, no matter how tenuously, these two shades of dignity. On one hand, it unmistakably gives voice to the humanistic demand for a democratic and citizen-led dignity, embodied in its call for the

CONCLUSION

Tunisian President to step down. But, on the other hand, "the notion of 'dignity' (*Karama*) refers first of all to the desire of the colonized subject to regain his humanity."[29] Its use was very much in line with an uprising of Black dignity. It is a clear matter of necessity: dignity or death. The movement's considerable success was likely due to its ability to respond to a wide set of existential needs—rather than democratic demands—all of which require a radical transformation of the political order.

As I indicated in the third chapter, one of the most striking and frequent expressions of Black dignity, an expression that bears the clear mark of necessity, can be seen in urban riots, most notably in what North American social scientists generally call "race riots." Riots are waged as the political expression of a pure necessity. While the phenomena of race riots may lie outside the conventional purview of social critique and political theory, political ontology and the paradigm of Black dignity are well positioned to illustrate their fundamental importance. Strikes and riots are often seen as two distinct ways of embodying struggle. The reflections on social movements detailed above point to a broader distinction, one that perhaps better reflects the current political environment. I am referring to the distinction between occupations and riots. Indeed, these two positions seem to constitute two distinct ways of existing in space, or even of interpreting spatiality itself.

The position of Guy Debord serves as a telling case study in this respect. His interpretation of the Watts Riots, offered in the heat of the moment in 1965, demonstrates how the European left routinely reframes foreign political events according to its own political experience. Sparked by a confrontation with police in an extremely segregated area of Los Angeles, these riots lasted seven days and left thirty-four people dead and a thousand wounded.[30] In an article published in *L'Internationale Situationniste* titled "The Decline and Fall of the Spectacle Commodity Economy," Debord spelled out his agenda: "The role of a revolutionary publication is not only to justify the Los Angeles insurgents, but to help elucidate *their justifications*, to explain in theory the truth sought by this kind of practical action."[31] Articulating his objectives in these terms, Debord is dispossessing those involved of any claims to truth, thus enacting a sort of *primitive accumulation of truth*. If "dispossession" seems like a fitting term here, it is because Debord is driven less by a desire to understand the riot than by a wish to identify with it politically. But if there are two things that a white man cannot fully identify with they are certainly Black suffering and Black violence. Debord thus finds himself adopting a position

193

described by Saidiya Hartman in regards to abolitionist discourse. He is speaking "not only for but literally in the place of"[32] rioters. Clearly, Debord's position discounts racial violence altogether, since this doesn't seem to concern him or his followers: "There was no *racial* conflict in this case: black people didn't attack white people who stood in their way, but only white police officers; nor did the solidarity of the black community extend to black storeowners or black drivers."[33]

No rigorous understanding of racial oppression can be achieved with such a simplistic view. Racial conflict shouldn't be confused, as it is here, with racist intolerance. And yet, Black consciousness—the self-consciousness of the rioters—shouldn't be perceived to be subsumed by a supposed racist hatred for white people. Race riots don't concern whiteness, but a Blackness that refuses the conditions of indignity in which it is imprisoned. As propelled by race as it is, the Black uprising isn't directed against "white people," but against the fundamental abjection of the Black condition itself. But all of this is lost on Debord, who insists on redefining the objectives of the riot in his own terms: "The uprising in Los Angeles was an uprising against the commodity, against the world of the commodity."[34] Seeing riots as the fight over access to commodities has a long history, of which Joshua Clover's work is but the latest example.[35] But this view overlooks a key ontological matter. Since the dawn of modernity, Black bodies have not occupied the structural position of consumers but that of commodities. For proof, look no further than the colonial era "Code Noir," Black Code, which defined Black people as "portable goods." As a result, Blacks often had to resort to violence to escape their objectified position and impose intersubjectivity. To avoid repeating Debord's mistake of neglecting the experience and motivations of Black rioters, we would do well to read today's riots from the perspective of this revolutionary history of Black dignity.

Debord's position comes into better focus when seen in the context of his own involvement in the May '68 protests in Paris. At the time, he was a member of the "Council for Maintaining the Occupations" (*Conseil pour le Maintien des Occupations*). The ontological meaning he gives to the notion of *occupation* helps explain his failure to understand the Watts riots. The ability to "occupy" a place such as the Sorbonne, which entails divesting it of its primary social function by turning it into a livable space, assumes a nonconflictual relationship with space. Judith Butler makes this point clear: "freedom of assembly may well be a precondition of politics itself, one that presumes that bodies can move and gather in an unregulated way, enacting their political demands in a space that, as a result, becomes public, or

CONCLUSION

redefines an existing understanding of the public."[36] Beyond mere institutional and democratic conformity, the political norms of "light dignity" described above assume what Jean Améry has referred to as "trust in the world": the certainty of not being killed simply for being in the wrong place. This trust in the world underlies Debord's gleeful politics, which is behind his claim, made in 1968, that "property was denied with everyone finding themselves at home everywhere."[37] Space becomes enchanted by occupation, as the refusal of alienated labor leads to the rediscovery of the virtue of play and celebration. Of course, taking stock of his own political moment, Debord also speaks about the riots that broke out in the Latin Quarter around the Sorbonne. But these riots were clearly an instrument used to secure the playground of the occupations.

Herein lies the key difference between the race riots for Black dignity and the May '68 politics of occupation. Unlike Debord and the *Internationale Situationniste* cohort, Black people cannot trust the world. When Debord calls these occupations a sort of "critique in action of the spectacle of non-life"[38] it is clear that by "non-life" he is referring to *ennui*, the feeling of discontent and uselessness afflicting the white middle class in the late twentieth century. This stands in stark contrast to the unrelenting form-of-death defining the Black condition, which demands a politics of necessity. Marxist-inspired interpretations of riots, from Debord to Badiou[39] and Clover, display the same elaborate refusal to consider that riots sparked by racist police violence could, quite simply, be uprisings against the structural violence of a racial state that deprives Black people of their humanity. For this reason, I don't share Debord's desire to identify some deeper truth that could explain the riots. Rather, it is imperative to stubbornly insist on the raw—and almost too obvious—necessity that triggered them. The traditional left is incapable of viewing the Black condition from an ontological perspective, for doing so would be to acknowledge the gulf dividing the experiences and interests of its supposed base and those of Black rioters whose radicality it seeks to appropriate. It would also mean leftist intellectuals would no longer be in a privileged position to reveal the fundamental truths driving the "practical action" of the rioters.

Black Dignity

As I've argued throughout this work, the concept of "Black dignity" is the cornerstone of an ethics rooted in the history of the oppressed.

195

In this respect, it goes against the grain of dominant political practices as well as those of practical philosophy. To be clear, this term doesn't simply refer to the "dignity of Black people," like some sort of feature or innate trait that belongs to them. "Black" is also meant to evoke a history that has remained for the most part in the dark, an underground or hastily dismissed history of dignity, which I hoped to expose. If the people grouped together today under the title "Black" figure prominently in this history, it is because they experienced modernity as an outright catastrophe. Black dignity is a dignity scarred by modernity, and therefore expressive of this history. A philosophical reflection founded on Black dignity responds to the urgency to reimagine an ethics where the history of conflict, inequality, and violence is confronted head-on. For it is this history that has beaten and brutalized humanity. My approach here challenges the dominant tendency in ethics to view subjects as neutral observers who exercise their free will to choose between various moral options or as creatures defined by compassion.

It should be borne in mind that violence stems principally from this very claim to neutrality. The omnipotent man in Pico della Mirandola, Kant's fetishization of the principal of non-contradiction, Habermas's emphasis on state power, or the condescending recognition advanced by Honneth all bear the illusion of reaching, through ethical reflection, a non-antagonistic essence of humanity. But this peaceful fantasy of a "human essence" makes conflict all the more apparent by refusing to acknowledge it, and, more forcefully still, by drawing a line between humanity and non-humanity. Given that the lives of those in the latter category are considered expendable, all conflict has seemingly been averted. As I have argued throughout this book, it is only by starting from singularity, rather than from a dogmatic universalism, and from acknowledging antagonistic relations, rather than replacing them with an illusion of harmony, that an ethics can do justice to human life as it really exists in history. As a result, the notion of dignity, far from being neutral and univocal, is by definition beset by contradictions, which express underlying political and social conflicts. In laying the groundwork for the notion of Black dignity, I suggested the metaphor of a battlefield, which is itself an act of position-taking. In this case, Black dignity is singularly positioned against various expressions of "light dignity."

Precarity and vulnerability are at the heart of this approach. One of the most striking aspects of the concept of dignity is that it remains indissociable with the experience of negativity. Someone who has weathered hardships is said to have kept their dignity. We speak

CONCLUSION

of dying or surviving with dignity. The existential experiences of indignity and dignity are inextricably bound together. African and diasporic histories are of invaluable significance in this respect as, from an Afro-decolonial perspective, indignity—the extreme point of negative experiences—precedes dignity and makes it visible. In its most radical meaning, indignity denotes a constant wavering between life and death; it evokes the unlivable, the moment when life is subsumed by death.

The dignity of the oppressed is made manifest in their struggle for a livable existence, but also in the history of this struggle. It takes form most prominently in a deep historicity, characterized by the unrelenting experience of social violence, the legacy of past struggles, and the presence of exterior markers that stubbornly betray an inescapable belonging to the zone of nonbeing. At root in this embrace of deep historicity is an essentialist project, which is to say, a politics of essence: the self-conscious reappropriation of heritages, specters, and archives, all of which are interwoven. These "survival histories" provide an indispensable resource, capable of enriching the present on an existential, intellectual, and affective level. To have dignity, in this respect, is to be haunted and inhabited by a past. James Baldwin was well aware of this fundamental dialectic: "That man who is forced each day to snatch his manhood, his identity, out of the fire of human cruelty that rages to destroy it knows, if he survives his effort, and even if he does not survive it, something about himself and human life that no school on earth—and indeed, no church—can teach. [...] If one is continually surviving the worst that life can bring, one eventually ceases to be controlled by a fear of what life can bring; whatever it brings must be borne."[40]

As indignity is the negation of human life, it must be confronted with the aim of abolishing it, of negating the negation. But, as necessary as this is for survival, this alone is not enough. Ethics and social philosophy, just like political action, must account for what is at stake in confronting the status quo. What is critique trying to accomplish? When "dignity" is the answer given by thinkers and activists taking up the Black cause, this means that negative experience is doubled by the self-conscious affirmation of a deep historicity and the presence of a collective memory that is needed to build a new humanity. In other terms, to criticize anti-Blackness without staking a clear position outside the values it represents and defends, or without drawing on the political traditions that have confronted imperialist violence through non-imperialist forms of existence, is to implicitly support the political ontology of the order

197

one seeks to combat, or to wait complacently for a messianic and nebulous "future," whose very ambiguity makes it all the more unassailable.

Black life is life as a form-of-death, which means it is always held in suspension, deprived of the possibility of self-realization. A nihilist interpretation might equate this state with powerlessness, but it would be wrong to do so. Only within European constructs of ontology is death seen as the absence of being, the absolute inexistence represented by nothingness. Black political ontologies have no use for such ideas. Black life as a form-of-death is haunted by specters, by the ruins of Black worlds ravaged by slavery, colonialism, and neocolonialism. The question of dignity is tied to the place of ancestors whose tortured ghosts bring both pain and the possibility of the new to the oppressed, like a sudden shift in perspective that allows one to mentally escape the prison of the present situation. Philosophy struggles to describe Black dignity. This is because Black dignity has been neglected throughout the history of thought under the hegemony of European concepts. Its troubling alterity has been domesticated to suit a Western humanism.

Art and literature struggle less with this problem. The first novel of the Franco-Congolese writer Wilfried N'Sondé, *The Heart of Leopard Children*, brings Black dignity into clear focus. The Black narrator is held in custody and subjected to violent interrogations. Dragged between his cell and the interrogation room, constantly beaten or made to undergo psychiatric exams, his powerless body—at the mercy of the sadistic pleasure of his jailers and the *libido sciendi* of supposed experts—is held in a form-of-death. But, from this body-prison, it isn't his mind that, as the cliché would have it, drifts beyond the prison walls. It is the prisoner who is visited by specters. He says as much to his executioner: "I'll take you to a place where we live side by side with the dead. I'll teach you to speak to them, just like they do with me in my head, and you'll close your eyes and see the light, yes there before you, a few inches from your forehead!"[41] In reality, his evanescent visitors are not only the dead. He sees childhood friends whose strategies of resisting death he recalls. Faith, madness, impossible escapes. But he is especially haunted by a young woman: his first love, who comes from a different background and who ends up despising him. And his own father, "the ancestor," who never comes alone but rather visits him with a crowd of others, as though accompanied by spirits.

For Saidiya Hartman, the slave's memory of Africa is like a phantom member that recalls less a temporal continuity than an abrupt rupture. This memory serves as a haunting reminder that an original plenitude is forever lost.[42] Serving as an Afro-descendant voice from the French projects, N'Sondé shows that memory's continuity isn't found in its content (songs and dances, landscapes and languages) but in its form and embodiment. In a form-of-death condition, memory results from the encounter with the disappeared, with ghosts and ancestors, the impact of which disrupts space and time. The particularity of this kind of memory owes less to the images that fill it than to the way it impacts one's existence. Africanness, Negritude—these are experienced like hauntings. And this haunting supports the life of the oppressed, never leaving them abandoned and alone. Legion is the name for Blackness since it is everywhere, nor will it ever be conquered:

> Captain, keep your airtight uniform on, firmly lace up your shiny black boots from the ankle up to the neck, pay attention to the openings, adjust your baseball cap and make sure it's pointed before your eyes before I lick you! I have the instinct of the bush. I'm thriving, endlessly regenerating. I have the heart of the jungle. Hidden within me is a force you could never imagine, a furnace with inexhaustible resources. With its support, I have regained my bearings, thanks to the wisdom of my forefathers. This is and remains my most loyal companion.[43]

The narrator of N'Sondé's novel observes the world in a state of collapse and the abandoned specters of wounded existences. Specters, along with dignity, carry Black people forward as they navigate the depths and despair of their living deaths. Stressing the role of dignity in Black ethics isn't meant to suggest that the form-of-death can be defeated or overcome, or that there exists an invincible core of Black vitality made to resist the assaults of imperial violence. Rather, it is meant to highlight the fact that this death itself contains a wealth of resources for persevering, fighting, creating. Being haunted in this way is similar to what the Algerian artist Kader Attia refers to as "reparation." Dignity is the perpetual reparation of Black existence. Never is this a matter of restituting an original wholeness. Instead, it allows us to identify the irreducibly irreparable part of ourselves, while at the same time revitalizing a fractured existence with a renewed sense of power.[44]

If Africans and their diasporas have survived the unrelenting blows of unspeakable violence while leaving their mark on all of modern culture, it is because they bear the legacy of ontologies for which death doesn't constitute a final limit absolutely distinct from life, but a passage, filled with entities that know how to navigate worlds.

199

DIGNITY OR DEATH

Slaveholders and colonizers forced slaves and the colonized to inhabit an arid hinterland bereft of life, but they didn't perish there because they knew *the depths of death*. This death is a refuge populated by terrifying beings, but also by potential allies. Ancestors are possessed by no one; for it isn't their sameness but their alterity that impacts us. Understood in this way, death is a reversible phenomenon that always already contaminates life. What underlies it and defines the humanity of the oppressed can never be deduced from any natural law, as Black infants are already swaddled in a form-of-death shroud. Black dignity cannot be discerned from the principals of moral law, for violence disfigures even reason itself. It doesn't benefit from any positive law, for the state doesn't protect Blacks but puts them to death. Black dignity has no legal status. It is defined and measured by the history of political, artistic, theoretical, philosophical revolts waged by Black people to affirm their negated humanity and the meaning they give it. May this history never give me peace. My dignity depends on it.

NOTES

Introduction

1   Frantz Fanon, *Black Skin, White Masks*, trans. Richard Philcox (New York: Grove Press, 2008), 190. Translation modified.
2   For him, this term refers above all to work done in the social sciences and to the "ontological turn" in contemporary anthropology, as can be seen in the work of Amade M'Charek, Annemarie Mol, or Eduardo Viveiros de Castro.
3   Walter D. Mignolo, *La Désobéissance épistémique. Rhétorique de la modernité, logique de la colonialité et grammaire de la décolonialité*, trans. Yasmine & Marc Maesschalck (Brussels: P.I.E. Peter Lang, 2015), 27.
4   Enrique Dussel, *The Invention of the Americas*, trans. Michael D. Barber (New York: Continuum, 1995), 41–42.
5   Tzvetan Todorov, *The Conquest of America: The Question of the Other*, trans. Richard Howard (Norman, OK: University of Oklahoma Press, 1999).
6   Nelson Maldonado Torres, *Against War: Views from the Underside of Modernity* (Durham, NC: Duke University Press, 2006).
7   Lewis R. Gordon, *An Introduction to Africana Philosophy* (Cambridge, UK: Cambridge University Press, 2008), 29.
8   Joaquim Romero Magalhães, "Africans, Indians, and Slavery in Portugal," *Portuguese Studies*, vol. 13, 1997, 143.
9   Frank B. Wilderson, *Red, White & Black: Cinema and the Structures of U.S. Antagonisms* (Durham, NC: Duke University Press, 2010).
10 Charles Pinderhughes, "Toward a New Theory of Internal Colonialism," *Socialism and Democracy*, vol. 25, no. 1, 2011, 235–256.
11 Kwame Ture & Charles Hamilton V., *Black Power: The Politics of Liberation* (New York: Vintage Books, 1992).
12 Calvin L. Warren, *Ontological Terror. Blackness, Nihilism and Emancipation* (Durham, NC: Duke University Press, 2018), 26–27.
13 Immanuel Kant, "Critique of Practical Reason" in *Practical Philosophy (The Cambridge Edition of the Works of Immanuel Kant)*, trans. Mary J. Gregor (Cambridge: Cambridge University Press, 1996).
14 Michel Foucault, *History of Sexuality, vol. 3: The Care of the Self*, trans.

201

NOTES TO PAGES 7–17

Robert Hurley (New York: Vintage Books, 1998); Judith Butler, *Giving an Account of Oneself* (New York: Fordham University Press, 2005).

15 James H. Cone, *The Spirituals and the Blues* (Maryknoll, NY: Orbis Books, 1991), 27–28. Cone's emphasis.

16 Vincent Lloyd, "Black Dignity," *Cross Currents*, vol. 28, no. 1, 2018, 78–79.

17 Landon Williams, "The Black Panther: Mirror of the People," *Black Panther Black Community News Service,* Jan. 17, 1970, 10.

18 Huey P. Newton, *Revolutionary Suicide* (New York, Penguin Books), 2009, 3.

19 Vincent Lloyd, "Black Dignity," 75.

20 Geoffrey Pleyers & Marlies Glasius, "La résonance des 'mouvements des places': connexions, émotions, valeurs," *Socio*, n° 2, 2013, 69.

21 Tommy J. Curry, "Canonizing the Critical Race Artifice: An Analysis of Philosophy's Gentrification of Critical Race Theory," in *The Routledge Companion to the Philosophy of Race*, eds. Paul Taylor, Linda Alcoff, & Luvell Anderson (New York: Routledge, 2017), 349–361.

22 bell hooks, *Ain't I a Woman: Black Women and Feminism* (New York, London: Routledge, 2015), 9.

23 Tommy J. Curry, "Killing Boogeymen: Phallicism and the Misandric Mischaracterization of Black Males in Theory." *Res Philosophica*, vol. 95, no. 2 (April 2018), 235–272.

24 Tommy J. Curry, *The Man-Not: Race, Class, Genre, and the Dilemmas of Black Manhood* (Philadelphia: Temple University Press, 2017), 55.

25 hooks, *Ain't I a Woman*, 13.

26 bell hooks, *Feminism is for Everybody: Passionate Politics* (Cambridge: South End Press, 2000), 17.

27 bell hooks, "Eating the Other: Desire and Resistance," in *Media and Cultural Studies Keyworks*, eds. Meenakshi Gigi Durham & Douglas M. Kellner (Malden: Blackwell Publishing, 2006), 375.

28 Asad Haider, *Mistaken Identity: Race and Class in the Age of Trump* (London: Verso, 2018), 76.

29 Alphonso Pinkney, *Red, Black, and Green: Black Nationalism in the United States* (Cambridge: Cambridge University Press, 1976).

30 Frank B. Wilderson III, *Afropessimism* (New York: Liveright, 2020), 14.

31 Lewis R. Gordon, "La 'Philosophie africaine' doit se définir en termes de projet intellectuel," *Critique*, n° 771–772, 2011, 626.

32 Frantz Fanon, *Alienation and Freedom*, ed. Jean Khalfa & Robert J.C. Young, trans. Steven Corcoran (London/New York: Bloomsbury, 2018), 204. Translation modified.

33 Luis Martinez Andrade, "*L'ego conquiro* comme fondement de la subjectivité moderne," *La Revue nouvelle*, n° 1, 2018, 30–35.

34 Lorenzo Chiesa, "Biopolitics in Early Twenty-First-Century Italian Theory," *Angelaki. Journal of the theoretical humanities*, vol. 16, n° 3, 2011, 1–5.

35 Nadia Yala Kisukidi, "Le 'missionnaire désespéré' ou de la différence africaine en philosophie," *Rue Descartes*, n° 83, 2014, 77–96.

36 Jared Sexton, "Afro-pessimism: The Unclear Word," *Rhizomes*, n° 26, 2016.

37 Warren, *Ontological terror*, 39.

38 Ibid., 37. In this passage, Warren is borrowing his terms from the closing paragraph of Fanon's *Black Skin, White Masks*.

NOTES TO PAGES 17–31

39 Frank B. Wilderson, "Blacks and the Master/Slave Relation," in Frank B. Wilderson et al., *Afro-Pessimism: An introduction* (Minneapolis: Racked & Dispatched, 2017), 25.

Part 1: Dignity Re-embodied

1 Patrice Lumumba, *May Our People Triumph: Poem, Speeches & Interviews*, ed. Paul Daniel Avarinth (CreateSpace Independent Publishing Platform, 2016). Translation modified.

Chapter 1: Decolonizing Moral Philosophy

1 Giorgio Agamben, *Remnants of Auschwitz: The Witness and the Archive*, trans. Daniel Heller-Roazen (New York: Zone Books, 2002), 66.
2 Ernst Kantorowicz, *The King's Two Bodies: A Study in Mediaeval Political Theology* (Princeton, NJ: Princeton University Press, 1997), 387.
3 Giovanni Pico della Mirandola, *Oration on the Dignity of Man: A New Translation and Commentary*, eds. Francesco Borghesi, Michael Papio, Massimo Riva (Cambridge: Cambridge University Press, 2012), 119.
4 Giorgio Agamben, *The Open: Man and Animal*, trans. Keven Attell (Stanford: Stanford University Press, 2004), 30.
5 Pico della Mirandola, *Oration on the Dignity of Man*, 169.
6 Ibid., 135. Translation modified.
7 Walter D. Mignolo, *The Darker Side of the Renaissance: Literacy, Territoriality & Colonization* (Ann Arbor: The University of Michigan Press, 2003), 69–71.
8 Pico della Mirandola, *Oration on the Dignity of Man*, 169.
9 William Shakespeare, *The Tempest* (1623), (London: Macmillan Collector's Library, 2019), 17.
10 Ibid., 20.
11 Kant, "What Is Enlightenment," in *Practical Philosophy*, 22.
12 It bears pointing out that this conception of dignity as belonging to all of humanity is already present in embryo in Cicero. Pico della Mirandola's contribution was to reframe it as a transformative and appropriative power. Peter Kemp, "Du bon usage de l'idée de dignité," *Diogène* 253 (2016), 91–96.
13 Kant, *Practical Philosophy*, 84.
14 As the philosopher Jay Bernstein explains, this contrast between price and dignity has its origin in Cesare Beccaria's *On Crimes and Punishments* (1764). J. A. Bernstein, *Torture and Dignity. An Essay on Moral Injury* (Chicago: University of Chicago Press, 2015), 38.
15 Éric Fiat, *Petit traité de dignité. Grandeurs et misères des hommes* (Paris: Larousse, 2012), 176.
16 Agamben, *The Remnants of Auschwitz*, 66–68.
17 Frantz Fanon, *The Wretched of the Earth*, trans. Richard Philcox (New York: Grove Press, 2004), 9.
18 Marcus Rediker, *The Slave Ship: A Human History* (New York: Viking, 2007), 18–19.

203

NOTES TO PAGES 31–42

19 Charles T. Davis & Henry Louis Gates, Jr., "Introduction: The Language of Slavery," *The Slave's Narrative* (Oxford/New York: Oxford University Press, 1991), xviii.

20 Immanuel Kant, *Observations on the Feeling of the Beautiful and Sublime and Other Writings*, eds. Patrick Frierson and Paul Guyer (Cambridge, UK: Cambridge University Press, 2011), 58–59.

21 Immanuel Kant, *Géographie*, trans. Michèle Cohen-Halimi, Max Marcuzzi, and Valérie Saroussi (Paris: Aubier, 1999), 327.

22 Immanuel Kant, "On the Different Races of Man," in *Race and the Enlightenment: A Reader*, ed. Emmanuel Chukwudi Eze (Malden, MA: Blackwell Publishing, 1997), 46.

23 As the philosopher Magali Bessone sums it up, "if the three non-white races lack cultivation, they also lack morality. Since access to the universal is empirically unequal, the cosmopolitical perspective concerns only the white race." Magali Bessone, *Sans distinction de race? Une analyse critique du concept de race et de ses effets pratiques* (Paris: Vrin, 2013), 46. See also Raphaël Lagier, *Les Races humaines selon Kant* (Paris: PUF, 2004).

24 Kant, *Géographie*, 318.

25 Kant, *Practice Philosophy*, 76. Kant's emphasis.

26 Keeanga-Yamahtta Taylor, *From #Blacklivesmatter to Black liberation* (Chicago: Haymarket Books, 2016), 3–4.

27 Jürgen Habermas, *The Future of Human Nature*, (Cambridge, UK: Polity Press, 2003), 37.

28 Jürgen Habermas, *The Crisis of the European Union: A Response*, trans. Ciaran Cronin (Cambridge, UK: Polity Press, 2012), 77–78.

29 Curry, "Killing Boogeymen," 239.

30 Habermas, *The Crisis of the European Union: A Response*, 81.

31 Ibid., 92.

32 Ibid., 100.

33 "The colonial world, as an offspring of democracy, was not the antithesis of the democratic order. It has always been its double or, again, its dark side. No democracy exists without its double, without its colony—little matter the name and the structure." Achille Mbembe, *Necropolitics*, Trans. Steven Corcoran (Durham, NC: Duke University Press, 2019), 26–27. Translation modified.

Chapter 2: Indignity

1 Thomas de Koninck, "Archéologie de la notion de dignité humaine," in Thomas de Koninck & Gilbert Larochelle, *La Dignité humaine* (Paris: PUF, 2005), 20–21.

2 Fanon, *Black Skin, White Masks*, 204. My emphasis.

3 Gilles Deleuze, *Proust and Signs*, trans. Richard Howard (Minneapolis: University of Minnesota Press, 2000), 97.

4 Ottobah Cugoano, *Thoughts and Sentiments on the Evil and Wicked Traffic of the Slavery: and Commerce of the Human Species, Humbly Submitted to the Inhabitants of Great Britain* (1787), (Ann Arbor, Michigan: University of Michigan Library, 2005), 10–12 https://quod.lib.umich.edu/e/eccodemo/K046227.0001.001/1:5?rgn=div1;view=fulltext

NOTES TO PAGES 42–50

5 Henry Louis Gates Jr., "Introduction," in Hannah Crafts, *The Bondwoman's Narrative* (New York: Grand Central Publishing, 2014).
6 Ramon Grosfoguel, "The Implications of Subaltern Epistemologies for Global Capitalism: Transmodernity, Border Thinking and Global Coloniality" in *Critical Globalization Studies*, eds. Richard P. Appelbaum & William I. Robinson (New York/London: Routledge, 2005), 284. See also Santiago Castro-Gomez, *La hybris del punto cero: ciencia, raza e ilustración en la Nueva Granada (1750–1816)*, (Bogotá: Editorial Pontificia Universidad Javeriana), 2005.
7 Mignolo, *La Désobéissance épistémique*, 74.
8 Jean Comaroff & John Comaroff, *Theory from the South: Or, How Euro-America is Evolving toward Africa* (Boulder, CO/London, Paradigm: 2012), 48.
9 Aline Helg, *Plus jamais esclaves! De l'insoumission à la révolte, le grand récit d'une émancipation (1492–1838)*, (Paris: La Découverte, 2016).
10 Olaudah Equiano, *The Interesting Narrative of the Life of Olaudah Equiano, or Gustavus Vassa, the African*. NP: https://www.amazon.com/Interesting-Narrative-Olaudah-Gustavus-African/dp/1499629605
11 Paul Gilroy, *The Black Atlantic: Modernity and Double-Consciousness* (London/New York: Verso, 2002).
12 Cugoano, *Thoughts and Sentiments*, 58.
13 W.E.B. Du Bois, *The Souls of Black Folk*, ed. Brent Hayes Edwards (Oxford: Oxford University Press, 2007), 135.
14 Warren, *Ontological Terror*, 15–16.
15 Davis & Gates Jr., "Introduction: The Language of Slavery," XXIII.
16 Orlando Patterson, *Slavery and Social Death. A Comparative Study* (Cambridge, MA/London: Harvard University Press, 1982).
17 Hannah Arendt, *The Origins of Totalitarianism* (Harcourt, 1973), 297.
18 Adriana Cavarero, *Horrorism: Naming Contemporary Violence*, trans. William McCuaig (New York: Columbia University Press, 2009), 9.
19 Ibid., 39.
20 Walter Benjamin, *Romantisme et critique de la civilisation*, trans. Christophe David & Alexandra Richter (Paris: Payot, 2010), 129.
21 Cavarero, *Horrorism*, 42.
22 Ibid., 117.
23 Arendt, *The Origins of Totalitarianism*, 207.
24 See also Kathryn T. Gines, *Hannah Arendt and the Negro Question* (Bloomington, IN: Indiana University Press, 2014), 86–87.
25 Ashis Nandy, *The Intimate Enemy: Loss and Recovery of Self under Colonialism* (Oxford, UK: Oxford University Press, 2009); Mathieu Renault, *Frantz Fanon. De l'anticolonialisme à la critique postcoloniale* (Paris: Éditions Amsterdam), 2011, 60.
26 Achille Mbembe, *Out of the Dark Night: Essays on Decolonization* (New York: Columbia University Press, 2021), 71.
27 The owner of human goods in the form of slavery can in effect exercise his rights of *usus* on them as well as those of *abusus*, as Equiano makes clear in a passage whose resemblance to the most disturbing depictions of the concentration camp will not be lost on today's reader: "I grant, indeed, that slaves are sometimes, by half-feeding, half-clothing, over-working and stripes, reduced so low, that they are turned out as unfit for service, and

NOTES TO PAGES 51–55

left to perish in the woods or expire on a dunghill." Olaudah Equiano, *The Interesting Narrative*, np.

28 Cugoano, *Thoughts and Sentiments on the Evil and Wicked Traffic of the Slavery: and Commerce of the Human Species, Humbly Submitted to the Inhabitants of Great Britain* (1787), 123.

29 What is true for the colony and the plantation is also true for the national socialist state, as Jean Améry illustrates in his reflections on torture and the insensitivity to the suffering inflicted on the "subhuman," which prove and display the veracity of racist ideology. Jean Améry, *At the Mind's Limits: Contemplations by a Survivor on Auschwitz and its Realities*, trans. Sidney Rosenfeld & Stella P. Rosenfeld (Bloomington, IN: Indiana University Press), 1980.

30 Thomas R. Gray, *The Confessions of Nat Turner* (1831), 5. https://docsouth.unc.edu/neh/turner/turner.html

31 Ibid., 12.

32 Ibid., 14.

33 Ibid., 11–12. Beyond its indisputable merits, *Birth of a Nation*, a film adaptation of Nat Turner's *Confessions*, greatly plays down these aspects of his story. The director, in fact, tries to make the reasons for the revolt immediately obvious and impossible to ignore for the viewer. He does this by overdramatizing the cruelty of Turner's master. Rather than explore the ethical and political dimension of Turner's narrative, this pedantic, stylized approach, though understandable, turns the inhumanity of slavery into an expository spectacle.

34 Cavarero, *Horrorism*, 73–74.

35 The critic Saidiya Hartman warned over twenty years ago that one may become numb to the violence endured by Black bodies by constantly turning this violence into spectacle. Saidiya V. Hartman, *Scenes of Subjection: Terror, Slavery, and Self-Making in Nineteenth-Century America* (Oxford, UK: Oxford University Press, 1997).

36 "But the life of the spirit is not the life that shrinks from death and keeps clear of devastation; —it is the life that endures death and preserves itself in it. Spirit gains its truth only when, in absolute disintegration, it finds itself. [...] spirit is this power only by looking the negative in the face, and by dwelling on it." G.W.F. Hegel, *The Phenomenology of Spirit* (1807), trans. Michael Inwood (Oxford: Oxford University Press, 2018), 16. http://ns210054.ovh.net/files/Georg%20Wilhelm%20Friedrich%20Hegel%20-%20The%20Phenomenology%20of%20Spirit%20%28Michael%20Inwood%20Translation%29.pdf

37 Ibid., 80.

38 Cugoano, *Thoughts and Sentiments on the Evil and Wicked Traffic of the Slavery: and Commerce of the Human Species, Humbly Submitted to the Inhabitants of Great Britain* (1787), 112.

39 Even though she remains very modest in her criticism, it is worth noting the important work of Ann Laura Stoler. See Ann Laura Stoler, *Race and the Education of Desire. Foucault's History of Sexuality and the Colonial Order of Things* (Durham/London: Duke University Press, 1995).

40 Michel Foucault, *"Society Must be Defended": Lectures at the Collège de France, 1975–1976*, ed. Arnold I. Davidson, trans. David Macey (New York: Picador, 1997), 254. My emphasis.

NOTES TO PAGES 55–63

41 Michel Foucault, *The History of Sexuality: Volume 1: An Introduction,* trans. Robert Hurley (New York: Vintage Books, 1990), 137.

42 Foucault, *"Society Must be Defended,"* 257.

43 Norman G. Finkelstein, *The Holocaust Industry: Reflections on the Exploitation of Jewish Suffering* (London/New York: Verso, 2001).

44 Françoise Vergès, *La mémoire enchaînée. Questions sur l'esclavage* (Paris: Hachette Littératures, 2006), 144.

45 "The lived experience of black people described by Fanon corresponded in some respects to the experiences I myself had lived as a Jew interned in a concentration camp." Jean Améry, "L'homme enfanté par l'esprit de la violence" (1971), trans. Julie-Françoise Kruidenier & Adrian Daub, *Les Temps Modernes,* n° 635–636, 2005, 175.

46 Jean Améry, *At the Mind's Limits: Contemplations by a Survivor on Auschwitz and Its Realities,* trans. Sidney Rosenfeld & Stella P. Rosenfeld (Bloomington: Indiana University Press, 1980), 16.

47 Michel Foucault, *"Society Must Be Defended,"* 253.

48 Giorgio Agamben, *Homo Sacer: Sovereign Power and Bare Life,* trans. Daniel Heller-Roazen (Stanford, CA: Stanford University Press, 1998); Roberto Esposito, *Terms of the Political: Community, Immunity, Biopolitics,* trans. Rhiannon Noel Welch (New York: Fordham University Press, 2013).

49 Jared Sexton, "People-of-Color-Blindness. Notes on the Afterlife of Slavery," *Social Text,* vol. 28, n° 2, 2010, 32.

50 Achille Mbembe, "Necropolitics" in *Necropolitics,* 66–92.

51 Achille Mbembe, *Sortir de la grande nuit* (Paris: La Découverte, 2010) 35 (passage not included in the English translation). See also Achille Mbembe, *"The Society of Enmity"* in *Necropolitics,* 42–65.

52 Léonora Miano, *L'Impératif transgressif* (Paris: L'Arche, 2016), 36.

53 Fabien Eboussi Boulaga, *Christianity without Fetishes: An African Critique and Recapture of Christianity,* trans. Robert R. Barr (Maryknoll, NY: Orbis Books, 1984), 106.

54 For this distinction between two deaths I am indebted to the work of the philosopher and classicist Jean Fallot. Jean Fallot, *Cette Mort qui n'en est pas une* (Lille: Presses Universitaires de Lille, 1993).

55 Jared Sexton, "The Social Life of Social Death: On Afro-pessimism and Black optimism," *InTension,* n° 5, 2011, 29.

56 Steve Biko, "We Blacks," in A. Stubbs, *I Write What I Like: Steve Biko: A Selection of his Writings* (London: Bowerdean Press, 1987), 30.

57 Bruce Bégout, *La Découverte du quotidien* (Paris: Allia, 2005), 38.

58 Steve Biko, "Black Consciousness and the Quest for a True Humanity," in A. Stubbs, *I Write What I Like: Steve Biko: A Selection of his Writings,* 89.

59 Fanon, *Black Skin, White Masks,* 15.

60 Ibid., 90. On everyday surveillance, see ibid., 18.

61 Frantz Fanon, *A Dying Colonialism,* trans. Haakon Chevalier (New York: Grove Press, 1965), 162.

62 Fanon, *Black Skin, White Masks,* 17.

63 W.E.B. Du Bois, *Darkwater: Voices from within the Veil* (1920) (Mineola, NY: Dover, 1999), 22.

64 Fanon, *Black Skin, White Masks,* 90.

65 To understand how this works in France, see Mathieu Rigouste, *La*

NOTES TO PAGES 63–71

Domination policière (Paris: La Fabrique, 2012), 163–164; for a Brazilian context, see Cleber Daniel Lambert Da Silva & Roger Anibal Lambert Da Silva "Violência e Repossessão do Sensível. Contribuição à Crítica Pós-Coloniala Partir da Obra do Rapper Carlos Eduardo Taddeo," in Carlos Frederico Miranda Medina, *et al.* (dir.), *Violencias en la posmodernidad: resistencias, paradigmas y conflictos en Latinoamérica* (Medellin: Sello Editorial Coruniamericana, 2015).

66 Léopold Lambert, *La Politique du bulldozer. La ruine palestinienne comme projet israélien* (Paris: Éditions B2, 2016), 8.

67 James Ferguson, *Global Shadows: Africa in the Neoliberal World Order* (Durham, NC: Duke University Press, 2006); John L. Comaroff & Jean Comaroff, "Law and Disorder in the Postcolony: An Introduction" in John L. Comaroff & Jean Comaroff (eds.), *Law and Disorder in the Postcolony* (Chicago: Chicago University Press, 2006); Norman Ajari, "L'état d'exception (post)colonial: généalogie et actualité d'une notion," *En Jeu. Histoire et mémoires vivantes*, n° 5, 2015, 33–44.

68 Frantz Fanon, *Toward the African Revolution*, trans. Haakon Chevalier (New York: Grove Press, 1967), 41.

69 Robin D. G. Kelley, "Thug Nation: On State Violence and Disposability" in Jordan T. Camp & Christina Heatherton (eds), *Policing the Planet: Why the Policing Crisis Led to Black Lives Matter* (London/New York: Verso, 2016), 32.

Chapter 3: Our Dignity Is Older than Us

1 Ernesto Laclau, *Emancipation(s)* (London/New York: Verso, 1996), 43.

2 Ernesto Laclau, *On Populist Reason* (London/New York: Verso, 2005), 96.

3 Jacques Rancière, *Hatred of Democracy*, trans. Steve Corcoran (London/New York: Verso, 2006), 56.

4 Hartman, *Scenes of Subjection*, 18.

5 Fanon opens *Black Skin, White Masks* by describing this distancing from a still raw suffering as both the source and necessary condition for his theoretical writing: "[These are] things I'm going to say, not shout. I've long given up shouting [...] This book should have been written three years ago. But at the time the truths made our blood boil. Today the fever has dropped and truths can be said without having them hurled into people's faces." xi–xiii.

6 Malcolm X, "Not Just an American Problem, but a World Problem," Address delivered in the Corn Hill Methodist Church, Rochester, New York, 16 February 1965. http://nationalhumanitiescenter.org/pds/maai3/community/text10/malcolmxworldproblem.pdf

7 Steve Biko, "We Blacks," in A. Stubbs, *I Write What I Like: Steve Biko: A Selection of his Writings*, 30.

8 Sadri Khiari, *Pour une politique de la racaille: immigré-e-s, indigènes et jeunes de banlieues* (Paris: Textual, 2006, 12.

9 Hartman, *Scenes of Subjection*, 65.

10 James H. Cone, *Martin & Malcolm & America: A Dream or a Nightmare* (New York: Orbis Books, 1991), 248.

208

NOTES TO PAGES 71–79

11 Ibid., 251.
12 Aimé Césaire, "Nègrerie. Conscience raciale et révolution sociale," Écrits politiques. 1935–1956, 33.
13 Léopold Sédar Senghor, *Ce Que Je Crois: Négritude, Francité et Civilisation de l'Universel* (Paris: Grasset, 1988), 22. Senghor's emphasis.
14 Stanislas Adotevi, *Négritude et Négrologues* (Paris: Union Générale d'Éditions, 1972).
15 Jean-Paul Sartre, "Black Orpheus," trans. John MacCombie, *The Massachusetts Review*, Vol. 6, No. 1, (Autumn 1964–Winter 1965), 16. Translation modified.
16 Fabien Éboussi Boulaga, "Le Bantou problématique" (1968), in *L'Affaire de la philosophie africaine. Au-delà des querelles* (Paris: Éditions Terroirs – Karthala, 2011), 44.
17 Jérémie Piolat, *Portrait du colonialiste. L'effet boomerang de sa violence et de ses destructions* (Paris: La Découverte, coll. "Les empêcheurs de penser en rond," 2011), 55.
18 Aimé Césaire, "Négreries. Jeunesse noire et assimilation" (1935), Écrits politiques. 1935–1956, 29.
19 Aimé Césaire, "*Tropiques*. Présentation" (1941), Écrits politiques. 1935–1956, 34.
20 Aimé Césaire, *Discours sur le colonialisme suivi du Discours sur la négritude* (Paris: Présence Africaine, 2004), 82.
21 Aimé Césaire, "Culture et Colonization" in *Presence Africaine: The 1st International Conference of Negro Writers and Artists, Paris, Sept. 1956*, 207. https://www.amherst.edu/system/files/media/0276/Aime_Cesaire__Culture _and_Colinisation.pdf
22 Fanon, *The Wretched of the Earth*, 2.
23 "'Races' don't exist in and of themselves, but rather in the mind as historically constructed categories." Pap Ndiaye, *La Condition noire. Essai sur une minorité française* (Paris: Gallimard, coll. "Folio," 2008), p. 39.
24 Bruno Latour, "Factures/fractures. De la notion de réseau à celle d'attachement" in André Micoud & Michel Peroni (eds.), *Ce qui nous relie* (La Tour d'Aigues, Éditions de l'Aube, 2000).
25 Kehinde Andrews, *Back to Black: Black Radicalism for the 21st Century* (London: Zed Books, 2019), 170.
26 Étienne Balibar, *On Universals: Constructing and Deconstructing Community*, trans. Joshua David Jordan (New York: Fordham University Press, 2020), 16. Balibar's emphasis.
27 Ibid, 17. Balibar's emphasis.
28 Fanon adds: "These bodies appear to embody respect for tradition, the cultural specificities, the personality of the subjugated people. This pseudo-respect in fact is tantamount to the most utter contempt, to the most elaborate sadism [...] The constantly affirmed concern with 'respecting the culture of the native populations' accordingly does not signify taking into consideration the values borne by the culture, incarnated by men. Rather, this behavior betrays a determination to objectify, to confine, to imprison, to harden." Fanon, *Toward the African Revolution*, 34.
29 Lewis R. Gordon, "Essentialist Anti-Essentialism, with Considerations from Other sides of Modernity," *Quadena*, n° 1, 2012.

209

NOTES TO PAGES 80–84

30 James H. Cone, *God of the Oppressed* (1975) (Maryknoll, NY: Orbis, 1997), 28.

31 Nathalie Etoke, *Melancholia Africana: The Indispensable Overcoming of the Black Condition*, trans. Bill Hamlett (London/New York: Rowman & Littlefield, 2019), 15.

32 Alain de Benoist, *Les Idées à l'endroit* (Paris: Éditions Libres Hatier), 1979.

33 Fabien Eboussi Boulaga, *Muntu in Crisis: African Authenticity and Philosophy* (Trenton, NJ: Africa World Press, 2014), 77.

34 Fanon, *The Wretched of the Earth*, 235.

35 Judith Butler, *Gender Trouble* (New York/London: Routledge, 2006).

36 Jacques Derrida, *Force de loi* (Paris: Galilée, 2005), 36.

37 Cone, *God of the Oppressed*, 191–192.

38 Homi K. Bhabha, *The Location of Culture* (London/New York: Routledge, 2004), 37. Bhabha's emphasis.

39 The most formidable and elegant expression of this unquestionably comes from a famous passage in Foucault's *The Archeology of Knowledge*: "I am no doubt not the only one who writes in order to have no face. Do not ask who I am and do not ask me to remain the same: leave it to our bureaucrats and our police to see that our papers are in order. At least spare us their morality when we write." Michel Foucault, *The Archaeology of Knowledge*, trans. A. M. Sheridan Smith (New York: Pantheon Books, 1972), 17. But the possibility of becoming weary of one's own civil identity requires not only having one's papers, but having them in order. Most of the texts analyzed in this book respond to a much more urgent and vital need: that of assuming an appearance that others can perceive as something other than the grimacing face of a monkey or the deformed features of a monster. The Franco-Algerian philosopher Seloua Luste Boulibina has a clear-eyed assessment of the problem: "Foucault was in Brazil only as a traveler and not as a resident, as a distinguished guest and not as an illegal migrant, as a white man and not as a black woman. This is doubtless why he dreamed, in writing, of not having a face or of losing his face. [...] For the resident, the illegal migrant, and the black woman, to have no face is neither an ideal nor a dream; it is an experience, a reality, a nightmare. There are therefore some who express themselves, on the contrary, in order to gain a face." Seloua Luste Boulibina, *Kafka's Monkey and Other Phantoms of Africa*, trans. Laura Hengehold (Bloomington, IN: Indiana University Press, 2019), 74.

40 Marc Maesschalck, *La Cause du sujet* (Bruxelles: P.I.E. Peter Lang, 2014), 241.

41 Sam Bourcier, "Le nouveau conflit des facultés: biopouvoir, sociologie et *queer studies* dans l'université néo-libérale française," *SociologieS* [online], 2016. Elsewhere, he has provided a strikingly lucid picture of this particular philosophic moment, which is worth citing in full: "The sweeping anti-foundational gestures of all these post-structural musings are, of course, the death of the subject, the impersonal character of power, the war waged à la Don Quixote against essentialism, the deconstruction of identity politics suddenly turned ultra-taboo in the 1990's U.S. academe, the unravelling of agency... [...] The spread of the fiction of *French Theory* by some (lesbian) American (post-) feminists in the 90s—including Butler—had the unexpected consequence of creating a paradoxical minority 'moral high ground' meant

NOTES TO PAGES 85–94

to call into question a fixed identity politics, which was seen as complicit with a hegemonic and normalizing position (officially, the gay assimilationist politics of the 90s). In a 1990s 'France,' this would have been putting the cart before the horse, given the way identity politics were—and continue to be (even if cracks are starting to show) hemmed in by politicians of all stripes—straight, gay or lesbian." Sam Bourcier, *Queer Zones* (Paris: Éditions Amsterdam, 2011), 183.

42 Fanon, *The Wretched of the Earth*, 6.
43 Sadri Khiari, *Malcolm X. Stratège de la dignité noire* (Paris: Éditions Amsterdam, 2013), 37.

Chapter 4: The Universal by Accident

1 *The Black Sash News*, vol. 16, n° 1, June 1972.
2 Basil Moore, "Black Theology: In the Beginning," *Journal for the Study of Religion*, vol. 4, n° 2, 1991, 19–28.
3 Basil Moore (ed.), *Black Theology. The South African Voice* (London: C. Hurst & Company, 1973).
4 Paget Henry, *Caliban's Reason. Introducing Afro-Caribbean Philosophy* (New York/London: Routledge, 2000). The turn to Caliban was in large part influenced by the Jamaican philosopher Lewis Gordon.
5 Silvia Federici, *Caliban and the Witch: Women, the Body and Primitive Accumulation* (Autonomedia, 2004).
6 Cornel West, *Democracy Matters: Winning the Fight against Imperialism* (New York: Penguin, 2004), 148. See also Mahamadou Lamine Sagna, *Violences, racisme et religions en Amérique. Cornel West, une pensée rebelle* (Paris: Karan, 2016), 52–53.
7 "When [Charles] Taylor says that the modern state has to make citizenship the primary principle of identity, he refers to the way it must transcend the different identities built on class, gender, and religion, replacing conflicting perspectives by unifying experience. In an important sense, this transcendent mediation *is* secularism. Secularism is not simply an intellectual answer to a question about enduring social peace and toleration. It is an enactment by which a *political medium* (representation of citizenship) redefines and transcends particular and differentiating practices of the self that are articulated through class, gender, and religion." Talal Asad, *Formations of the Secular: Christianity, Islam, Modernity* (Palo Alto: Stanford University Press, 2003), 5.
8 See Luis Martinez Andrade, *Écologie et libération. Critique de la modernité dans la théologie de la liberation* (Paris: Van Dieren, 2016), 29.
9 Henri Pena-Ruiz, *Qu'est-ce que la laïcité?* (Paris: Gallimard, coll. "Folio," 2003), 31.
10 Philippe Pignarre, "Apprendre à échapper aux alternatives infernales," *Mouvements*, n° 32, 2004, 40. See also Philippe Pignarre & Isabelle Stengers, *Capitalist Sorcery: Breaking the Spell*, trans. Andrew Goffey (New York: Palgrave Macmillan, 2011).
11 Vincent Delecroix, *Apocalypse du politique* (Paris: Desclée de Brouwer, 2016), 51.
12 Cugoano, *Thoughts and Sentiments on the Evil and Wicked Traffic of the*

211

NOTES TO PAGES 95–104

Slavery: and Commerce of the Human Species, Humbly Submitted to the Inhabitants of Great Britain (1787), 56.

13 Henri Pena-Ruiz, *Qu'est-ce que la laïcité?*, 27.
14 Ibid., 97.
15 Ibid., 101.
16 Asad, *Formations of the Secular*, 7.
17 On the use of the notion of theodicy in critical theory, see Gordon, *Disciplinary Decadence*, 91.
18 Alain Badiou, *Saint Paul: The Foundation of Universalism*, trans. Ray Brassier (Stanford, CA: Stanford University Press), 6.
19 Rudolf Bultmann, *History and Eschatology: The Presence of Eternity* (New York: Harper Torchbooks, 1955), 44.
20 Alain Badiou, *Théorie du sujet* (Paris: Seuil, 1982), 56.
21 Slavoj Žižek, *The Fragile Absolute—or, Why is the Christian Legacy Worth Fighting For?* (London/New York: Verso, 2000), 99.
22 Slavoj Žižek, *The Puppet and the Dwarf: The Perverse Core of Christianity*, (Cambridge, MA: MIT Press, 2003), 130.
23 Pena-Ruiz, *Qu'est-ce que la laïcité?*, 25.
24 Žižek, *The Puppet and the Dwarf*, 99.
25 Badiou, *Saint Paul*, 66.
26 Fabien Eboussi Boulaga, *Christianity without Fetishes*, 17.
27 Bruno Chenu, *Le Christ noir américain* (Paris: Desclée, 1984), 86.
28 Badiou, *Saint Paul*, 71.
29 Mehdi Belhaj Kacem, "Antiscolastique et philosophie," *Textes inédits* (Paris: Les Presses du réel, 2016), 254.
30 Ibid., 258. Belhaj Kacem's emphasis.
31 Du Bois, *The Souls of Black Folk*, 173.
32 "Death is not a destiny but a choice, as is shown by the fact that we can be offered, through subtraction of death, the choice of life." Badiou, *Saint Paul*, 73.
33 James H. Cone, *God of the Oppressed*, 115. Cone's emphasis.
34 Hartman, *Scenes of Subjection*, 66.
35 Sophie Wahnich, *In Defense of the Terror: Liberty or Death in the French Revolution*, trans. David Fernbach (London/New York: Verso, 2012).
36 Alain Badiou, *Ethics: An Essay on the Understanding of Evil*, trans. Peter Hallward (London/New York: Verso, 2001), 12. Translation modified.
37 Enrique Dussel, *Ethics of Liberation: In the Age of Globalization and Exclusion*, trans. Eduardo Mendieta, Camile Pérez Bustillo, Yolanda Angulo & Nelson Maldonado-Torres (Durham/London: Duke University Press, 2013), 205.
38 Theodor W. Adorno, *Negative Dialectics* (1973), trans. E.B. Ashton (New York/London: Routledge, 2004), 18.
39 Cugoano, *Thoughts and Sentiments on the Evil and Wicked Traffic of the Slavery: and Commerce of the Human Species, Humbly Submitted to the Inhabitants of Great Britain* (1787), 148.
40 Gary Wilder, *Freedom Time. Negritude, Decolonization and the Future of the World* (Durham, NC: Duke University Press, 2015); Souleymane Bachir Diagne, *Bergson postcolonial. L'élan vital dans la pensée de Léopold Sédar Senghor et de Mohamed Iqbal* (Paris: CNRS Éditions, 2011); David Alliot, *Aimé Césaire: Le Nègre universel* (Gollion, Infolio, 2008).

NOTES TO PAGES 104–115

41 Judith Butler, "Competing Universalities" in Judith Butler, Ernesto Laclau, Slavoj Žižek, *Contingency, Hegemony, Universality: Contemporary Dialogues on the Left* (London/New York: Verso, 2000), 163.
42 Étienne Balibar, *On Universals*, 14–15.
43 Ibid., 132–133.
44 Adorno, *Negative Dialectics*, 152.
45 Badiou, *Saint Paul*, 12. Badiou's emphasis.
46 Améry, *At the Mind's Limits*, p.33.
47 Given his unrestrained heroization of those who resist torture and his championing of their valor in *Ethics*, Alain Badiou remains incapable of grasping the truth Améry exposes.
48 Badiou, *Saint Paul*, 99.
49 Slavoj Žižek, *The Puppet and the Dwarf*, 132–133.
50 Steve Biko, "Black Souls in White Skins," in A. Stubbs, *I Write What I Like: Steve Biko: A Selection of his Writings*, 24.
51 Marco Dell'Omodrame, "Anibal Quijano et la saturation coloniale" in Maxime Cervulle, Nelly Quemener & Florian Vörös (eds.), *Matérialismes, Culture & Communication. Tome2: Cultural studies, théories féministes et décoloniales* (Paris: Presses des Mines), 2016.
52 Kant, *Groundwork of The Metaphysics of Morals*, in *Practical Philosophy*.
53 Bernard Doray, *La Dignité. Les debouts de l'utopie* (Paris: La Dispute, 2006), 55.
54 "The neotenic infant [...] would find himself in the condition of being able to pay attention precisely to what has not been written, to somatic possibilities that are arbitrary and uncodified: in his infantile totipotency, he would be ecstatically overwhelmed, cast out of himself, not like other living beings into a specific adventure or environment, but for the first time into a *world*." Giorgio Agamben, *Idea of Prose*, trans. Michael Sullivan & Sam Whitsitt (Albany, NY: State University of New York Press, 1995), 96, Agamben's emphasis. See also Dany-Robert Dufour, *Lettres sur la nature humaine à l'usage des survivants* (Paris: Calmann-Lévy, 1999); Marc Levivier, "L'hypothèse d'un Homme néoténique comme 'grand récit' sous-jacent," *Les Sciences de l'éducation – Pour l'Ère nouvelle*, n° 44, 2011, 77–93.
55 Judith Butler, *Frames of War: When Is Life Grievable?* (London/Brooklyn: Verso, 2009), 14.
56 Cornel West, *Prophesy Deliverance! An Afro-American Revolutionary Christianity* (Louisville: Westminster John Knox Press, 2002), 17.
57 Doray, *La Dignité*, 59.

Chapter 5: A Theology of Black Dignity

1 Saidiya V. Hartman, *Lose Your Mother: A Journey along the Atlantic Slave Route* (New York: Farrar Straus Giroux, 2006).
2 Jacob Taubes, *"Le temps presse." Du culte à la culture*, trans. Mira Köller & Dominique Séglard (Paris: Seuil, 2009), 346.
3 Gilroy, *The Black Atlantic: Modernity and Double-Consciousness*, 36. Gilroy's emphasis.
4 Cone, *The Spirituals and the Blues*, 3. Cone's emphasis.
5 Ibid., 6.

213

NOTES TO PAGES 115–124

6 LeRoi Jones, *Blues People: Negro Music in White America* (New York, HarperCollins, 1963), 29.

7 Etoke, *Melancholia Africana*, xx–xxi.

8 Cornel West, "A Prisoner in the Night of the American Empire: Dialogue with Gabriel Rockhill" in *Politics of Culture and the Spirit of Critique: Dialogues*, eds. Gabriel Rockhill & Alfredo Gomez-Muller (New York: Columbia University Press, 2011), 114.

9 Rediker, *The Slave Ship: A Human History*.

10 Hartman, *Scenes of Subjection*, 44.

11 Jean Baudrillard, *Consumer Society* (London/Thousand Oaks/New Delhi, Sage Publications: 1998), 134.

12 Rediker, *The Slave Ship: A Human History*, 239.

13 I'd like to thank the choreographer James Carlès for bringing this pertinent example to my attention.

14 Philippe Lacoue-Labarthe, *Poetics of History: Rousseau and the Theater of Originary Mimesis*, trans. Jeff Fort (New York: Fordham University Press, 2019), 66. Lacoue-Labarthe's emphasis.

15 Eduardo Viveiros de Castro, "Le marbre et le myrte: de l'inconstance de l'âme sauvage" in Aurore Becquelin & Antoine Molinié-Fioravanti (eds.), *Mémoire de la tradition* (Nanterre, Publications de la Société d'Ethnologie, 1993).

16 Sexton, "The Social Life of Social Death," 28.

17 Steve Biko, "Some African Cultural Concepts," in A. Stubbs, *I Write What I Like: Steve Biko: A Selection of his Writings*, 43–44.

18 Cone, *The Spirituals and the Blues*, 30.

19 James H. Cone, *The Cross and the Lynching Tree* (Maryknoll, NY: Orbis Books, 2011), 138.

20 Bruno Chenu, *Dieu est noir. Histoire, religion et théologie des Noirs américains* (Paris: Le Centurion, 1977), 79.

21 Du Bois, *The Souls of Black Folk*, 132.

22 Chenu, *Dieu est noir*, 94.

23 Achille Mbembe, *On the Postcolony*, trans. A.M. Berrett, Janet Roitman, Murray Last, & Steven Rendall (Berkeley/Los Angeles: University of California Press, 2001), 239.

24 James H. Cone, *Black theology and Black Power* (Maryknoll, NY: Orbis Books), 1989, 74–75.

25 Chenu, *Le Christ noir américain*, 28–30.

26 Chenu, *Dieu est noir*, 119.

27 West, *Prophesy Deliverance!*, 97–98.

28 Chenu, *Dieu est noir*, 128.

29 Ibid., 137.

30 Ibid., 182.

31 The anthropologists Jean and John Comaroff see today's Pentacostalism as indicative of the neoliberal development of religion: "Bold color advertisements for BMWs and lottery winnings adorn altars; tabloids pasted to walls and windows carry testimonials by followers whose membership was rewarded by a rush of wealth and/or an astonishing recovery of health. [...] This shift is endemic to the new religious movements of the late twentieth century. For them, and for their many millions of members, the Second Coming evokes not a Jesus who saves, but one who pays dividends. Or, more

NOTES TO PAGES 124–130

accurately, one who promises a miraculous return on a limited spiritual investment." Jean Comaroff & John Comaroff, "Millenial Capitalism: First Thoughts on a Second Coming." *Public Culture* (2000), 12.2, 314.

32 Cone, James H., *A Black Theology of Liberation* (Maryknoll, NY: Orbis Books, 2010), 19. See also Gordon, *Disciplinary Decadence*.

33 Cone, *God of the Oppressed*, 39.

34 Cone, *Black theology and Black Power*, 88.

35 Enrique Dussel, *History and Theology of Liberation: A Latin American Perspective*, trans. John Drury (Maryknoll, NY: Orbis Books, 1976).

36 Cone, *The Cross and the Lynching Tree*, 95.

37 Bruno Chenu, *L'Urgence prophétique. Dieu au défi de l'histoire* (Paris/ Bayard: Le Centurion, 1997), 13.

38 Cone, *The Cross and the Lynching Tree*, 61. See also Cone, *Martin & Malcolm & America*.

39 Gilles Deleuze & Félix Guattari, *Kafka: Toward a Minor Literature*, trans. Dana B. Polan (Minneapolis/London: University of Minnesota Press, 1986), 16.

40 Jacob Taubes, *Occidental Eschatology*, trans. David Ratmoko (Stanford CA: Stanford University Press, 2009), 26.

41 Max Weber, *The Sociology of Religion*, trans. Ephraim Fischoof (Boston: Beacon Press, 1991), 46.

42 Sylvie Barnay, *La Parole habitée. Les grandes voix du prophétisme* (Paris: Seuil, coll. "Points"), 2012.

43 West, *Prophesy Deliverance!*, 6.

44 "Dialectical logic is a logic of history, giving rise to the eschatological interpretation of the world. This logic is determined by the question of the power of the negative, as posed by apocalypticism and Gnosis. Apocalypticism and Gnosis form the basis of Hegel's logic, which is often discussed but seldom understood. The connection between apocalyptic ontology and Hegelian logic is neither artificial nor an afterthought. Hegel, as a young theologian, worked out his way of thinking from the New Testament. The young Hegel's early, profound essays are closely modeled on the text of the Gospels. Here we can trace the way in which Hegel's dialectical mode of thinking is awakened, and how he grows into that mode by studying sentences in the Gospels, breaking the mold of Aristotelian, rational logic." Jacob Taubes, *Occidental Eschatology*, 36.

45 West, *Prophesy Deliverance!*, 108.

46 Cone, *God of the Oppressed*, 84.

47 Bernard Aspe, "C'est la veille," in *Kénose. Revue philosophique & politique*, n° 0, 2014, 22.

48 Giorgio Agamben, *The Highest Poverty: Monastic Rules and Form-of-Life*, trans. Adam Kotsko (Stanford, CA: Stanford University Press, 2013), 105.

49 Cone, *God of the Oppressed*, 35.

50 Ibid., 123. Cone's emphasis.

51 Cone, *The Cross and the Lynching Tree*, 75.

52 Cone, *Black Theology and Black Power*, 68.

53 "[Eckhart's] thought fluctuates between the demands of a law: voluntary disappropriation and impoverishment; and the description of a state: the original liberty which man has never lost at the basis of his being. The concept of releasement includes these two aspects." Meister Eckhart, *Wandering Joy:*

NOTES TO PAGES 130–138

Meister Eckhart's Mystical Philosophy, trans. Reiner Schürmann (Great Barrington, MA: Lindisfarne Books, 2001), xix.

54 Aimé Césaire, "Introduction à la poésie nègre américaine" (1941), *Écrits politiques. 1935–1956*, 36.

55 Cornel West, "A Philosophical View of Easter" (1980), *The Cornel West Reader* (New York: Basic Civitas Books, 1999), 420.

56 Etoke, *Melancholia Africana*, 47–48.

57 Cone, *The Cross and the Lynching Tree*, 161–162.

58 Cone, *Black Theology and Black Power*, 26. Cone's emphasis.

59 Louis Althusser, "Ideology and Ideological State Apparatuses (Notes Towards an Investigation)" in *Essays on Ideology*, trans. Ben Brewster (London/New York: Verso, 1993), 44. Translation modified.

60 Ibid., 51.

61 Cone, *A Black Theology of Liberation*, 18.

62 Søren Kierkegaard, *Fear and Trembling*, eds. C. Stephan Evans & Sylvia Walsh, trans. Sylvia Walsh (Cambridge: Cambridge University Press, 2006), 52.

63 Kierkegaard, *Fear and Trembling*, 61.

64 Cone, *God of the Oppressed*, 200.

65 Bruce Bégout, *De la décence ordinaire* (Paris: Allia, 2017), 17.

66 Cone, *A Black Theology of Liberation*, 21.

67 Ultimately, only Black people are in a position to authentically affirm Max Stirner's famous expression from *The Unique and Its Property*—"I have founded my cause on nothing"—since in a society fueled by anti-Blackness, founding oneself on one's own Black dignity is, strictly speaking, to found oneself on nothing, on emptiness—on the zone of nonbeing.

68 Cone, *God of the Oppressed*, 2.

69 Cone, *A Black Theology of Liberation*, 16.

70 Cone, *The Cross and the Lynching Tree*, 139. Cone's emphasis.

71 Cone, *God of the Oppressed*, 131–132.

72 Chantal Mouffe, *The Democratic Paradox* (London/Brooklyn: Verso, 2009), 104.

Chapter 6: Ubuntu

1 An earlier version of this chapter first appeared as "Née du désatre. Critique de l'ethnophilosophie, pensée sociale et africanité" in *AUC Interpretationes*, vol. V, n. 1, 2016, 115–29. I am grateful to Fabio Bruschi for allowing its republication.

2 Gilles Deleuze & Félix Guattari, *What Is Philosophy?*, trans. Graham Burchell & Hugh Tomlinson (London/New York: Verso, 1994), 85.

3 Marcien Towa, *Essai sur la problématique philosophique dans l'Afrique actuelle* (Yaoundé: Éditions CLE, 1981).

4 Jean-Loup Amselle, *L'Occident décroché: enquête sur les postcolonialismes* (Paris: Stock, 2008).

5 See, respectively, Mbembe, *On the Postcolony*, 183, and Peter Trawny, *Heidegger et l'antisémitisme*, trans. Julia Christ (Paris: Seuil, 2014). If we trust Trawny's portrait of him, Heidegger can quite legitimately be seen as a Germanic ethnophilosopher. But the ethnophilosophy that embraces an

NOTES TO PAGES 138–147

imperialist project like that of the Third Reich is of a different racist nature than the one that seeks only to re-humanize traditions of thought that have been destroyed by political and cultural domination.

6 Giorgio Agamben, *Qu'est-ce que Le Commandement?*, trans. Joël Gayraud (Paris: Payot), 2013, 8–9.

7 Séverine Kodjo-Granvaux, *Philosophies africaines* (Paris: Présence Africaine, 2013), 26.

8 Paulin Hountondji, "Knowledge as a Development Issue" in Kwasi Wiredu (ed.), *A Companion to African Philosophy* (Malden, MA/Oxford, UK: Blackwell Publishing, 2004), 529.

9 Stanislas Adotevi, *Négritude et Négrologues*, 54.

10 Paulin Hountondji, *African Philosophy: Myth and Reality*, trans. Henri Evans & Jonathan Rée (Bloomington, Indiana: Indiana University Press, 1983).

11 Ibid., 60.

12 J. C. Carothers, *The African Mind in Health and Disease: A Study in Ethnopsychiatry* (Geneva: World Health Organization, 1953).

13 Hountondji, *African Philosophy: Myth and Reality*, 84.

14 Hountondji, *African Philosophy*, 107.

15 Marcien Towa, *Essai sur la problématique philosophique dans l'Afrique actuelle*, 25–26.

16 Clarence E. Walker, *We Can't Go Home Again: An Argument about Afrocentrism* (Oxford, UK: Oxford University Press, 2001). Despite an otherwise convincing critique, the absence of empathy and understanding of the politico-existential sources of the Afro-centrist project (which is a North American variant of sub-Saharan ethnophilosophy) ensnares Clarence Walker in a confrontation he cannot see past.

17 Achille Mbembe, *De La Postcolonie*, XI.

18 Anthony Mangeon, *La Pensée noire et l'Occident* (Paris: Sulliver, 2010), 103.

19 Hountondji, *African Philosophy: Myth and Reality*, 154. A bit later, he speaks of the Althusserian idea of a "class struggle in theory." But this is only to shoot it down as he mocks Althusser's disciples of self-critique who put him on trial for his "theoretical abstractions" in the 60s. But whether he followed or resisted the Althusser turn is of little importance here. What matters is being attentive to the needs of the African situation, with a deliberate "return to the things themselves" that these needs demand.

20 Gordon, *Disciplinary Decadence*, 69.

21 Kwame Anthony Appiah, *In My Father's House: Africa in the Philosophy of Culture* (Oxford, UK: Oxford University Press, 1992), 106.

22 Eboussi Boulaga, *Muntu in Crisis*, 37.

23 Hountondji, *African Philosophy: Myth and Reality*, 166.

24 Eboussi Boulaga, *Muntu in Crisis*, 77.

25 Ibid., 29. Translation modified.

26 Antonio Gramsci, "L'anti-Croce (cahier 10)," *Textes* (Paris: Éditions Sociales), 1983.

27 Towa, *Essai sur la problématique philosophique dans l'Afrique actuelle*, 75.

28 Eboussi Boulaga, *Muntu in Crisis*, 143.

29 Ibid., 149.

30 Ibid., 170.

31 Ibid., 234.

NOTES TO PAGES 147–154

32 Drucilla Cornell, *Law and Revolution in South Africa: Ubuntu, Dignity and the Struggle for Constitutional Transformation* (New York: Fordham University Press, 2014), 150.

33 "All liberation theology stems from trying to make sense of human suffering when those who suffer are the victims of organized oppression and exploitation, when they are emasculated and treated as less than what they are: human persons created in the image of the Triune God, redeemed by the one Savior Jesus Christ and sanctified by the Holy Paraclete. This is the genesis of all liberation theology and so also of black theology, which is the theology of liberation in Africa. Black theology has occurred mainly in Southern Africa, where blacks have had their noses rubbed in the dust by white racism, depersonalized them to the extent that they have—blasphemy of blasphemies—come to doubt the reality of their own personhood and humanity. They have often come to believe that the denigration of their humanity by those who oppress them is the truth about themselves." Desmond Tutu, "The Theology of Liberation in Africa," in *Philosophy of Religion*, eds. Eleonore Stump & Michael J. Murray (Malden, MA/Oxford, UK: Blackwell Publishers, 1999), 258.

34 Desmond Tutu, *God has a Dream: A Vision of Hope for Our Time* (New York: Image, 2005), 25–26. Tutu's emphasis.

35 Ibid., 38.

36 Michael Battle, *Ubuntu: I in you and you in me* (New York: Seabury Books, 2009), 25.

37 Kant, *Practical Philosophy*, 55.

38 Tutu, *God Has a Dream*, 78. Tutu seems here to be giving a literal reading of Kant, and there is strong reason that Tutu is drawing directly on him. But, by failing to make any mention of law while speaking about the relational character of ubuntu, he is, perhaps unwittingly, marking a significant departure from Kant.

39 Eboussi Boulaga, *Christianity without Fetishes*, 114.

40 Tutu, *God Has a Dream*, 97.

41 Cone, *Black Theology and Black Power*, 53.

42 Cone, *God of the Oppressed*, 135–136.

43 Tutu, *God Has a Dream*, 36–37.

44 Kora Andrieu, *La Justice transitionnelle. De l'Afrique du Sud au Rwanda* (Paris: Gallimard, coll. "Folio"), 2012, 233–234.

45 Michael Battle, *Reconciliation: The Ubuntu Theology of Desmond Tutu* (Cleveland: The Pilgrim Press, 1997).

46 Desmond Tutu (ed.), *Amnistier l'apartheid. Travaux de la Commission Vérité et Réconciliation*, trans. Sylvie Courtine-Demany, Charlotte Girard, Philippe-Joseph Salazar (Paris: Seuil, 2004), 171.

47 Tutu, *God Has a Dream*, 53.

48 Desmond Tutu, *No Future without Forgiveness* (New York: Doubleday, 1999), 54–55.

49 Cornell, *Law and Revolution in South Africa*, 112.

50 Souleymane Bachir Diagne, "Philosophie africaine et Charte africaine des droits des hommes et des peoples," *Critique*, n° 771–772, 670–671.

51 Julius K. Nyerere, *Socialisme, démocratie et unité africaine* suivi de *La Déclaration d'Arusha*, trans. Jean Mfoulou (Paris: Présence Africaine, 1970), 27.

NOTES TO PAGES 155–161

52 Eboussi Boulaga, *Muntu in Crisis*, 9.
53 Margaux Schild, "En Afrique du Sud, les attaques contre les fermiers blancs ravivent les tensions raciales," *Paris Match Belgique*, 8 March 2017 (available at https://parismatch.be/actualites/societe/15392/afrique-du-sud -fermiers-blancs-apartheid).
54 Jean Comaroff & John Comaroff, *Theory from the South*, 36–37.
55 Leslie London, "The 'dop' system, alcohol abuse and social control amongst farm workers in South Africa: a public health challenge," *Social Science & Medicine*, vol. 48, n° 10, 1999, 1407–1414.

Part 3: Forms-of-death in the European Necropolis

1 Original lyrics: Leur haine envers nous est omniprésente / Comment oublier tout ce qu'on représente? La voix du Négro vient du bloc / Je suis le bébé de ma mère, un oubli de mon père / Un enfant issu de l'immigration / Je ne suis pas communautaire / Mais autour de moi tout est sombre, des tours de béton à la population / Ça vend la mort juste en bas de la maison, des fan-tômes hantent le tiekson / La hass prend le dessus sur ma vision / Les représentants de la nation parlent de nous / qu'en période d'élection / Iblis es ten constante érection / Je vis la mélodie de cette malediction.

Chapter 7: Recognition and Dignity

1 Patrick Capps, *Human Dignity and the Foundations of International Law* (Oxford, UK/Portland, OR: Hart Publishing, 2009), 82.
2 Bruno Latour, *Down to Earth: Politics in the New Climatic Regime*, trans. Catherine Porter (Cambridge, UK: Polity Press, 2017), 1.
3 Étienne Balibar, "Racism and Crisis" (1985), in Étienne Balibar & Immanuel Wallerstein, *Race, Nation, Class: Ambiguous Identities*, trans. Chris Turner (New York: Verso, 1991).
4 For the Puerto Rican sociologist Ramon Grosfoguel, the coloniality of power "refers to a crucial structuring process in the modern/colonial world-system that articulates peripheral locations in the international division of labor with the global racial/ethnic hierarchy and Third World migrants' inscription in the racial/ethnic hierarchy of metropolitan global cities." Ramon Grosfoguel, "The Epistemic Decolonial Turn: Beyond Political-Economy Paradigms," *Cultural Studies*, vol. 21, n° 2–3, 2007, 219–220.
5 Sabelo J. Ndlovu-Gatsheni, *Coloniality of Power in Postcolonial Africa: Myths of Decolonization* (Dakar: CODESRIA, 2013), x.
6 William Reno, *Warlord Politics and African States* (Boulder, CO/London: Lynne Rienner Publishing, 1998), 35.
7 Ferguson, *Global Shadows*, 23.
8 "Some private companies lobby in a thinly veiled way for mining operations, including diamond mining and oil extraction, in unstable countries. This was the case in the 1990s in countries such as Sierra Leone, Angola, or the Democratic Republic of Congo (formerly Zaire). These countries' involvement in the immoral and murky game of some multinationals only serves to prolong the conflicts plaguing each country." Pascal Le Pautremat,

219

NOTES TO PAGES 161–166

"Mercenariat et sociétés militaires privées: expressions divergentes de la privatisation des conflits?", *Inflexions*, n° 5, 2005, 144.

9 Ferguson, *Global Shadows*, 203–204.

10 Staatsprojekt Europa, *L'Europe des flux. Migrations, travail et crise de l'Union Européenne* (Paris: Eterotopia France, 2017), 35.

11 Lucia Le Maquis, *Nous ne ferons pas marche a rière! Luttes contres la frontière franco-italienne à Vintimille 2015–2017* (Le Mas D'Azil Niet! Éditions, 2017), 27.

12 Judith Butler & Athena Athanasiou, *Dispossession: The Performance in the Political* (Cambridge, UK: Polity Press, 2013), 167.

13 Étienne Balibar, *Droit de cité* (Paris: PUF, 2002), 36–37.

14 Bertrand Ogilvie, *L'Homme jetable. Essai sur l'exterminisme et la violence extreme* (Paris: Éditions Amsterdam, 2012), 73–74.

15 Babels, *De Lesbos à alais: Comment l'Europe fabrique des camps* (Neuvy-en-Champagne, Le Passager Clandestin, 2017), 62.

16 Angela Davis, *Freedom is a Constant Struggle: Ferguson, Palestine, and the Foundations of a Movement* (Chicago: Haymarket Books, 2016), 57.

17 Jade Lingaar, "Ghassan Hage: 'Les réfugiés sont traités comme des déchets non recyclables,'" Mediapart.fr, 23 octobre 2017 (available at https://www.mediapart.fr/journal/culture-idees/231017/ghassan-hage-les-refugies-sont-traites-comme-des-dechets-non-recyclables).

18 Ghassan Hage, *Is Racism an Environmental Threat?* (London: Polity, 2017), 50.

19 Vitally Lubin, "Libye, Mauritanie, partout dans le monde... Stop à l'esclavage des Noirs," *Negus*, n° 4, December 2017, 9–10.

20 Alex Panzani, *Une prison clandestine de la police française (Arenc)*. (Paris: Maspero, 1975).

21 Babels, *De Lesbos à Calais*, 46.

22 Francesco Fistetti, *Théories du multiculturalisme. Un parcours entre philosophie et sciences sociales* (2008), trans. Philippe Chanial & Marilisa Preziosi (Paris: La Découverte, 2009), 14–15; Haud Guégue & Guillaume Maloche, *Les Théories de la reconnaissance* (Paris: La Découverte, 2014); Didier Fassin, *Life: A Critical User's Manual* (Cambridge, UK/Medford, MA: Polity Press, 2018).

23 Glen Sean Coulthard, *Red Skin, White Masks: Rejecting the Colonial Politics of Recognition* (Minneapolis/London: University of Minnesota Press, 2014), 17. Coulthard's emphasis.

24 Charles Taylor, "The Politics of Recognition," in *Multiculturalism: Examining the Politics of Recognition*, ed. Amy Gutmann, (Princeton, NJ: Princeton University Press, 1994), 25.

25 Honneth supports the idea that recognition is inherently positive on several occasions, such as when he argues that it is a matter of "turning in an affirmative manner toward the existence of the other person or other group" while remaining impartial. This definition, which arbitrarily decrees the essentially positive nature of recognition, seeks to preclude any analysis of the negative side of recognition. It is naïve to ignore that all concepts, including that of dignity, have a dark side. Nowhere does the two-sided nature of recognition appear more clearly than in the ἀναγνώρισις (*anagnorésis*), or recognition in Aristotelian theater, where love and hate swap positions. Honneth cannot avoid this problem by evoking the specificity of the German term

NOTES TO PAGES 166–172

"anerkennung," which is less ambiguous than the French or English term. Even if the term "recognition" was replaced by a more unambiguously positive term, the asymmetry Fanon has called attention to remains. Axel Honneth, "La reconnaissance comme idéologie" (2004), *La Société du mépris. Vers une nouvelle théorie critique*, trans. Olivier Voirol, Pierre Rusch & Alexandre Dupeyrix (Paris: La Découverte, 2008), 253.

26 Fanon, *Black Skin, White Masks*, 89. My emphasis.
27 Ibid., 89–90.
28 Ibid., 92.
29 Ibid., 94.
30 Ibid., 95.
31 Emmanuel Renault, *The Experience of Injustice: A Theory of Recognition*, trans. Richard A. Lynch (New York: Columbia University Press, 2019), xvii.
32 Maldonado-Torres, *Against War*, 129.
33 Axel Honneth, *The Pathologies of Individual Freedom: Hegel's Social Theory*, trans. Ladislaus Löb (Princeton, NJ: Princeton University Press, 2010), 44. Translation modified.
34 Axel Honneth, "Invisibility: On the Epistemology of 'Recognition,'" trans. Maeve Cooke & Jeff Seitzer, *Proceedings of the Aristotelian Society, Supplementary Volumes*, vol. 75 (2001), 111.
35 Ibid., 126.
36 Axel Honneth, *The Struggle for Recognition: The Moral Grammar of Social Conflicts*, trans. Joel Anderson (Cambridge, MA: MIT Press, 1996), 145.
37 Kierkegaard, *Fear and Trembling*, 46.
38 Honneth, *The Pathologies of Individual Freedom: Hegel's Social Theory*.
39 Honneth, *The Struggle for Recognition: The Moral Grammar of Social Conflicts*, 58–59. I think Honneth is deceiving himself when he calls his own theory "post-traditional."
40 Louis Carré, *Axel Honneth: Le droit de la reconnaissance* (Paris: Michalon, 2013), 37.
41 Honneth, "La reconnaissance comme idéologie," 249–250.
42 Aimé Césaire, *A Tempest*, trans. Richard Miller (New York: Ubu Repertory Theater Publications, 1992), 21.
43 Fanon, *Black Skin, White Masks*, 196.
44 Louis Carré, *Axel Honneth*, 102.
45 "If, however, we have a certain propensity to insist on this point, it is in reality because we wish, in the case of Nazism, to mark our suspicion and scepticism [*sic*] of the hasty, crude, and usually blind accusation of *irrationality*. There is, on the contrary, a *logic of fascism*. This also means that a *certain logic is fascist*, and that this logic is not wholly foreign to the general logic of rationality inherent in the metaphysics of the Subject." Philippe Lacoue-Labarthe & Jean-Luc Nancy, "The Nazi Myth," trans. Brian Holme, *Critical Inquiry*, vol. 16, no. 2, 1990, 294. Lacoue-Labarthe's and Nancy's emphasis. Slavoj Žižek takes a very different approach to make a similar argument about the intrinsic rationality of totalitarianism, emphasizing the parallel between Stalin's form of governance and Kant's practical reason. Slavoj Žižek, *Did Somebody Say Totalitarianism? Five Interventions in the (Mis)Use of a Notion* (London/New York: Verso, 2002).
46 Achille Mbembe, *Critique of Black Reason*, trans. Laurent Dubois (Durham, NC: Duke University Press, 2017), 119.

NOTES TO PAGES 172–175

47 Lewis R. Gordon, "Fanon on Decolonizing Knowledge," in *Fanon and the Decolonization of Philosophy*, eds. Elizabeth A. Hoppe & Tracey Nicholls (Lanham, MA: Lexington Books, 2010).

48 Fanon, *Black Skin, White Masks*, 199.

49 Lewis R. Gordon, *Fanon and the Crisis of European Man* (New York/London: Routledge, 1995), 23; Gordon, *Disciplinary decadence*.

50 Alain de Benoist, *Le Moment populiste* (Paris: Pierre Guillaume de Roux, 2017), 14.

51 Fanon is skillfully playing with two meanings of the term "comparison" here in two languages. First, in French, he is following Rousseau's lead, as described in the *Second Discourse*: "If this were the place to go into details, I could easily show how, even without the Government's intervention, inequality of prestige and authority becomes inevitable among Private Individuals as soon as, united in one Society, they are forced to compare themselves one with the other and, in the continual use they have to make of one another, to take account of the differences they find. [...] I would show how much this universal desire for reputation, honors, and preferment which consumes us all exercises and compares talents and strengths, how much it excites and multiplies the passions and, in making all men competitors, rivals, or enemies, how many reverses, how many successes, how many catastrophes of every kind it daily causes by leading so many Contenders to enter the same lists [...]."Jean-Jacques Rousseau, *'The Discourses' and Other Political Writings*, trans. Victor Courevitch (Cambridge: Cambridge University Press, 1997), 183–184. The second meaning, unique to West Indian Creole, was pointed out to me by the Guadeloupean playwright Gerty Dambury: "to be 'comparison' in Creole is to a certain extent to find yourself where you shouldn't be, to get caught up in something that doesn't concern you. We also have an expression: 'comparison as salted cod tail', cod being what black people added to their meals that were lacking a bit of 'flesh' as we say in Creole ('flesh' being meat or fish...). Not having the means to purchase meat, people kept dry and salted cod tail to season vegetables, which means that cod tail ended up everywhere, including being added to food where it didn't belong. Comparison, 'rantra', all these words signal then that fact that you are forcing yourself to be in a place where you are neither expected or welcome (which fits with Fanon's definition: black people seeking recognition)." Gerty Dambury, email to author, March 9, 2019.

52 Fanon, *Black Skin, White Masks*, 185–186.

53 Axel Honneth, "A Social Pathology of Reason: On the Intellectual Legacy of Critical Theory," trans. James Hebbler, in *Pathologies of Reason: On the Legacy of Critical Theory* (New York: Columbia University Press, 2009), 41.

54 Georg Lukacs, *History and Class Consciousness: Studies in Marxist Dialectics*, trans. Rodney Livingstone (Cambridge, MA: The MIT Press, 1971), 86–87.

55 Fanon, *Black Skin, White Masks*, 190.

56 Judith Butler, *Subjects of Desire: Hegelian Reflections in Twentieth-Century France* (New York: Columbia University Press, 2012), 110.

57 This same conclusion could be drawn from the introduction to Hegel's *The Phenomenology of Spirit*, as Jean-Clet Martin has shown: "I can,

NOTES TO PAGES 175–182

for instance, simply classify all the buds of the apple genus and describe their characteristics as opposed to pear trees. They are certainly not the same flowers; their respective charts do not entirely align. But this exterior difference neither defines an apple or a pear tree. It doesn't account for the way a bud becomes a flower, then becomes a fruit whose seeds open for the future tree that will shatter them. In the first case, we are dealing with a simple difference of comparison: that between apples and pears, differences between classes or species. Hegel is more interested in studying the bud and noting internal differences, the occasionally violent transition as it becomes a flower and, then, a fruit capable of replacing it." Jean-Clet Martin, *Une Intrigue criminelle de la philosophie. Lire la* Phénoménologie de l'Esprit *de Hegel* (Paris: La Découverte, 2009), 25.

58 Fanon, *Black Skin, White Masks*, 132. Translation modified.

59 Carré, *Axel Honneth*, 111–113.

60 Fanon, *Toward the African Revolution*, 3.

61 "If there is something to forgive, it would by what is called in religious discourse the mortal sin, the worst, most unforgivable crime or wrongdoing. Hence the aporia that can be described in its dry and implacable formality, in its mercilessness: forgiveness only forgives the unforgivable. One can or should forgive, there is only forgiveness, if forgiveness is possible, at the site of encounter with the unforgivable." Jacques Derrida, *Foi et Savoir* suivi de *Le Siècle et le Pardon* (Paris: Seuil, 2000), 108.

62 Fanon, *Black Skin, White Masks*, 197.

63 Ibid., 195–196.

64 Ibid., 191.

65 Alexandre Kojève, *Introduction to the Reading of Hegel*, trans. James H. Nichols Jr (Ithaca/London: Cornell University Press, 1969), 9.

66 Michel Agier, *Les Migrants et nous. Comprendre Babel* (Paris: CNRS Éditions, 2016), 15.

67 Fanon, *The Wretched of the Earth*, 139.

68 Ibid., 144.

69 Étienne Balibar, *La Proposition de l'égaliberté* (Paris: PUF, 2010).

70 Fanon, *The Wretched of the Earth*, 139.

71 Aimé Césaire, *Discourse on Colonialism*, trans. Joan Pinkham (New York: Monthly Review Press, 2001), 70.

72 Fassin, *Life: A Critical User's Manual*, 78.

73 Thomas Lindemann & Julie Saada, "Théories de la reconnaissance dans les relations internationales. Enjeux symboliques et limites du paradigme de l'intérêt," *Cultures & Conflits*, n° 87, 2012, 7–25.

74 Robert H. Jackson & Carl G. Rosberg, "Why Africa's Weak States Persist: The Empirical and the Juridical Statehood," *World Politics*, vol. 35, n° 1, 1982, 1–24.

75 Fanon, *Black Skin, White Masks*, 201.

76 Aimé Césaire, *Toussaint Louverture: la Révolution française et le problème colonial* (Paris: Présence Africaine, 1981), 228.

77 Louis-Georges Tin, *Esclavage et Réparations. Comment faire face aux crimes de l'histoire* (Paris: Stock, 2013), 19.

78 Ibid., 20.

79 Michelle Alexander, *The New Jim Crow: Mass Incarceration in the Age of Colorblindness* (New York: The New Press, 2010).

NOTES TO PAGES 183–191

Conclusion

1 Aimé Césaire, *Discours sur le colonialisme* followed by *Discours sur la négritude*, p. 81.
2 Frank B. Wilderson, *Red, White & Black.*
3 Rediker, *The Slave Ship: A Human History*, 43.
4 Élise Fontanaille-N'Diaye, *Blue Book* (Paris, Calmann-Lévy, 2015), 135.
5 Léonora Miano, "Noire hémoglobine," in Léonora Miano (ed.), *Marianne et le garçon noir* (Paris: Pauvert, 2017), 11–12.
6 The term first appeared with its current theoretical acceptation in 2003 in a conversation between Frank Wilderson and Saidiya Hartman. Hartman used it to refer to a set of conditions shared by Black North Americans and Black Africans. Saidiya V. Hartman & Frank B. Wilderson, "The Position of the Unthought," *Qui Parle?*, vol. 13, n° 2, 197.
7 Greg Thomas, "Afro-Blue Notes: The Death of Afro-pessimism (2.0)?", *Theory & Event*, vol. 21, n° 1, 2018, 282–317. A similar critique can be found, in a more anecdotal mode, in Annie Olaloku-Teriba, "Afro-pessimism and the (un)Logic of Blackness," *Historical Materialism*, vol. 26, n° 2, 2018 [online].
8 Ibid., 307.
9 Ibid., 308.
10 Frank B. Wilderson, "Blacks and the Master/Slave Relation," 20–21.
11 Aimé Césaire, *Toussaint Louverture*, 33.
12 Mario Blaser, "Political Ontology," *Cultural Studies*, vol. 25, n° 5, 2009, 879.
13 Louis Sala-Molins, *Le Code Noir ou le calvaire de Canaan* (Paris: PUF, 2007), 241.
14 Christina Sharpe, *In the Wake: On Blackness and Being* (Durham, NC: Duke University Press), 2016, 74.
15 Orlando Patterson, *Slavery and Social death*, 38.
16 Claude Meillassoux, *The Anthropology of Slavery: The Womb of Iron and Gold*, trans. Alide Dasnois (London: The Athlone Press, 1991), 106–107. Meillassoux's emphasis.
17 Ibid., 112. Meillassoux's emphasis.
18 Orlando Patterson, *Slavery and Social Death*, 3.
19 Wilderson, *Red, White & Black*, 54–55.
20 Wilderson, "Blacks and the Master/Slave Relation," 30.
21 R. A. Judy, "For Dignity: Tunisia and the Poetry of Emergent Democratic Humanism," *boundary 2*, vol. 39, n° 1, 2012, 12. See also Mohamed-Salah Omri, "A Revolution of Dignity and Poetry," *boundary 2*, vol. 39, n° 1, 2012, 137–165.
22 Ahmet Insel, "Quand l'identité victimaire renforce la violence et menace la civilité," in Étienne Balibar et al., *Violence, civilité, révolution. Autour d'Étienne Balibar* (Paris: La Dispute), 2015, 161. (https://www.researchgate.net/publication/350604891_When_victime_identity_reinforces_violence_and_threatens_civility)
23 Ibid., 175–176.
24 Ibid., 179.
25 Elsa Dorlin, *Se Défendre. Une philosophie de la violence* (Paris: La Découverte, coll. Zones), 2017.

NOTES TO PAGES 191–199

26 David Marriot, *Haunted Life: Visual Culture and Black Modernity* (New Brunswick, NJ: Rutgers University Press, 2007), 2.
27 Butler & Athanasiou, *Dispossession: The Performance in the Political*, 196.
28 Fanon, *Black Skin, White Masks*, 199.
29 Michaël Béchir Ayari, "The People's Revolution: The Shifting Terrain of Politics. From the Ills of Poverty to the Will to 'Dignity': the Tunisian Revolution of January 2011," trans. JPD Systems, *Revue Tiers Monde*, n° 5 HS, 2011, 211. See also Michaël Béchir Ayari, "Non, les révolutions tunisienne et égyptienne ne sont pas des 'révolutions 2.0,'" *Mouvements*, n° 66, 2011, 56–61.
30 Janet Abu-Lughod, *Race, Space and Riots in Chicago, New York and Los Angeles* (Oxford, UK: Oxford University Press, 2007), 199.
31 Guy Debord, "Le déclin et la chute de l'économie spectaculaire-marchande" (1965), *Œuvres* (Paris: Gallimard, coll. "Quarto"), 2006, 703. Debord's emphasis.
32 Hartman, *Scenes of Subjection*, 18.
33 Guy Debord, "Le déclin et la chute de l'économie spectaculaire-marchande," 704. Debord's emphasis.
34 Ibid.
35 Joshua Clover, *Riot. Strike. Riot. The New Era of Uprisings* (London: Verso, 2016).
36 Judith Butler, *Notes Toward a Performative Theory of Assembly* (Cambridge, MA/London: Harvard University Press, 2015), 160.
37 Guy Debord, "Le commencement d'une époque" (1969), *Œuvres*, 918.
38 Ibid., 919.
39 Alain Badiou, *Le Réveil de l'histoire. Circonstances 6* (Paris: Lignes, 2011).
40 James Baldwin, *The Fire Next Time* (New York: Vintage Books, 1993), 98–99.
41 Wilfried N'Sondé, *The Heart of the Leopard Children*, trans. Karen Lindo (Bloomington/Indianapolis: Indiana University Press, 2016), 7.
42 Hartman, *Scenes of Subjection*, 73–74.
43 N'Sondé, *The Heart of the Leopard Children*, 77.
44 Kader Attia, *Repair* (Paris: Blackjack éditions, 2014). Attia's fascinating 2016 documentary "Reflecting Memory" draws a parallel between the themes of haunting and reparation. Essentially, any reparation implies two hauntings: that of the situation before the rupture (the origin) and that of the situation of the reparation (the destroyed being).

INDEX

Adler, Alfred 12
Adorno, Theodore 102, 105, 168
Adotevi, Stanislas 140
Africa
  Bantu conception of dignity 112
  and Black political ontology 185
  colonialism, and "useful" and
    "useless" Africa 160–161,
    162, 164
  genocide in Southwest Africa 184
  neocolonial land enclosures 161
  pan-African revolutionaries 182
  religious practices 136
  sovereignty and African states 180
  structural adjustment programs 63
African Americans
  civil rights movement 15, 124–126
  and dignity 71–72
  and the Jim Crow laws 182
  music 114–120
  see also Black liberation theology;
    slavery
African philosophy 15–16, 136–156
  and colonialism 136–137
  ethnophilosophy 139–145
  Muntu 146–147, 154, 155
  and pluralism 144–145
  tradition in 146–147
  unanimity 140–141, 144–145
  and Western philosophy 138–139
  see also ubuntu
Africana studies 4, 10, 12
AfriForum 156

Afro-decolonial philosophy 6, 11–12,
    38, 39
  and asymmetric recognition 170
  critique of Habermas 36
  critique of Kant 30, 34
  and dignity 7, 8–9, 44, 45,
    109–112
  and essence 81
  and indignity 56
Afro-Prophetism 126–131
  community-centered position 127
  dialectical position 127–128
  minority position 126–127
Afrocentrism 142
Afropessimism 16–18, 71, 185
Agamben, Giorgio 14, 23–24, 27, 29,
    48, 57, 186
  and African philosophy 138
  conceptions of life and death 58
  on Franciscan theology 129
agency and essence 80
Agier, Michel 177–178
Algeria 78, 112
alienation
  and asymmetric recognition 173
Althusser, Louis 131–132, 133
American Indians see Native
    Americans
Americas, conquest and colonization
    4–5, 22, 48, 50, 80
  and slavery 6–7
Amery, Jean 57, 105–106, 195
Amselle, Jean-Loup 138

226

INDEX

Andrews, Kehinde 77
Angola 161
anti-dialectical philosophy 98
anti-essentialism 11
anticolonial movements 21
antiracism 1, 3, 21
antisemitism 97
Appiah, Kwame Anthony 143
appropriation and dignity 13
Arendt, Hannah
  on dignity 13, 47, 48, 50, 51
  and racism 40–41, 48–50, 53
Armstrong, Louis 134
Asad, Talal 92, 95
Aspe, Bernard 129
assimilation
and asymmetric recognition 172–173
  and Negritude 74
  asymmetric recognition 166,
    168–176
Attia, Kader 199
Augustine, St. 52
Auschwitz 48–49, 106
autobiography *see* slave narratives
autonomy and dignity 13, 22, 26,
    27–30

Bachelard, Gaston 141
Back-to-Africa movement 9
Badiou, Alain 15, 96–97, 98–100,
    101, 102, 103, 105, 106, 131,
    195
Baldwin, James 102, 197
Balibar, Étienne 15, 77–78, 80,
    104–105, 108, 178
  on migration policy 162
Baraka, Amiri 115
barbarism 106
Baudrillard, Jean 116
Ben Ali, Zine el-Abidine 190
Benjamin, Walter 48, 49
Bhabha, Homi 83–84
Biko, Steve 59, 60, 69, 70, 79, 89,
    107, 112
biopolitics 55, 57, 58
birth
  and Black political ontology
    186–189
Black bodies
  and lynchings 130

and modernity 183
and slavery 117–119, 189
Black dignity 17–18, 192–200
  battlefield metaphor for 196
  and death 17, 198–200
  and race riots 193–195
  and the Tunisian Revolution
    192–193
Black essence 77, 79–80
Black Europeans
  double consciousness of 45
Black liberation theology 109, 112,
    113–114, 120–136, 154
  Afro-Prophetism 126–131
  and Black political ontology 185
  the call of dignity 131–136
  and prophetic interpellation
    132–135
Black Lives Matter 1, 107–108
Black men
  Habermas on 36
  religion and the free Black man 46
Black nationalism 9, 10, 11, 12
Black Panthers 8, 10
Black political ontology 17, 184–190,
    195, 198
Black power
  dignity as 85
  politicization of 68–69
Black Power movement 15, 126
bodies *see* Black bodies
Bolk, Louis 27
border controls
  and migration policy 161–162
Bourcier, Sam 84
Brown, Michael 33–34, 36, 64
Bultmann, Rudolf 97
Butler, Judith 11, 104, 109, 161, 186,
    194–195

Cabral, Amílcar 182
Canguilhem, Georges 141
Capicia, Mayotte 12
capitalism
  and Black slavery 183–184
  and the migrant crisis 159, 162
Cavarero, Adriana 47–48, 49–50, 51,
    52, 53
Césaire, Aimé 79, 181
  A Tempest 90, 171

227

INDEX

Césaire, Aimé (*cont.*)
　on African American religion 130
　and Black political ontology 185
　Discourse on Colonialism 51, 179
　and Negritude 67, 72, 73–76, 77, 90, 104, 183
Charles X, King of France 181–182
Chauvin, Sébastien 2
Chenu, Bruno 120, 121, 122
China 136
Christian University Movement (South Africa) 89
Christianity 15, 99–101, 113–114
　and African religion 121
　the Bible 113, 123
　　Abraham's sacrifice 132–134
　　and the call of dignity 131–136
　Christian eschatology 58, 119–120
　Constantinian Christianity 90–91, 95–96
　and ethnophilosophy 139
　and love 149–152
　materialist Christology 129, 131
　and Paul the Apostle 96–101, 105
　Pentecostalism 124
　prophetic 90, 93–94, 125
　　Afro-Prophetism 126–31
　and slavery 93–94, 99, 100–101, 113–114, 120–123, 125
　　the conversion of slaves 122
　in South Africa 89
　and ubuntu 148–152
　urban churches 123–124
　and White theology 121–122, 124–125
　see also Black liberation theology; Jesus Christ; political theology
citizenship
　and recognition theory 165
　sovereignty and dignity 179
civil rights movement 15, 124–126
civil society and individuals 133
class
　and Negritude 73
　and race 10
clericalism 92–93, 94, 96
Clover, Joshua 194, 195
colonialism
　and African philosophy 136–137, 143, 145

　and asymmetric recognition 172
　and the Black Code 194
　and Black life as a form-of-death 198
　and Black political ontology 189
　colonial racism 55–56
　and genocide 56, 184
　the hidden horror of 46–54
　and Negritude 74, 75
　and violence 74, 136
coloniality and racism 61
Comaroff, Jean and John 44
communism
　and Christianity 97, 98
　Eurocentric 103
communitarianism 98
comparison
　and asymmetric recognition 175
Cone, James H. 7, 15, 69, 89, 112, 147, 171
　and Black liberation theology 113, 124–126, 126, 129–130, 134–135, 136
　on Black music 114–115, 119, 120
　on dignity 71–72, 80, 150, 151
　on the ethics of Black slaves 83
　on the politics of the resurrection 100–101
Conrad, Joseph 49, 50
Constantinian Christianity 90–91, 95–96
constructivism 11
continental philosophy 12
Cornell, Drucilla 147, 148, 154
Coulthard, Glen Sean
　Red Skin, White Masks 165
creolization 11
critical theory 2, 4, 11–12
　and Black liberation theology 129
　and secularism 96
Cugoano, Ottobah 22, 41–42, 43, 45, 49, 50–51, 53–54, 60
　and the power of the negative 102–103
　and prophetic Christianity 93–94

Davis, Angela 163
Davis, Charles T. 46
death
　and Black dignity 17, 198–200

228

INDEX

and Black theology 100
and life, and Black dignity 17
and necropolitics 14, 58–59, 75
social death and slavery 17,
187–190
Debord, Guy 193–195
decolonial essentialism 84
decolonization politics 1
decolonizing moral philosophy 12–13
deconstruction 2, 12, 14, 82–85
deep historicity of dignity 14, 67,
76–82, 95, 107, 108, 197
dehumanization
and African philosophy 142, 143
and Black music 115
and dignity 9, 13, 17, 38, 150,
177, 195
and slavery 40, 50
Delacroix, Vincent 93
Delany, Martin 11
Deleuze, Gilles 2, 41, 84, 126, 136
deliberative democracy 21
Derrida, Jacques 2, 11, 78, 82, 83,
84, 167, 176
Descartes, René 74
Dessalines, Jean-Jacques 181
diasporic consciousness 80
Diderot, Denis 5
difference, politics of 85
dignity 65–85
Bantu conception of 112
as Black power 85
critical history of 12–13, 21–39
Habermas 13, 21, 22, 34–38, 39
humanism 24–27
Kant 13, 21, 22, 27–34
premodern 23–24, 29
and deconstruction 14, 82–5
deep historicity of 14, 67, 76–82,
95, 107, 108, 197
demands of 65–67
ethics of 7–9, 15, 70
and freedom 66, 70, 95
and indignity 39, 65, 196, 197
light dignity 192–193, 195
and love 149–152
and Negritude 14, 67, 72–76
and the politics of recognition 16
and prophetic interpellation
132–135

and secularism 94–95
shades of 190–195
sovereigndignity 16, 176–182
the struggle of 67–72
and ubuntu 15–16, 147–155
and universality 109–112
Diop, Cheikh Anta 185
Doctors Without Borders 163
Doray, Bernard 111
Dorlin, Elsa 191
Douglass, Frederick 31
Du Bois, W.E.B. 45–46, 62, 79, 100,
115, 121, 185
Dussel, Enrique 4, 5, 6, 92, 102

Eboussi Boulaga, Fabien 15, 58,
73, 81, 138–139, 143–144,
145–147, 155, 185
and the hermeneutics of Muntu
146–147
on love 149
electoral politics
in the Global North 135
Ellison, Ralph 169
empty signifiers (Laclau) 66, 70
epistemological point zero 42–43, 44,
81–82
equality and dignity 66, 70, 171
Equiano, Olaudah 22, 44–45, 49,
53–54, 60
Esposito, Roberto 14, 57
essentialism
anti-essentialism 14, 84, 85
decolonial 84
and deep historicity 76–81
ethical conflicts
and dignity 36–38
ethno-relativist discourse 81–82
ethnophilosophy 139–145
unanimous hypothesis 140–141
Etoke, Nathalie 80
Eurocentrism 34, 57, 80, 84, 103
and death 100
and universality 108, 172
European nation-state
and secularism 95

Fanon, Frantz 31, 34, 49, 57, 62, 64,
69, 79
and Black political ontology 185

229

INDEX

Fanon, Frantz (*cont.*)
  Black Skin, White Masks 1, 12, 40,
    60, 166–167, 181, 192
  on dignity and love 150
  A Dying Colonialism 61, 75, 81
  on ethno-relativism 81–82
  on French Algeria 78
  and Negritude 14, 73
  "The North African Syndrome"
    176
  on the politics of essence 77
  and recognition theory 16,
    165–167, 169, 170–171, 173,
    174, 175–176, 177
  on sovereignty and dignity 178,
    179–180, 182
  on universality 111–112
  The Wretched of the Earth 30, 75,
    178
fascism 172
Fassin, Didier 179
Federici, Silvia 90
feminism 9–10, 191
Fiat, Éric 29
films about slavery 116–117
Fischer, Eugen 184
fixation 165–168
Floyd, George 1, 36
Foucault, Michel 2, 11, 13, 57, 84
  on racism 40–41, 55–57
France
  colonialism and "useful" and
    "useless" Africa 160–161,
    162
  May '68 protests in Paris
    194–195
  refugees 163
freedom
  and Black theology 100–101
  and dignity 66, 70, 95
French Revolution 101
Freud, Sigmund 12
Frontex 161

Garvey, Marcus 7, 11
Gates, Henry Louis 46
gender
  and patriarchal violence 191–192
  and racism 9–10
  see also women

genocide 13, 50, 55, 56, 57, 58, 64
German Enlightenment 21
Germany
  colonialism and genocide in
    Southwest Africa 184
  Nazism (National Socialism) 13,
    48–49, 101–102, 184
Gilroy, Paul 11, 45, 114
Global North 21, 43, 44, 61,
    160–161
  and asymmetric recognition 176
  post-political society 135
  and refugees 163–164
  and sovereignty 180
Global South 43, 44
  and African philosophy 138
  and asymmetric recognition 176
  migration 160, 161, 164
"Go Down Moses" (spiritual) 134
Gordon, Lewis 6, 12, 143, 173
Gramsci, Antonio 145
Gray, Thomas 51, 52
Guattari, Félix 126, 136
Guevara, Ernesto 112

Habermas, Jürgen 13, 21, 22, 34–38,
    39, 154, 196
Hage, Ghassan 163
Haider, Asad
  *Mistaken Identity: Race and Class
    in the Age of Trump* 11
Haitian revolution 71, 181–182
Haitian society, racism in 185
Hall, Stuart 11
Hamilton, Charles 6
Harlem Renaissance 104
Harlem riots 69, 71
Hartman, Saidiya 71, 116, 118–119,
    194, 198–9
Haywood, Harry 11
Hegel, Georg 5, 12, 54, 104, 133,
    181
  and African philosophy 138
  Phenomenology of the Spirit
    127–128, 169
  and recognition theory 165, 167,
    168–169, 169–170, 174–175
Heidegger, Martin 138
Henry the Navigator, Prince 6
Henry, Paget 90

230

INDEX

historical epistemology 141
history, philosophies of
and African philosophy 138
Hobbes, Thomas 154, 169
Holiday, Billie 120, 124
Holocaust 98, 184
homophobia 106
Honneth, Axel 16, 177, 181, 196
on asymmetric recognition
168–170, 171, 173, 174, 176
and recognition theory 165
hooks, bell
*Ain't I a Woman: Black Women
and Feminism* 9–10
Horkheimer, Max 48, 168
horrorism 47–48, 51–53, 54
Hountondji, Paulin 15, 138, 139,
144, 145
African Philosophy 140–143
Hughes, Langston 7
human neoteny 27, 109–110, 148,
186
human rights
and asymmetric recognition 175
and secularism 95
humanism
African 22, 154–156
and anti-humanism 84
Renaissance conception of dignity
24–27, 34
humanitarianism
and dignity 177–178
Hume, David 31
hybridity 11, 83–84

identity, deconstruction of 83–84
ideology, Althusser on 131–132
IMF (International Monetary Fund)
63, 161, 181
imperialism
and sovereignty 180–181
indigenous people
and recognition theory 165
indignation
as an affirmation of dignity 8–9
indignity 13–14, 39–64
and Black liberation theology 130
and Black music 115–119
and Black political ontology
189–190

and dignity 39, 65, 196, 197
everyday experiences of 59–64
the hidden horror of colonialism
46–54
and insensitivity 50–51, 53–54
and necropolitics 14, 57–59
and power 54–59
and slave narratives 39, 41–46
individuals
and civil society 133
Insel, Ahmet 190–191, 192
insensitivity
and indignity 50–51, 53–54
Islam 78
Israel 63

James, C.L.R. 183
Jefferson, Thomas 134
Jesus Christ
and Black liberation theology
128–130
martyrdom 126
resurrection 99–101, 131
Jews 56, 101–102, 105–106, 184
and Black liberation theology 126,
129
Christianity and Judaism 96–98
justice
and dignity 66
indeconstructibility of 82–83

Kacem, Mehdi Belhaj 100
Kagame, Alexis 139, 142
Kant, Immanuel 5, 13, 21, 22, 37,
44, 109, 111, 169, 196
on autonomy and dignity 27–30,
148
on Black Africans and slavery 22,
30–33, 34
*Groundwork of the Metaphysic of
Morals* 28
on love and moral law 149
*Observations on the Feeling of the
Beautiful and Sublime* 13
"What Is Enlightenment?" 27
Kantorowicz, Ernst 23
Kelley, Robin 64
Khiari, Sadri 85
Kierkegaard, Søren 124, 170
Fear and Trembling 132–134, 134

INDEX

King, Martin Luther 7, 71, 126
kingship and dignity 23
Kojève, Alexandre 177
Kymlicka, Will 165

Lacan, Jacques 11
Laclau, Ernesto 65–66, 70
Lacoue-Labarthe, Philippe 117–118
Lambert, Léopold 63
Las Casas, Bartholomé de 4–5
  History of the Indies 6, 49
Latin America 135
Latour, Bruno 159
legal understandings of dignity
  in Habermas 34–35
Lesbos
  Moria camp 163
liberal democracy
  Habermas on 36, 37
liberal individualism 154–155
liberation theology
  Shiite 112
Libya 180–181
life and death
  and necropolitics 14, 58–59, 75
  and racist fixation 167–168
light dignity 192–193, 195, 196
Lloyd, Vincent 7–8
Louverture, Toussaint 54, 181, 182
love, relational ethics of 149–152
Lukacs, Georg 174
Lumumba, Patrice 11, 19, 182

Macchiavelli, N. 169
Maesschalck, Marc 84
magic
  and *dignitas* 26
Malcolm X 8, 10, 69, 71, 85, 126
Maldonado-Torres, Nelson 168–169
Malian empire 154
Mandela, Nelson 147, 152–153
Mannoni, Octave 12
Maran, René 12
Marcionism 97
Marx, Karl 65–66, 112
Marxism 11, 12, 65–66
  and Negritude 73
materalist Christology 129, 131
Mbembe, Achille 14, 50, 57–58, 172
  "Necropolitics" 57–58

MCD (Modernity/Coloniality/
  Decoloniality) 4–6
Meeropol, Abel 120
Meillassoux, Claude 17, 187–188
memory
  and Black dignity 197, 198–199
  deep historicity of 76, 80–81
  and slave narratives 46–47
  vigilent memory 146
Mengele, Joseph 184
Miano, Léonora 58, 184–185
Mignolo, Walter 43
migration *see* refugees
minority pronouncements 105–106
misogyny 10
modernity
  and African philosophy 136
  and Black dignity 196
  and deep historicity 80, 81
  and racism 13–14, 50
  and secularism 96
  and slave narratives 43
  and theology 89
monasticism 129
morality and dignity
  in Habermas 36–37
  in Kant 29, 32–33
Mouffe, Chantal 65, 135
multiculturalism 16, 160, 164
  and recognition theory 168
Muntu 146–147, 154, 155
music
  Black music 114–120
Mutant, Isaac 155

Namibia 184
Native Americans 4–5, 6, 22, 48, 50,
  54–55, 118
Nazism (National Socialism) 13,
  48–49, 101–102, 184
Ndlovu-Gatsheni, Sebelo 160
necropolitics 14, 16, 57–59, 63, 75,
  173
negativity
  and Black dignity 196–197
  Hegel on 127–128
  politics of 101–103
Negritude 14, 67, 72–76, 77, 90,
  104, 183, 199
  and ethnophilosophy 140

232

INDEX

neoliberalism 135
neoteny 27, 109–110, 148, 186
Newton, Juey
  Revolutionary Suicide 8
Niebuhr, Reinhold 134
nihilism 82
Nkrumah, Kwame 11, 139, 182
N'Sondé, Wilfried
  The Heart of Leopard Children
  198–199
Ntwasa, Sabelo
  Essays in Black Theology 89
Nyerere, Julius 154

Palestinians 55, 56, 63
Panafricanism 9, 11, 12, 76, 79, 185
Parks, Rosa 124, 131
particularity of Black Lives 103–108
Patterson, Orlando 17, 46, 187
Paul the Apostle 96–101, 105
Peele, Jordan 117
Pena-Ruiz, Henri 92, 94–95, 98
Pentecostalism 124
personhood, Kant's conception of
  29–30, 32, 33
Pico della Mirandola, Giovanni 13,
  21–22, 28, 37, 80, 84, 196
  Oration on the Dignity of Man
  24–27
Piolat, Jérémie 74
Plato 142
pluralism 81
  and African philosophy 144–145
point zero epistemology 42–43, 44,
  81–82
police checkpoints 61
police violence 132, 182, 183
  and indignity 63, 64
  murders of Black people 33–34,
  36, 64, 134
political ontology *see* Black political
  ontology
political theology 14–15, 89–103
  Black theology 90, 93–94, 96–103
  clericalism 92–93, 94, 96
  liberation theology 109, 112,
  113–114, 120–136
  the post-political 135
  Prospero as political theologian
  96–103

secularism 14–15, 91–96, 136
  ubuntu 15–16, 139, 147–155
  see also Christianity
political violence 47–49, 59, 172
populism 65–6
postcolonial regimes 160–161
postcolonial theory 12, 83–84
postmodernity 2
poststructuralism 2, 11, 12, 67, 85
power
  colonial power and migration
  159–160
  dignity as Black power 85
  and ethno-relativism 82
  and indignity 54–59
  politicization of 68–70
  and politics 67
  state power and religion 93
precarity 109, 152, 186, 196
prophetic Christianity 90, 93–94, 125
  Afro-Prophetism 126–131
prophetic interpellation 132–135
Prosser, Gabriel 123

Quakers 122

race
  critical theory of 3
  and the migration 159, 164
race riots
  and Black dignity 193–195
  Harlem 69, 71
racial dehumanization *see*
  dehumanization
racial violence
  and indignity 39–40, 50
  and the particular 107
  slave revolts 51–54
racism
  Arendt on 40–41, 48–50
  and asymmetric recognition 171,
  172–173
  and Black political ontology 185
  and colonialism 48–50
  and daily indignity 59–64
  Foucault on 40–41, 55–57
  and gender 9–10
  and modernity 13–14
  racist fixation 166–168
Rancière, Jacques 67–68, 135

233

INDEX

reciprocity
  and recognition theory 170
recognition theory 16, 160, 164–176,
  196
  asymmetric recognition 166,
    168–176
  fixation 165–168
  and sovereigndignity 16, 176–182
reconciliation
  and ubuntu in South Africa
    152–155
Rediker, Marcus 117, 183–184
refugees 16, 159–164, 166
  European migrant policy 159–160,
    161–164, 180–181
  migrant camps 162–163, 164
  and recognition politics 166,
    173–174, 177–178
  recycling disposable lives 160–165
religion
  and Black dignity 15
  and the free Black man 45–46
  see also Black liberation theology;
    Christianity; political theology
Renaissance understanding of dignity
  21, 24–27
Renault, Emmanuel 168
Reno, William 160
representation, politics of 1–2
respect
  and dignity 22, 29–30
restorative justice 154
Roman republic and *dignitas* 23, 24
Romani 56
Rousseau, Jean-Jacques 52
  Social Contract 186–187

Sala-Molins, Louis 186–187
Sankara, Thomas 182
Sartre, Jean-Paul 12, 14, 167
  and Negritude 72–73
Schmitt, Carl
  Political Theology 94
science
  and African philosophy 141–142
secularism 14–15, 91–96, 98, 136
  and clericalism 92–93
  and ubuntu 151
self-fashioning
  and human dignity 24, 26

Senghor, Léopold 72–73, 104, 140
Sepúlveda, Juan Genes de 4–5
Sexton, Jared 57, 58–59, 118, 185,
  188
Shakespeare, William
  The Tempest 26, 90
Shariati, Ali 112
Sharpe, Christina 187
slave narratives 39, 41–46, 43, 44–46
  and abolitionist movements 42, 46
  and indignity 50–51
  and memory 46–47
  see also Cugoano, Ottobah;
    Equiano, Olaudah; Turner, Nat
slavery
  abolitionists 31, 42, 122
  and Afropessimism 17
  and American colonization 5–6
  and asymmetric recognition 168,
    170–171
  Black dignity and death 200
  and Black music 115–118
  and Black political ontology
    186–189
  and capitalism 183
  and Christianity 93–94, 99,
    100–101, 113–114, 120–123,
    125
  and dehumanization 13
  and dignity 7, 83, 134, 200
  ethics of Black slaves 83
  films about 116–117
  fugitive slaves 46
  and indignity 39
  Kant on Black Africans and slavery
    22, 31–32
  medicine-men 121
  and the migrant crisis 159
  modern slavery 164
  and the politicization of Black
    suffering 67–68
  slave rebellions 51–54, 84, 123,
    181–182
  see also transatlantic slave trade
social immanence
  and asymmetric recognition
    175–176
social invisibility 169, 170
social movements
  and universality 104

INDEX

South Africa
African National Congress 152–153
Black Theology: The South African Voice 89
Blackness in 189
Christian University Movement 89
colonization 49, 50, 53
Dookoom and black agricultural laborers 155–156
and the politics of the particular 107
racism 60
Truth and Reconciliation Commission (TRC) 16, 152–154
ubuntu in 147–149
sovereigndignity 16, 176–182
state violence
and dignity 35–36
and European immigration policies 16
Strange Fruit (Billie Holiday) 120, 124
strategic essentialism 79
suffering
Black suffering and music 117–118
politicization of 68, 70
suicide
and state power 179

Tanzania 154
Taubes, Jacob 113, 127
Taylor, Charles 165–166, 169
Tempels, Placide 139, 140
terrorist violence 47–48
thanatopolitics 14, 57, 58, 63
theology *see* political theology
Thomas, Greg 185
Till, Emmett 124, 131, 134
Torres, Nelson Madonado 5
torture 105–6
Towa, Marcien 136, 139, 142, 144, 145
tradition
and recognition theory 170
transatlantic slave trade
and Afro-Prophetism 127
and Afropessimism 17, 184–185
and Black bodies 117

and Black political ontology 187, 189
and colonial capitalism 50
and dehumanization 13
and the discourse of deconstruction 84
and human dignity 31
and indignity 39, 48
and prophetic Christianity 93–94
slave narratives 44–45
transindividuality 181
Travis, Joseph 52–53
Tubman, Harriet 8
Tunisian Revolution 190, 192–193
Ture, Kwame 6
Turkey
Gezi movement 190–191
Turner, Nat 8, 51–54, 54, 60, 99, 101, 123, 156
Tutu, Archbishop Desmond 15, 139, 147–149, 150, 151, 152, 155

ubuntu 15–16, 139
and loving thy neighbour 147–152
in South Africa 152–155, 156
United Kingdom
and migrant crisis 163
United Nations
definition of genocide 56
universal voluntarism 105, 108
universality
and dignity 109–112
and political theology 14–15, 89–103
and recognition 172
and the particular 98, 103–108

Valladolid debate (1550) 4–5, 6, 61
Venegas, Alejo 25
verbal abuse
and fixation 166–167
Vesey, Denmark 8, 123
victimized identities
and the Gezi movement 190–191
vigilant memory 146
violence
attacks on South African farms 155–156
and Black dignity 196, 198, 199–200
and Black political ontology 186

235

INDEX

violence (*cont.*)
  colonial 74, 136
  gender and patriarchal violence
    191–192
  and indignity 41, 47–8, 60, 63–64,
    65
  lynchings 63–64, 120, 124–125,
    129, 134
  political violence 47–49, 59, 172
  and secularism 95
  and uprisings of dignity 190–191
  see also police violence; racial
    violence
Voltaire 5

Warren, Calvin 17
Washington, George 134
West, Cornel 90, 93, 110, 115–116,
  119, 122, 125, 127
Western philosophy

and African philosophy 138–139
and Black dignity 198
white supremacists 62, 64, 107–108
  and African American religion 113
  and Black music 116
  and the migrant crisis 159
Wilderson, Frank 12, 183, 185, 188,
  189
Wilson, Darren 33–34
witchcraft, colonial 26
women
  Black women, sexism and racism
    9–10
  Habermas on the violation of
    human dignity 35
  and politicization 67–68
World Bank 63, 161

Žižek, Slavoj 15, 96, 97–99, 98, 101,
  102, 103, 105, 106, 131